GREEN GROWS IVY

GREEN

GROWS

IVY

McGRAW-HILL BOOK COMPANY, INC.

Ivy Baker Priest

NEW YORK   TORONTO   LONDON

GREEN GROWS IVY

Copyright © 1958 by Ivy Baker Priest.

Printed in the United States of America.
All rights reserved. This book
or parts thereof may not be reproduced
in any form without written permission
of the publishers.

Library of Congress Catalog Card Number: 58-13015

FIRST EDITION

To Roy and our children,

without whose encouragement

all of this

would not have been possible—

and to my mother and father,

who set the ivy

the way it should grow

ACKNOWLEDGMENTS

At the conclusion of a recent speech I made, a member of the audience came up to me and said, "You really ought to write a book." I confessed that I had been thinking of writing one for some time, but the pressure of official duties left little time for other work. At last the impulse grew too strong to be resisted. But this book could not have been completed without the assistance of Alfred Toombs and without the aid and counsel of my editor, Ray Pierre Corsini, whose understanding has been so keenly attuned to my work.

I

THE April night seemed to be filled with the peculiar magic which spring works in Washington, as nowhere else.

Along the wide streets the trees had put out their first, fresh green leaves. Daffodils nodded in profusion in the parks and the magnolia blossoms burst with beauty. From the vast lawn around the White House came the warm, sweet smell of the awakening earth.

Spring's spell seemed to hover over the White House dining room where we were seated. Tall, pencil-thin candles sent flickering gleams darting across the white damask and were reflected back by the gold table service. Just two places from me sat a genial, magnetic figure, the President of the United States. Ranged around the table were such well-known Americans as Senator and Mrs. Robert A. Taft, Senator and Mrs. William Knowland, ex-Ambassador and Mrs. Joseph E. Davies, Senator Frank Carlson, and a few others who had been invited by the President to honor the daughter of the President of Brazil.

I found myself staring at the place card in front of my plate, which said:

Ivy Baker Priest, Treasurer of the United States.

Suddenly, I was overwhelmed by the wonder of it all. And my thoughts went racing back through the years . . . back to Coalville and Bingham Canyon, the somber little mining towns where I had lived my girlhood . . . back to days when there was not enough money for food and clothing, or any of the basic amenities of living.

In the halo around the candles' gleam, I seemed to see the faces of some who had been kind to me and of a few who had been less than kind—and, as clearly as if she were there, I felt my mother's presence in the room. I have often had these intuitive, almost psychic experiences and I hoped desperately that Mother could know that I was dining that night in the White House, just two places away from the President of the United States. For it was she, more than anyone else, who had made all this possible.

Even after the dessert plates had been removed, and the ladies had retired for coffee to the Red Room, the strange spell seemed to linger with me. It was 1953, shortly after the administration in which I was to have the honor of serving had taken over, and it was my first White House dinner. As the ladies chatted with Mrs. Eisenhower, my thoughts drifted away again in the presence of history which haunted the small drawing room, with its red brocade walls, gold mirrors, and crystal chandeliers. Here had sat Madison, Jackson, Lincoln, Teddy Roosevelt, and others whose names were written large on the pages of history. When I spoke to the President's wife, whom I had come to know so well during the campaign, I found myself calling her "Mrs. Eisenhower."

2

"Remember, Ivy," she whispered to me, "it's still 'Mamie.' "

But I just couldn't call her Mamie there in the White House.

When the men joined us, President Eisenhower came over to chat with me.

"Well, Mrs. Priest," he asked pleasantly, "how are you enjoying your new job?"

"I'm enjoying it immensely, Mr. President," I replied—unable to use the familiar "Ike." "But at the moment, I'm just so overwhelmed to be here . . . I never expected to get anywhere near the White House."

His face broke into that familiar grin.

"I know just how you feel," he said. "Neither did I."

Since that night, I have dined with queens and princes, Cabinet members and ambassadors, captains of industry and leaders of world thought. This is not because I have found the right toothpaste to assure social success or because I have taken a charm course. It's just that I happen to hold a public office and Washington protocol precipitates me into rarefied circles which would not otherwise be open to me. Though I've become acclimated, I have never ceased to wonder how this all came to be.

Recently, I was seated next to Norman Vincent Peale at a luncheon. He turned to me and said:

"Mrs. Priest, the people I have known in this world who have achieved things have all overcome some great handicap to reach their goal. I hope you won't mind my asking you . . . what was yours?"

"You promise not to laugh?"

"I promise."

"Poverty," I replied without hesitation.

3

"And now you are in charge of all that money," he said and laughed heartily.

There probably is a certain irony in the fact that the journey which carried me to my post as custodian of the world's greatest storehouse of treasure began in poverty. For, long before I ever dreamed of taking *potage julienne* from pastry-thin Meissen cups, I had supped on thin soup served in thick pottery. Before I found myself seated between admirals and nobles, my dinner partners were the miners who ate at my mother's boardinghouse. I felt at ease in either company—for I love people, wherever I find them.

My signature has appeared on bills which have a value running into billions of dollars, but personally I have been able to hang on to very few samples of the product.

The day that a committee of the United States Senate held a hearing prior to my confirmation as Treasurer of the United States, someone asked facetiously:

"Does your personal checkbook always balance, Mrs. Priest?"

"It has to," I admitted without hesitation. "There's no margin for error in my bank account."

But I've learned there are treasures that money cannot buy, and these have enriched my life. My work in politics and in government has been secondary to my job as a homemaker. My career grew out of a desire to be a better mother and to assume the responsibilities of community life. There have been rugged times, but I have satisfied myself that a wife and mother can, and should, have an active life outside her household.

When, in the course of a bid for public office a few years ago, I was subjected to what I felt was an unfair charge of neglecting home and hearth to go into politics, I told the voters frankly:

"It is because of my children that I am running for Con-

4

gress. Someone is going to have to take this responsibility if our children are to grow up in the kind of world we want."

However, women in politics and in government are not yet taken quite seriously by the opposite sex. When my appointment as Treasurer was announced, the press made much of the fact that for the second time a woman had been named to fill such an "unfeminine" post, and some wits had a field day with my name.

"The new Treasurer is going to sign the money Ivy Baker Priest," wrote one reporter. "It figures. A baker should know what to do with the dough."

Another said, "We don't know the religion of the new lady Treasurer. But one thing is certain—there will be a Priest on every bill."

"Her name is Ivy. Isn't that the green stuff that grows and grows?" commented a third wag.

But women were apparently gratified by the appointment and a good many wrote to congratulate me. One of them said she hoped that a precedent had now been established. Why not honor the distaff side still further, she asked, by printing the portraits of women, as well as men, on our money? "We women ought to put first things first," I replied in an attempt at humor. "Why should we mind if men have their faces on the money, as long as we get our hands on it?"

My parents, who accumulated very little of "the green stuff that grows," made the best of a hard life without whimpering. They taught me a realistic optimism.

"There are doers and done-fors," my father told me. "You'll soon find out which you'll be, my girl."

Although there have been times when I have felt like a "done-for," I have always managed, with God's help, to rally. It has seemed that I was being moved through life, as if some great, unseen hand were taking me across a chessboard, each

5

move carefully planned and fitted in with the next. It has been, as my mother said whenever I faced temporary defeat, "all for the best."

But those words of Mother's meant little to me as a child, especially when disaster struck my family, as it did one quiet Sunday afternoon in 1912.

I was playing with paper dolls in the front yard of our clapboard house in the mining village of Grass Creek, near Coalville, Utah. Suddenly, there was a deafening roar in the distance and the sky grew black. The force of an explosion scattered my paper dolls in all directions.

Afraid that flying debris would injure me, Mother rushed out into the yard to get me, then froze in her tracks. A piece of heavy metal was flying straight at me. Just then I bent down to pick up a doll and the fragment sailed over my head. Mother was petrified. Had I not stooped at the moment, I would have been killed.

"My dolls are blowing away!" I screamed. "My dolls are blowing away!"

Recovering from her paralysis, Mother snatched me up and carried me into the house. I was still whimpering for my dolls, as she sat me down with my younger brothers, Fearnley and Max, beside her.

Some time later we heard the sound of heavy footsteps on our porch. Several men, carrying a stretcher, pushed through the door.

"Boiler blew," said one. "Where must we lay him down?"

My father lay on the stretcher, gasping for breath, his face white and twisted with pain.

"Bill's gone for Doc," said one of the stretcher-bearers.

With no outcry or visible sign of shock, Mother went to work to make Dad comfortable.

"Whustlin' in the kitchen again, 'e was," she said, taking

6

grim note, in her rich Scottish Midlands accent, of another violation of one of her lengthy list of superstitions. "When 'e leaves 'ere in th' morrnin', I neverr know whuther 'e'll walk 'ome or be carried 'ome."

When the doctor arrived, he strapped up several broken ribs and said that Dad would be fit to go back to work again in a few days. His fellow workers agreed that this was a minor miracle. For the ancient boiler which Dad had been tending in the mine works that afternoon had exploded with force enough to shake the town. He had been knocked into a corner by the blast and a heavy iron door had wedged between the two walls, thus shielding him from a bath of live steam.

It was the first, but not the last, time that Dad was brought home on a stretcher. He was what, in these days, we call accident-prone. Friends used to say that he was the luckiest unlucky man alive. While he was fit for duty again within a week, he discovered that he had literally blown the job. With the boiler gone, there was no other work for him—and so we moved on from Coalville.

One dark night in 1913, in the midst of a raging blizzard, we arrived in Bingham Canyon, Utah. I was seven years old and sat with my face pressed against the cold window of our railway coach, peering into the snow-spangled blackness outside. In the depths below the station, I could see the orange glow of kerosene lanterns in the windows of the small frame houses. Above the eerie moan of the winter wind, I could hear the muffled roar of an occasional dynamite explosion and the deep rumble of ore cars crossing a trestle.

I looked to my father, sitting next to me, for reassurance. He was a big man, broad-shouldered and heavy-muscled, with black hair and kindly gray eyes that could be stern and piercing when he was displeased. When he smiled back at me, I felt that everything was all right. But then, the train

7

began to turn slowly—and I grasped his arm with fright.

"It's all right," he said soothingly. "They're just turning the train around so it can go back to Salt Lake City."

I burst into tears.

"I don't want to stay here," I sobbed. "This is the end of the world. Even the train has to turn around and go back."

If my parents felt dismay as they arrived in this strange, out-of-the-way place to start a new life with three small children and no visible resources, they did not show it. Even had they known what sharp blows of fate would be dealt our family there, I doubt that they would have turned back. For Mother and Dad would also have known that they had love and faith enough to see us through.

Their characters had been hewn out of the stern stuff of reality. My father, Orange Decatur Baker, had been a farm boy, the son of one of the first non-Indian babies born in Tooele County, Utah. His grandfather, a blacksmith, had come west with the first Mormon settlers. Dad had been raised on the fertile, but arid, soil of southern Utah. His father had two wives—successively, not simultaneously—and there were sixteen children in his family. How many times, in later years, I have wished that I could be sure of the votes of all the descendants of those sixteen Bakers!

When my father, the eldest of the first marriage, had reached the fifth grade, it was decided that he had sufficient education, and he took his place beside the men in the fields. But he had a good mind and, by reading constantly, he improved it. According to the Mormon custom, he went abroad as a missionary for the church when he was twenty-one. He spent eighteen months in England and became a convert himself—to the charms of a young English woman from Yorkshire who was to become my mother.

The daughter of an iron puddler, my mother, Clara Fearnley, came from what my father considered a small family—

8

only nine children. Her mother's people, the Lloyds, had owned the iron foundry where my grandfather worked as a laborer. The family—descendants of the haughty Stuarts of Scotland—had disowned Grandmother when she made a marriage they considered beneath her station.

Left motherless in childhood, Mother had gone to work in the home of a Church of England parson. The music she heard there, the fine furnishings she saw, the clothes the women wore, gave her a taste for the better things in life that remained with her always, as did the Anglican customs of the household. We were, I would guess, the only Mormon family in town that had fish for dinner on Fridays and celebrated the Lenten season and other principal holidays on the Church of England calendar.

Mother's younger sister, Gert, had already migrated to Utah with a Mormon family. When Dad got back home, he left the farm and took a job as a gold miner. After he had saved enough money, he sent a ticket to his Clara in England, and she sailed on the same ship that had brought him home. A few weeks after her arrival in October, 1904, they were married in the Mormon temple at Manti and settled in the little town of Kimberley, where I was born on September 7, 1905. Though I didn't have a silver spoon in my mouth, at least I was born on top of a gold mine. But the gold vein played out and we moved on. I was to see very little gold until they handed me the key to Fort Knox.

Hard years in hard places had prepared my parents for whatever might await them in Bingham Canyon. We went to a hotel that first night and Dad found a job the next day, working in one of the copper mines. He came whistling into our hotel room, tossed his hat jauntily on the bed, and said:

"I've found just the place for us to live."

"Now take yer 'at off that bed and stop whustlin' indoors," said Mother sternly. "It's no wonder ye're gettin' blown up."

I think that Dad deliberately violated Mother's superstitions just to tease her. So he picked up his hat and brushed the bed off carefully.

"An' what sort of 'ouse 'ave ye found? 'As it a yarrd forr th' children?"

"The biggest yard in town."

The rambling frame house which Dad had found did, in fact, have the largest yard in town. The house had all the grace and style of a cow barn, but it was surrounded by about the only piece of level ground in that part of Bingham. Most of our neighbors' houses were built up the side of the canyon, so that one back yard became another front yard, or ran under the stilt-supported front porch of the next house.

It was my notion that, since we had the yard, I should get busy and do some playing. But Mother said we'd have to clean the house first and get our curtains up.

"Ye know, th' windows of yer 'ouse tell a lot about ye," she explained. "Nice, clean currtains tell people they can expect a warrm welcome inside. But them as care not aboot theirr windows care not aboot much else."

One day, while she was fixing Dad's lunch, she asked me to watch Fearnley and particularly baby Max, who was just a toddler. My mind was still on the hopscotch game outside, as I sat there glowering at my two charges.

"It's Ivy's turn," I heard someone yell outside.

It didn't seem to me that those two little boys could get into much mischief in five minutes, so I tiptoed out the door and took my turn at the game.

When I returned to the living room, I heard Max screaming with pain. Mother was bending over to pick him up, and my face flushed with guilt. The little fellow had found a can of the lye water Mother had been using in scrubbing and had dipped his hand in it. When his fingers burned, he put them in his mouth to ease the pain.

Intent on quick rescue, Mother did not panic for an instant.

"Crack some eggs and give me the whites . . . quickly," she ordered.

She began forcing these down the baby's throat. "Run for the doctor," she cried a moment later.

As I raced out the door, I passed my father. "What's the hurry?" he asked.

Sick with dread, I didn't pause to answer. I found the doctor and he hurried home with me, holding my hand reassuringly.

But there was little he could do at the moment. Max had swallowed enough of the caustic to burn his esophagus badly. Mother's calm, prompt action had saved his throat from irreparable damage. But he could not swallow and it became necessary to insert a rubber tube in his throat so that he could take nourishment. But as new tissue grew, it would close the rubber tube, and Max was in danger of dying from malnutrition.

For months, we carried the helpless child around on a pillow, going from doctor to doctor. Our savings went for medical bills, but still there was no cure. Mother never scolded me for my terrible lapse that day. She didn't have to. For I knew. She had been counting on me and I had let her down.

Little Max seemed to be fading away. Every time I looked at him in his crib, I was stricken with remorse. Though I was only seven at the time, his accident made an indelible impression on me. Ever since then I have been overcome by a sense of guilt whenever—even through circumstances beyond my control—I've been unable to keep a promise or commitment.

When hope for Max was almost gone, our prayers for his recovery seemed to be answered. Aunt Gert wrote that our old family doctor in Coalville, where she still lived, had successfully treated a similar case. Her hope soaring, Mother immediately took the baby to Dr. French, who had delivered Max. The cure devised by this country practitioner, with meager resources at his disposal, proved to be highly effective. He inserted a silver tube in Max's throat, and this allowed new tissue to grow. Eventually his throat was restored to normal.

When he was able to run and play again, I felt that he was my special charge and never let him out of my sight. He took a delight in hiding from me. Once, I panicked at losing him and scoured the house, frantically calling his name. Suddenly, I heard a cackle from on high. Looking up, I saw the taffy-headed imp swinging on top of a door, his blue eyes sparkling with mischief. "See me up here!" he screeched, pleased as Punch with his prowess. I couldn't scold him— for I was too delighted by this sign of his recovery.

The family resources were still drained from the long siege with Max when we were rapped by another hammer blow. Dad was brought home from the mine on a stretcher again. Mother took one look at him and again sent me racing for the doctor. In those days few people had telephones, and a child running downhill to Dr. Straupp's office was a familiar sight.

When the doctor came in, Mother told him, " 'E put 'is left leg in 'is trousers first this mornin'—I knew somethin' bad would 'appen."

"It's a broken leg," the doctor said. "He'll be out for at least three months."

They had a very simple arrangement about insurance and unemployment compensation in those days. If you stopped working, your pay stopped. It saved paper work but it was a little hard on the people. Mother—with three children at home now and another on the way—didn't bat an eyelash.

"We'll just 'ave to make the best of it," she announced.

I remember looking at her with open-mouthed wonder.

Her slender body was erect and the wealth of light-brown hair piled in a knot on the top of her head increased the illusion of regality about her. Her sparkling blue eyes mirrored her determination. Everything about her seemed to reflect strength and confidence in an emergency. If there was energy enough for worrying, she would use it instead to meet the problem.

How we were to meet this particular problem I did not know. With Dad out of work and so many mouths to feed, things seemed hopelessly black. At the age of eight I began to feel the responsibility of the eldest child and tried to think of ways to earn money. The few pennies I picked up baby-sitting, running errands, and washing dishes added to the family purse like grains of sand to the beach.

One evening, two of Dad's friends, both bachelors, stopped by to see him when their shift was over. Mother, who would invite people to dinner as easily as she'd say hello, insisted that they stay for a bite with us. After dinner, I was washing dishes and listening to Dad talking with his friends in the next room.

"O.D., your wife's a mighty fine cook. Wouldn't mind eating her food regular," one of them remarked. Then he had an afterthought. "Why don't we board here at your house?"

Dad had a way of thinking everything over carefully. He was fond of the game of checkers—and he made every move in life with the same careful deliberation that went into a move at checkers. I peeked out and saw that his gray eyes were thoughtful as he considered this suggestion carefully as a judge. But before he could make up his mind—and when he made it up, nothing would change it—Mother spoke up:

"It's a fine idea. It'll 'elp us over th' 'ump."

Father nodded his assent. After all, these two men were friends. What could be more natural than to have them in for meals? And so it was that Mother opened a boarding-house.

It meant added work for me—watching the youngsters,

setting the table, and climbing up on a stool to do the dishes at night. I preferred washing to drying, and later, as my brother Fearnley grew old enough to help me, I always gave him his choice. "Either I will wash the dishes and you can dry them, or you can dry and I'll wash." This arrangement worked well for a while until "Bake," as we called him, got wise to my ruse. "You always give me my choice," he complained. "But you never say for *me* to wash." After that, Dad had us draw straws to settle the argument. Actually, we didn't mind the chore too much, when we could listen to the boarders talking.

One of our boarders, Joe Bannock, was the most colorful and entertaining storyteller I have ever met. Had he done everything he claimed, he would have had to be older than Methuselah. But he kept Dad in good spirits with his tall stories.

During his wanderings, Joe had run into a mining man, popularly known as "Silver Jack," who had struck it rich in the early high, wide, and handsome days. According to Joe, Silver Jack had built a garish mansion in Salt Lake and had developed the eccentricities that only the very rich can afford. His interests had gone beyond the mines he owned to real estate, banking, sheep raising, and various other enterprises. One cold, wintry night he came in from his sheep camp to keep an appointment. Unshaven, wearing shabby mackinaw and levis, he paced up and down in front of an office building, as he waited for his friend. From time to time, he peered into a jewelry shop to look at a clock. A policeman who'd kept his eye on this seeming vagrant, came up and said, "Move on, bud! You've loitered long enough. Just get moving."

Later, his friend asked, "For gosh sake, why didn't you tell the cop you owned that building?"

"Oh, no," said Silver Jack. "If I had, he would have run me in for sure."

One Christmas Eve he came in from the mines in his rough clothes, walked into a jewelry store, and demanded a diamond necklace as a gift for his wife. The flustered clerk said, "Sorry, sir. We have no diamond necklaces in stock."

"You got diamonds, ain't you?" said Silver Jack.

"Well, yes, unmounted ones."

"Trot 'em out. Let's look 'em over."

When the clerk brought out an assortment of gleaming stones, the miner demanded, "Why can't you just string 'em together? You know how. I want this necklace by tomorrow for my wife's Christmas."

"But we haven't time. Our man would have to work all night," the clerk protested.

"Get him started—I'll pay whatever it costs."

Next morning there was a magnificent necklace of oddly assorted diamonds under the Christmas tree for Silver Jack's plain wife Sarah. And, the story goes, she mistook them for rhinestones.

One night, while Joe Bannock was holding forth with one of these tales at the dinner table, there was a knock at the door. Mother opened it and found a ragged stranger, sporting a heavy beard, standing outside.

"Mrs. Baker, I understand you take in boarders," he said.

Mother wasn't entirely sure that she wanted this boarder and her reply was rather evasive.

"Well, lady, I know some people that say if'n you'd let me stay here, I'd really have myself a good place. I know I don't look very good right now, but I been out of work. I just come here from Butte and I got me a job, but I need a place to stay and somebody to feed me till I get my first payday."

I could see Mother's eyes fill with sympathy, as she listened to this hard-luck story. Without a word, she ushered him into the dining room for supper. Joe and the other boarders were regarding the new arrival with skepticism, and we noted that his black work-pants were crudely patched with pink thread.

"If ye'll leave yer trousers when ye go to work in th'

morrnin', I'll see if I can't put a patch on them," Mother said.

He turned around with quiet dignity and said:

"That's right kind of you, Mrs. Baker. But, you see, I ain't got another pair to wear to work."

His name, he told us, was Shea. He was one of those drifters of the old West, moving from mining town to mining town, as the whim or the work dictated. There was something of the grand gentleman about Mr. Shea, however. His courtly manners endeared him to all of us, but they caused Joe to look upon him with dark suspicion.

Mr. Shea was invariably on time for meals and, while he kept his beard and had only the one pair of trousers, he was always clean. He laughed heartily at Joe's stories, and had long talks with Dad on the historical and scientific books which Dad loved to read.

When payday came, the boarders appeared promptly to settle their bills. But when dinner was served, there was no sign of Mr. Shea. As the others sat down at the table, they shot knowing glances at each other. Mother kept going to the window, saying anxiously:

"Oh, dear, I hope he didn't have an accident."

"Don't worry, Mrs. Baker. Nothin's 'appened to that bloke," said George Corliss, an English miner who had drifted out West in search of work and had been delighted to find a fellow countrywoman who could serve him his favorite beef steak and kidney pie. " 'E's just took off with yer board money," George added.

"Now, George," Mother admonished. "Mr. Shea's a trustworthy man, that 'e is. I'd stake my life on 'im."

"Ye're a trustin' woman, that you are," Joe Bannock shot back, and launched into one of his whoppers. "Ye know, that Shea 'minds me of a feller I worked with up in Butte. Wandered out on payday when that big blizzard uz on in '88," said Joe. "Didn't find him until spring thaw. Unnertaker started lookin' through his pockets, seein' it'd been payday when he strayed off. Fella sat up and tole 'im to set 'em up for the house. Had so much alkyhol in him, kep' him from freezin' all winter."

Dad started to join the boarders in a good laugh, but he saw the dark look on Mother's face and kept quiet.

Mr. Shea didn't appear that night at all and next morning Mother was still fussing and worrying. I knew she wasn't upset about his bill, but was genuinely concerned for his safety. When he failed to appear that evening, Mother said nothing—but her manner was grim. Dinner was almost over when there came an unmistakable knock on the door.

Mother opened it and there stood a tall, clean-shaven man, dressed in new clothes and holding a bunch of flowers and some packages.

"Why, Mr. Shea!" she exclaimed in astonishment. "I didn't recognize you."

"It's me all right," Mr. Shea said, moving in to present the flowers to Mother, a toy to Max, and candy to Fearnley and me.

"Why, thank ye, Mr. Shea, that's mighty thoughtful of ye," said Mother. "Ye look nice in yer new clothes. If ye'd like to leave me that other pair of pants, maybe I could put a patch on them."

"Mrs. Baker, there just wouldn't be no use in doin' that. I bought another pair."

Then he went into the dining room, where he was treated to some good-natured ribbing by his fellow boarders.

After he'd enjoyed a hearty meal and lit up his battered old pipe, Mr. Shea gave an account of his disappearance. With his first pay burning a hole in his pocket, he'd taken off for a shopping spree and "a bit of high livin'" in Salt Lake City.

"But I sure didn't spent my board money," he said, taking

a brand-new leather purse out of his pocket. As he counted some money into Mother's hand, she looked around with an I-told-you-so air, pleased by her ability to size people up.

Turning to Dad, Mr. Shea said, "Mr. Baker, I been tellin' the fellows how good your wife feeds us and I reckon I could bring you some new boarders, if'n it'd help out."

Before Dad could answer, Mother, who'd come in with a platter of food, spoke up. "That'd be nice, Mr. Shea. How many would it be?"

"Oh, I reckon about fifteen more."

I stopped midway in a bite of chocolate. That would mean twenty for dinner every night. I could just see mountains of dishes piling up for me to wash.

"Glad to he'p out, Mrs. Baker. Seein's you and Mr. Baker was so good about takin' me in."

"Don't mention it, Mr. Shea. Everybody needs 'elp now and then," said Mother. "Fifteen extra—that would be a lot of mouths to feed. I'll 'ave to get a 'ired girl to 'elp in the kitchen." Looking at me with an understanding smile, she added, "Ivy cawn't do all those dishes by 'erself."

At that I relaxed and happily finished my bite of chocolate.

Indeed everything was going to be for the best. Trust Mother to see to that.

My unquestioning faith in Mother reflected her deep faith in God. But hers was a dynamic faith, tempered by practical realism. From her store of adages for every occasion came one of her favorite sayings: "The Lord will provide. But 'e does need an 'elpin' 'and."

II

MOTHER'S pragmatic, homespun philosophy seemed to work. And so did her tireless hands. In short order operation boardinghouse was going full blast. For the next few years Mother capably ran this growing concern, and also took time out to increase her family with another son and two little daughters.

Mother, two hired girls, and I labored mightily to stay ahead of the assembled appetites. Three meals a day would cost a miner one dollar, and for that he would expect—and would get—first-class fare. Those were the days when the butcher would give you calf's liver to feed the cat and throw meaty soup bones in with the ten-cents-a-pound sirloin, without charge. There was enough profit margin in our operation, anyway, to keep us solvent.

By the age of twelve I had practically a full-time job. At 5 A.M., I would tumble out of bed in my cold room, slip into long underwear, black bloomers, black stockings, and the plain cotton dress which I always wore to school. I had just the one. I would submit to the torture of having my hair braided tight and knotted on top of my head by Mother and then the day's work would begin.

There was the breakfast table to set and then there were sandwiches to make for the men's lunch buckets. The first boarders would appear for breakfast at 6 A.M. and no sooner had they gone clomping off to work than another shift— just leaving the mines—would sit down. They would eat huge bowls of steaming mush, eggs with either ham or chops, and polish this off with hot cakes or hot homemade bread, spread with Mother's elderberry jelly.

Then I'd see that my sleepy-eyed brothers and sisters ate their breakfasts and afterward shepherd them to school. When I got home in the afternoon, it would be time to set the table for the first supper shift—served at four o'clock for the men who worked in the early evening. Then came supper again for the day workers who were emerging from the mines.

When the miners had left, we would have our family hour in the living room, gathered close to the big black stove in winter. Dad, dignified and grave, would lead us in prayer, thanking God, in his resonant voice, for the blessings which had been bestowed that day and entreating for strength and wisdom to achieve our aims. Our family prayers became something of a daily accounting to the Deity and each of us came to know how we had succeeded or failed in using the talents entrusted to us. As a little girl, I could imagine that God was present in our living room each night, listening and nodding His approval—or sometimes sighing with disappointment—as a new chapter in the life of the Baker family unfolded. We grew up feeling that God was almost like a member of our family.

From Dad, and in the Mormon Sunday school which we all attended, we learned the tenets of our sustaining faith. It was to spread this Mormon belief that my father had gone to England as a missionary, he told us. He would read us notes from the journal he had kept then and he made us feel his own pride in having been selected to undertake the mission. This practice of sending young Mormons abroad began soon after the church was founded by Joseph Smith, the Vermont farm boy who became the Latter-day Saints' first prophet. Thousands of people were brought over from Europe to settle in Utah through the missionaries' efforts.

Then Dad would tell us stories of the pioneering days which he had heard from his father and grandfather—who knew intimately of the hard struggle that followed the trek of the Mormon caravan from Illinois to the barren flats of Utah. The tall, bearded, austere figure of Brigham Young and the other leaders of this singularly American faith became so well known to us that they were almost like neighbors.

Before going to bed, Mother and I would start packing lunch buckets for the men who went to work after midnight on the graveyard shift. We would make hot coffee and leave it on the stove, with doughnuts and cake on the table—and then we'd tumble into bed.

Mother managed to preserve her serenity in the face of all things, save one. It was the mud, the dark oozing mud that filled the unpaved streets of our town during the winter thaws and spring rains.

Bingham Canyon was built between the steep walls of two mountains. We would hardly see the sun before ten o'clock, and by four o'clock it had sunk below the canyon's rim. The Kennecott Copper Company operated the world's largest open-pit copper mine at the top and other companies had underground mines nearby. Streams of water from the mountains poured through town in ditches—which had become open sewers.

So when it rained hard, or when the snows melted in the spring, the ditches would overflow and Bingham would become a morass.

"Ye'd think they'd put doon wooden walkways," Mother would say indignantly, as she surveyed her floors.

With the children, plus twenty or thirty miners, tramping in and out of the house every day, she had more reason than most housekeepers to complain about the muddy streets.

Mother was determined to do something about it, in spite of the general feeling of women in town that conditions must be accepted as they were. There was still something of the aura of the old Wild West about the place. Main Street was lined with drinking and gambling halls, the largest of which was the Copper King Saloon. On paydays, the canyon would echo with the songs, shouts, and clinking glasses of celebrants—and Constable Si Jones, who weighed 300 pounds and was quick as a cat, was kept on the jump. Of course, we children were not supposed to know about the street populated by a lively colony of painted ladies.

The town was inhabited by colorful characters whose names had been earned in some fantastic episodes in years past—Paddy the Priest, Monkey Motion Davis, Smiler Shelley, and others. Through the unpaved streets rumbled wagons loaded with ore, which sometimes got away, running down steep hills and over the unfortunate horses which drew them. None of the skinners who handled these huge teams was more skilled than one-armed Joe Hamilton, who drove the big beer wagon with eight head of horses—and could unload beer kegs with his one arm.

The business houses along Main Street gave the town its stability. J. C. Penney had opened in Bingham the fourth of what was to be his great chain of stores. There were various small enterprises, mostly in one-story, frame buildings, operated by local folks. The big general store was the Bingham Mercantile. Its owner, C. C. Adderley, was always ready to lend a sympathetic ear, and quite often unlimited credit, to those who were down on their luck.

22

By and large, luck in Bingham ran from bad to worse. Mining was a hazardous job, and in many local homes the breadwinner was laid out with what was commonly called "miner's con." It was, in fact, silicosis, a fatal lung ailment caused by particles of dust.

There were regular mine disasters. When a mine whistle would sound to signal trouble underground, we would freeze in our tracks and wonder who was working that shift.

The whistle wailed its mournful warning one day, when I was home from school for lunch. Mother paused anxiously for a moment and turned white as a sheet. For she knew that Dad had gone underground with two of the mine bosses to inspect a stope that was in danger of collapse. But, instead of rushing to the scene, Mother stayed at home. She kept me with her that afternoon on some pretext—I guess she just wanted company. It wasn't long before a neighbor appeared to tell us:

"He's all right, Mrs. Baker. Mighty lucky. But he's still down there, tryin' to save the others."

We waited fifty-six agonizing hours before Dad finally emerged from the mine. He had escaped by a miracle, although Mother gave some of the credit to the fact that when he had spilled the salt that morning, she had thrown some over her left shoulder. Dad had been the last man in a party of five to enter the dangerous part of the mine. He heard a loud cracking sound and shouted:

"Come on, men . . . we better get out!"

Then the stope collapsed with a roar and Dad was blown out to safety, like a cork popped out of a bottle. Joe Norden and Dan Eden, two of the mine bosses, and two Mexican workers had been trapped inside. Dad refused to leave the scene and led the rescue party to the trapped men. Three were dead, but he helped save Joe Norden's life.

When disaster struck, Mother always seemed to emerge

as leader of the relief activities. Sometimes there would be snow slides and entire houses would be buried. Twice we had fires which wiped out half the houses in Bingham. Mother would be in the thick of it, organizing the distribution of food and clothing to the stricken and arranging temporary housing for the homeless.

There could have been few places on earth where so many different races and creeds were crowded into such a small area as Bingham. Yet we all lived in harmony. When tragedy occurred, we came together like members of a single family. Between times, we had no inclination to note differences in skin coloring or religious creeds. Mother was almost worshiped by some of the foreign-born whom she guided through the strange customs of their adopted land.

My constant playmates were three girls—one Swedish, one Greek, and one Japanese—and an Irish boy. Perhaps in large cities you'll find such mixtures—Poles, Finns, Mexicans, Italians, Swedes, and Greeks—but seldom do you encounter such a melting pot in a small town.

So it was that our house became the social hub of the town. There was always plenty of company, for Mother would sweep through town inviting anyone she met to come for dinner—and bring his friends. Later, she would pay a return call, gathering up more friends along the way. Those who asked Mother to dinner always expected her to bring two or three guests of her own and she returned this multiple hospitality in kind.

Our yard, too, always overflowed with children. The Baker family alone would have filled most yards—for there were seven of us by this time. In addition to Fearnley and Max, there were now Lloyd, a dependable, studious boy; the winsome little girls, Gertrude and Lynn; and Keith, the baby brother. Sometimes Mother would look out the kitchen window and say happily:

"I think I could count fifty children out there—and it's good to know wherre me own are."

We had the run of the house, and when the boys got hungry they could bring their friends in and cook what they liked on the coal stove which was kept going around the clock.

As we grew up, the yard was not big enough to hold us, and the whole town became our playground. I became a tomboy, partly in self-defense. I had to ride herd on my younger brothers, and paper dolls no longer attracted me as much as outdoor games.

The sports in which we engaged were, I suppose, no more dangerous than Russian roulette. We played follow-the-leader over the girders and machinery in the old mill. We scrambled like monkeys up the trestles of the ore railways which towered over town, or borrowed our father's work gloves to swing by our hands from the big ore buckets which swept at dizzying heights from one mountaintop to the next. Running up the sides of the canyon to the railway station were dual-track tramcars, something like San Francisco cable cars. When a car going up would pass one going down on the adjoining track, we would leap from one to the other.

The mud on the streets, which bothered Mother so much, did not stand in the way of our fun. In fact, there was a mudhole on Main Street where the miners would toss coins just to watch the boys scramble for them. The drainage ditches provided us with further amusement. Sometimes the boys would succeed in catching a live rat along the banks of the ditches. Once I captured a live white rat sunning itself on the bank, and was the heroine of our own junior league for days after.

But, no matter what pleasures we found in drainage ditches and mud, Mother was determined to clean up the town. You might say it was mud that got us into politics.

She found a willing political ally in our family physician, Dr. Straupp. A short, roly-poly man, who was constantly chewing a cigar and whose coattails always seemed to be flying out as if he were rushing off on an emergency case, Dr. Straupp happened to be a Republican—which was the party Mother had chosen to support.

Dr. Straupp took a dim view of the way the town was being run by the Democratic incumbents and would boom out his criticisms in ringing tones. In Mother he found a sympathetic listener and, what was even better, a willing and dedicated political collaborator. The good doctor wanted to run for mayor of Bingham and Mother encouraged the notion.

"Now if ye werre to promise to put doon wooden sidewalks, ye'd have everr housekeeperr in the toon behind ye," she pointed out.

The doctor launched his campaign on a solid platform— wooden sidewalks for Bingham. Mother tried to get Dad interested in the local political situation, but he had found a couple of good new checker players and was not inclined to let the campaign interfere with his favorite recreation. So Mother took to the hustings herself, rounding up the solid support of her friends among the foreign-born. This involved having them registered as voters, which sometimes meant she had to get their citizenship established.

Naturally, I became involved in this matter. I was official errand-runner . . ."Ye go, Ivy. I'd send one of th' boys, but ye know 'ow much mud they bring back." I was also in demand as a baby watcher, while Mother marched parents down to establish them as voters.

The campaign generated a certain amount of steam, with opposition coming not only from the Democrats, who held local offices, but also from some of Dr. Straupp's colleagues, who thought he should stick to maternity cases and surgery. But Mother and the doctor, between them, managed to stir Bingham up that year and election day was a high-voltage affair. I spent the day around the polls, my heart skipping with the excitement of it all. When it came time to tally the vote and our candidate, Dr. Straupp, was declared the winner, I felt as elated as a kingmaker.

Dr. Straupp's generous praise of Mother's work in the local campaign helped to start Mother on a lifelong, if part-time, political career. In time, she became a well-known figure in political circles. Visiting candidates would always seek her out, and her support in an election year was highly prized. On the Fourth of July, she could usually be found on the speakers' platform when the festivities got under way. She didn't make speeches, but the politicians wanted to let everyone in town know that they were Clara Baker's friends.

The announcement, one year, that our Fourth of July speaker would be the Republican congressman from our district created considerable excitement. Congressman Elmer O. Leatherwood was a man of commanding presence and was an orator of the old school. They need not have bothered inventing the loudspeaker, or even the radio, for the likes of Mr. Leatherwood. He could make himself heard from one end of the district to the other, if the wind was right.

For weeks in advance of the big celebration, we were in such a high state of excitement at home that we failed to take notice of the important and inevitable signal that the family had gone broke again. We had pork shanks and beans two nights in a row without anyone's understanding the significance.

The boarders had faded out of our life temporarily, for Dad had been doing well. He had decided to gamble on becoming a "leaser." He would take over a section of mine which had not been worked. If it turned out to be rich with ore, he would hire helpers and we would enjoy a period of feast. Otherwise, we would face a time of famine.

There was neither moaning nor weeping around our house to signal the transition from feast to famine or back again. We learned to read certain signals, however. A piece of new furniture or the announcement that one or another of us was going to start music lessons would indicate that Dad was doing well enough to be able to gratify Mother's enthusiasm for the finer things of life, like those she had known in the English parsonage. Or we would find Dad with his nose in a new book on world history. Mother delighted in serving roast beef and Yorkshire pudding, or spring lamb with her special mint sauce, when there was enough money. The trip down the economic roller coaster would be ushered in quietly by the appearance of cheap cuts of meat—usually pork and beans or a stewing hen.

Just as the Fourth of July approached, the good things disappeared from the menu and we found ourselves on our famine diet. Far from daunting us, it whetted our appetites for the events of the holiday. For there were to be small cash prizes awarded in various contests and, when there was cash at stake, you could be sure the Baker kids would be in there trying.

We were up early that Fourth. Main Street was decked with flags, and the bunting on the platform in front of the Bingham Merc flapped smartly in the cool breeze that blew down the canyon. Barefoot and free of all responsibility for the day, I trooped down the street with my three younger brothers in tow to wait for the band to assemble and start playing. Bingham wasn't much for fireworks. Since dynamite shook our windows round the clock, we found the absence of explosions a novelty on the Fourth.

The sun was well up over the rim of the canyon when

the adults began to gather. Mother was seated on the Bingham Merc platform next to the congressman, and I stood there gazing at her erect young figure with pride. Mayor Straupp was there, discoursing enthusiastically upon the future of our town, and the other good doctors of Bingham were also platform guests. With a gesture of *noblesse oblige*, the mayor introduced them all for a few words, and then Congressman Leatherwood delivered a speech which rattled the windows.

After his sonorous oration, we all paused for refreshment. Vendors pushed their way through the crowds hawking, "Peanuts, chewing gum, candy, soda pop!" We all stuffed ourselves while waiting for the contests of skill to begin.

Congressman Leatherwood stayed close to Mother as the games got under way. He applauded vigorously when she won the first prize of five dollars in the ladies' nail-driving contest.

My little sister Gertrude easily won the egg-and-spoon race and I noticed that, while she turned in her spoon, she palmed the egg for her breakfast next morning. If we kept on doing this well, we'd be able to have one more roast-beef-and-Yorkshire-pudding dinner before Mother took in boarders again.

In the pie-eating contest, Fearnley and Max really had no competition. There's nothing like a hungry fighter, they say—unless it's a hungry pie-eater. Those boys, with their hands behind their backs, could dig into a blueberry pie and consume it in nothing flat, let the juice trickle where it might. Gert turned her breakfast egg over to me long enough to win the sprint for younger girls, and Max—carrying a weight handicap of the homemade pies he'd eaten—streaked home first in the younger boys' foot race.

Congressman Leatherwood was obviously getting a great deal of pleasure out of the Baker family's success. He would shake hands gravely with my brothers and sisters, as they collected their money prizes, and would tell Mother what a wonderful family she had. I had the feeling that Congressman Leatherwood was going to carry Bingham by a record vote next year, even if Mother had to conduct naturalization classes in Finn Hall.

I approached my foot race with confidence. I had won it regularly in other years and I was pretty sure I could even win a race against the boys. This would boost our income for the day to over twenty dollars—more than enough for roast beef, and roly-poly for dessert.

I got off to an early lead in the race, sailed down the course easily, and, near the finish line, glanced back to see how close the nearest runner was to me. Then it was I stumbled. I was almost close enough to roll across the line. Instead I tried to crawl. I didn't make it in time.

All I had to show for my effort was a badly skinned knee, made worse by crawling. Disconsolately, I limped away, not even glancing back to see the congressman congratulating the girl who had won. I was just looking for a gopher hole to crawl into.

Over at the horse trough, I washed off my injured knee and then sat down to pout. Idly I watched the boys throwing themselves into the final event of the program. They were trying to climb a greased pole to reach the top prize of the day—a five-dollar bill which was stuck at the top.

I noticed that each boy seemed able to get up a little higher than his predecessor, and felt that I could climb higher than any of them, if only girls were allowed in the contest. But it was considered too unladylike. Sure, it would be easy, I told myself. Every boy who went up wore off some grease and so the next one went a little higher. Suddenly, a bright idea came to me and, forgetting about my skinned knee, I rushed over to pull my brothers out of line, and took them aside for a little briefing. I noticed that Congressman Leatherwood had his gimlet eye on us.

Dropping the boys back to the end of the line, I put Lloyd, the youngest, ahead of the other two, and dusted his shirt with dirt. He made it higher than anyone else. Then I sent Max on up, covered with dirt again—and he nearly reached the top.

Then Fearnley, the strongest of the boys, started his assault upon Mount Everest. He got up as far as Max without much trouble, since there was now plenty of dirt on the pole. Holding on with one hand, he reached into a trouser pocket for a handful of dirt and got enough of a grip to get up higher. Then he reached into another pocket, and I held my breath as he climbed up and grabbed the bill.

There was a cheer from the crowd as he started down, and Congressman Leatherwood reached out to shake Fearnley's greasy hand, but prudently let it go with a pat on the back. Mother came up smiling proudly.

Suddenly the congressman put his arm around me.

"Smart girl you've got, Mrs. Baker," he boomed to Mother. "She ought to go into politics."

I had never been so proud. For this seemed the highest form of praise to my young ears. Watching Mother in action and being errand girl at the polls provided me with valuable experience. I was learning that politics wasn't just a sport, or a glamorous public show either. It was hard work and serious business. And a political career—if ever I could aspire to one —seemed the ultimate in glorious achievement.

III

IT was said that there was only one way to grow in Bingham Canyon—straight up. I followed the pattern as I entered my teen years. I was tall, gangly, and awkward—endowed with all the soft feminine charm of a bean pole.

Most of my best friends were still boys. I sat in the back of the classroom with the male scholars, to get a better vantage point for tossing spitballs. When a plot was hatched to slip out of school on April 1, leaving only an "April Fool" note scribbled on the blackboard for our teacher, I was in the thick of it. That was the day we raided the Greek confectionery on Main Street. The proprietors were strangely unconcerned when we snatched up candy off the trays on the counter. We found out soon enough why they were so complacent. The bonbons were filled with garlic, red pepper, vinegar, and other soft centers concocted for April Fools' Day. To cap the climax, our teacher routed us out of the movie we had crashed and marched us back to class without further ado.

"April Fool," she said sweetly.

32

When Halloween mischief was afoot, I was generally in the midst of it. My brother Fearnley, with his penchant for getting into trouble, was the architect of most of our fiendish Halloween plans. Having tipped over most of the outhouses in town one Halloween, Fearnley decided it would look suspicious if ours were left upright. So, as a sort of afterthought, he led the assault on the little structure behind the Baker house. How was he to know that Father was lurking inside at the time—waiting for someone to try this feat?

My Dad was a man who kept a tight rein on his temper. When he heard charges against the boys, he would never punish them until the next day—when his temper had cooled off. I remember a trip to Salt Lake City when we had eleven flat tires—without evoking a single curse from Dad. But getting trapped inside the overturned outhouse that night made him angrier than we had ever seen him. Perhaps he was so enraged that he was afraid to ask the boys where they had been at the time, but nothing was said.

As I grew into adolescence, I was imbued with the notion that, to win the esteem of the opposite sex, you must be able to excel at their own games.

It was natural, then, that my heroine among the stars whose images flickered across the screen at the Princess Theater was neither America's sweetheart, Mary Pickford, nor the famous siren, Theda Bara. My ideal was Pearl White. She was the absolutely indestructible heroine of the serial thriller, *The Perils of Pauline*, an episode of which was shown at each Saturday matinee. She was the original cliff-hanger—a pretty blonde pursued by men, but more than a match in agility, stamina, and brains for all the burly villains who made her life one long, hair-raising adventure.

Why couldn't I be as daring and seductive as the dashing Pearl? This urge became especially strong when a new boy came to town. A handsome twelve-year-old man of the world from Salt Lake, he had all the appeal of a city boy for a small-town girl. I was determined to impress him.

So, with the boys of our gang acting as stooges, I organized the greatest of all the Perils of Pauline, to be enacted live and in full color. My friends were gleefully cast in the roles of the villains, while the new boy was to be the hero, waiting at the end of the chase to ride away with me into the sunset.

After giving me a short head start, the gang mounted broomstick steeds and charged after me. The whoops they let out were so realistically bloodcurdling that I began to wonder what would happen if this band of spurned friends actually did catch up with me.

But this was no impromptu affair. I scrambled up a row of heavy nails which I had driven in the woodshed, and climbed out onto the roof. Then I jumped to the roof of another building and clambered up on top of our porch. The villains, showing appropriate rage and frustration, discovered the way I had taken to the shed roof and now appeared to be closing in.

Sliding down the porch pillars, I raced to a sheer cliff and made my way, by a carefully explored route, to the top. As they followed me and clumsily clambered up the cliff, I jumped to a tree and poised for the final daring feat. I intended to swing out in a graceful arc with a rope tied to one of the branches, and land at the feet of my hero—who was waiting with an extra, saddled broomstick. There would follow a shy exchange of smiles and we would trot away together —as Pearl did to the strains of the Spring Song trilled out by the piano player in the pit.

I leaped at the rope—and missed. Down the hill I tumbled, more like Jill than Pauline, and wound up in a cloud of dust at my hero's feet. Instead of a beaming smile, I was greeted by a loud guffaw. What was worse still, the villains all gave up their pursuit and rolled on the ground, doubled up with laughter. What had started as high drama had turned into a Mack Sennett comedy. I never looked that boy in the eye again. Every time he saw me coming, he would snicker.

Surely, I thought, there must be a more effective way to impress the boys. As a tomboy I was just one of the gang and they weren't inclined to spare my girlish feelings. Even if I could beat them at their own games, they would only resent me. In the days that followed I reflected earnestly on my changing relationship with the opposite sex. Other girls were attracting beaux by different means. There was my closest friend, Miriam Eskelson, a doctor's daughter, for instance. She dressed beautifully and had that confident air about her which seemed to attract everyone.

But then, I reflected, Miriam came from a home where everything seemed to be pleasant and normal—no feast or famine, no train of brothers and sisters to watch—and she had a mother who had beautiful taste and plenty of time to sew. I was at the stage, I realize now, when children become ashamed of their families.

One day, I was taking the train to Salt Lake City and was standing on the platform dressed in my Sunday best. Then I saw Mother running up the long flight of stairs from the bottom of the canyon. She arrived breathless and handed me the ticket I had forgotten. She had rushed out in her house dress, her hair a little disarranged. And instead of appreciating what she had done, I just stood there wishing she'd go back home before anyone saw her that way.

And while other mothers were home entertaining the weekly card club, my mother was out working for Dr. Straupp's reelection as mayor. That year, my younger brother, Keith, was still an infant. Dr. Straupp had come booming into the house one day, his broad forehead deeply lined with worry.

"Clara," he shouted, "we're in trouble. You've just got

to drop everything and come along with me, if we're going to win this election."

"Now, doctorr, ye know yerrself that I've got a nurrsin' baby that's got to be fed everr' three 'ourrs."

"What do you think I've got a hospital for, woman?" he demanded impatiently. "Now bring your baby and come along."

So they took Keith to the hospital and put him in the care of a nurse. Then they started out to visit all Mother's friends, to make sure they were registered and would vote. Every three hours, they would rush back to the hospital so that Mother could nurse the baby.

In later years, of course, I could laugh at these "humiliations" and blush a little at my own callowness. But they seemed at the time to be as dreadful a social handicap as my personal appearance.

Mother still insisted on braiding my hair and tying a huge ribbon in it. I still had only one dress for school—oh, sometimes I would own two. Mother ordered us into long underwear and black stockings at the first sign of frost and we were not allowed to put on light underclothes until summer.

"Never change a clout 'til May's out," Mother would repeat firmly, whenever we protested that other youngsters were already in summer clothes.

The only way I could hope to conceal the dreadful long underwear from my school mates was to pull my long johns up out of my stockings and tuck the legs up inside my bloomers.

One day, I was late leaving home after lunch and ran all the way back to school. When I rushed breathlessly into class, everyone started to laugh. Even the teacher put her face behind a book to cover her smile. Finally, the girl next to me pointed to one of my legs. I saw that my long underwear had unrolled over the outside of my stocking. Though deeply humiliated, I made a great show of indifference, tucked the underwear back in, and walked haughtily out of the class.

Naturally, no child enjoys being scoffed at. Psychologists today attribute later success to early frustrations—I believe they call it compensation. Perhaps the childhood ridicule we suffer toughens us and increases the ambition to amount to something. At any rate, in my daydreams I saw myself achieving fame and fortune in the outside world, and returning triumphantly to the old home town, to the blare of trumpets and cheers of crowds. I'd be a stylish lady, of course, dressed in something far more alluring than the riding breeches and open-front shirt affected by my former heroine, Pearl White.

While I longed for fine feathers, I couldn't drum up any interest in making them myself. Our high-school sewing class was a great bore to me. I must admit that I became a nuisance, talking constantly and keeping others from their needlework. Finally, the teacher lost patience and said, "If you'd pay attention and stop chattering, you could learn to sew and wouldn't have to come to school in those awful things you wear."

My response was to get up and leave the class in high dudgeon. Once I was outside the door, tears of mortification began to flow, and I ran home to pour out the story to Mother. Like a hen with her chick in tow, she marched me back to school to see the principal, Mr. Neilson, a bald, heavy-set man who looked at you with penetrating eyes when you came to his office. You didn't invent excuses for Mr. Neilson when you were in trouble—you told him the exact truth. He listened attentively to my complaint about the sewing teacher and then called her in to apologize to Mother.

I was none too happy about tattling on teacher. But the family honor had to be upheld. Mother did all she could for us on her limited means—and no one could insult her with impunity.

37

This episode proved to be a boon in disguise. My sewing teacher gave me up as a hopeless case and I was allowed to take Spanish instead. It was a relief to switch from plying a ladylike needle to conjugating irregular verbs.

Looking back on my school days does not fill me with pride. Though I liked reading, I preferred my father's books to school texts. Homework often went by the board, while I read with more gusto than discrimination—everything from history, biography, geology, and other heavy books way beyond my comprehension, to *Little Women*, *Jane Eyre*, and Zane Grey westerns. During a long quarantine for smallpox that affected all of us, I went straight through all twenty volumes of *The Book of Knowledge*. Had this welter of information stayed with me, what a fortune I might have made on the quiz shows that dominate the air waves today.

At school I managed to get good marks—by studying my teachers more than my lessons. By catering to their special whims I made better grades than I deserved. For instance, our history instructor was a stickler for dates. So I would skim-read an assignment, making sure to memorize all the important dates, from 1066 to 1776. Another instructor liked nothing better than a good argument. When I failed to do my homework, I would precipitate a class debate—and he'd forget all about calling on us for lessons. One morning, he threatened to fail me for not doing a book report. Having counted on his forgetfulness, I reminded him that he had not kept his promise to order the book for me.

When he urged us all to go to college and study psychology, if possible, he glanced at me meaningfully. "As for you, Ivy—I don't think the psychology will be necessary."

To my foolish young ears this sounded like flattery. It was only in later years that I realized I had really outwitted myself by outwitting my teachers—for good grades did not a scholar make.

The part of the school year that we enjoyed most, of course, was the Christmas vacation. In our family each youngster was allowed to request just one present from Santa. We had enough sense to keep our wishes within reach of the family budget. In my first year in high school, I lost interest in pocket knives, ball bats, and jump ropes of other years. I knew exactly what I did want, however.

And it was there under the tree that Christmas morning— an imitation leather hatbox. I was filled with awe. Picking it up, I walked dreamily to my room. I posed languidly at the mirror, dangling the hatbox from my arm, and conjuring up beautiful visions of Lady Ivy, until Mother called to say that the roast goose was on the table.

Of course, I didn't possess a single hat to put in the box— but it was a start in the right direction.

My great dream was to be an actress, and the realization of this burning desire seemed within reach when the Salt Lake *Telegram* announced a movie contest for a film to be made in Salt Lake. The roles were to go to those who received most "votes," based on the number of subscriptions they sold to the newspaper.

I started through Bingham like one of those cold winter winds which somehow managed to creep through doors and windows. I got into every house, all right; and, perhaps because my mother and dad were so well liked, I sold scores of subscriptions. To my own great consternation, I finished up with the second lead in the movie.

My confusion was nothing, however, compared to that of the movie people when they saw me. What could they do with a gangly girl of fourteen as second lead in a movie? But they thought of something and put me into one big scene where I danced in a beautiful, but abbreviated, costume.

Of course, the film had to be shown in Bingham, where the only movie house was owned by the Cheslers, our close friends and neighbors. I was so excited on opening night that I couldn't eat a bite of dinner. I sat in the dark theater, which was packed with those who had made my quick rise to stardom possible, waiting for my big scene. Suddenly I danced out on the screen, and there was a moment of silence. Then the audience broke into howling laughter.

Towering on the screen like an animated beanstalk, I seemed to consist mostly of scrawny legs and sharp elbows. How awful I looked! I wanted to run away and hide in a dark hole. If only they would stop showing the picture—but it kept on and on and so did the laughter. Unable to bear any more of it, I slipped out of the theater before the movie was over, crept home, and cried myself to sleep.

By morning, I steeled myself to face the teasing I would get at school. . . . But at least the movie was not a total loss. One of those who had won a part was a girl named Fay Wray. The director gave her a terrible dressing-down and told her she would never get anywhere in the movies. She went on to prove his judgment wrong, of course.

Those were difficult years, for I was going through the troubled transition from girlhood to womanhood. And the psychology that worked on the teachers had no effect whatever on the boys.

I despaired of ever getting a date. At high-school dances I would sit on the sidelines with other wallflowers, watching the popular girls float by with their swains. When a boy had the courage to dance with me, I towered over him like a swaying Amazon. And the bravado with which I covered my self-consciousness did nothing to enhance my charm. Sensing my unhappiness, Mother was determined to help me.

Luckily, Dad hit a rich streak during my sophomore year. This touched Mother off on a shopping spree, but her enthusiasm outran her judgment. She brought home what she thought was an elegant outfit for the next school dance—a bright yellow satin dress with ruffles, a pale green moiré coat, and a green bonnet with a rakish feather at the side. For the price of this costume she could have bought me five or six much-needed school dresses—but that was Mother's way.

Looking like a Maypole in yellow ruffles, I set out for the dance, with hope in my heart and Mother's praises ringing in my ears. But, alas, it took more than gold satin to make me belle of the ball.

One gallant youth did ask me to dance toward the end of the evening. Very much flustered, I blushed and stammered my way through the number, feeling like a flamingo in hoop skirts.

The next morning, in the locker room at school, I overheard some girls laughing about me.

"That Jim'll do anything on a dare," one of them giggled. "I bet he'd dance with Pinhead Nielson, if you dared him."

"Did you see her face?" asked another girl. "She looked so surprised! That's what I got a kick out of."

After I recovered from this humiliation, I realized that I owed those girls a debt for a lesson I have never forgotten. For I resolved then and there never to participate in a joke or action which would hurt anyone else's feelings. Today, I still feel so drawn to the lonely and neglected that whenever I see anyone standing alone at a gathering I introduce myself and make sure the man or woman meets my friends.

It is easy to look back upon my painful adolescence with the hindsight of adulthood and say those years were good for me. But I believe this is true. The hard knocks took a lot of the tomboy cocksureness out of me. I wondered, when I saw the advantages that other girls had, why it was that some had so much and others so little. It was not easy to take it when the kids laughed at me and made fun of my clothes. But such trials become insignificant in retrospect and I suppose they helped develop a resistance to adversity.

Mother and my Aunt Gert felt that I needed new interests and friends. So Aunt Gert, who was now living in Salt Lake City, suggested that I spend the school year with her and attend the Latter-Day Saints High School, coming back to Bingham for weekends.

Aunt Gert was like a second mother to all of us, and we had visited back and forth all through the years of my childhood. She was heavier than Mother, but her figure was supple and slim-legged, and she could do a Highland fling or Scottish sword dance as gracefully as any slender young thing. Her manner was sharper than Mother's, but she spoke with the same rich accent and respected the same set of beliefs and superstitions. She had the habit of ripping out an occasional "damn," causing Dad to look up and raise his eyebrows with surprise.

Her husband, Uncle Lije, was a tall, spare, dour man who seldom spoke. Dad said this was because Aunt Gert never stopped talking and, if so, it was a comfortable arrangement. Uncle Lije hardly uttered more than three sentences in the course of an evening and usually these gems of thought went unheard by Aunt Gert—for she was quite hard of hearing. She would see Uncle Lije's lips moving and demand:

"What'd 'e say? Is 'e talking aboot me again?"

Life at Aunt Gert's house was something of an education in itself. She and Uncle Lije had once operated a small confectionery store where the business consisted largely of "a penny's worth of this and a penny's worth of that." They enjoyed a hearty respect for the penny ever after and when a dollar came into the house it was treated like royalty—and was expected to stay for a long time. In the morning, Aunt Gert would study the grocery ads in the paper and start out on a shopping tour. She would travel any distance to save three cents and come home to announce triumphantly:

"Got a real barge-in today in 'amburrgerr."

"You mean 'bargain,' Aunt Gert," I would say.

"I call it barge-in," she would reply, with a firm snap of her head.

We lived in the kitchen at Aunt Gert's—saving heat and wear and tear on the good furniture. They had a parlor, furnished in Aunt Gert's version of overstuffed elegance, but no one ever went in there except to look at it. After twenty years, the furniture was still as good as new.

The big school in Salt Lake, with its thousands of students, was quite a change from our Bingham schoolhouse. And to a small-town girl, the large, wonderfully clean, and well-laid-out city seemed like a veritable Utopia. Situated in a lush valley at the foot of the snow-capped Wasatch mountains, it had broad tree-lined streets, well-kept houses and lawns, beautiful gardens and parks. Towering above the city was the marble, domed state capitol, and below it stood the historic Mormon Temple with the gold statue of the angel Moroni shining atop its spire.

I marveled over the tall buildings with their glittering electric signs, wandered dreamily through the well-stocked department stores, and sat entranced through the vaudeville acts at the Pantages and Orpheum theaters—whenever Aunt Gert, who also loved the theater, felt that a special treat justified the price of admission.

The year at Salt Lake must have rubbed some rough edges off the self-conscious schoolgirl. When I returned home, Bingham seemed smaller and more confined than ever. I missed the bright lights and the hustle and bustle of the big city. A glimpse of broader horizons only increased my longing for faraway places.

When an invitation came to visit an old friend in San Francisco, I was beside myself with excitement.

"It will only be for the summer," I said, pleading with Mother to let me go. "We can afford it, can't we? It won't cost anything to stay at the Eskelsons' and I'll be careful—"

"Now 'old it a bit!" Mother cut short my outburst. "Ye'll have to ask yer father."

Dad was in the living room, with little Keith cradled on his knees, and I noticed he was reading a new book. This, coupled with the fact that Mother was making steak-and-kidney pie, was proof that prosperity was back. When I broached the subject to Dad, he thought it over carefully.

"San Francisco's a long way," he said finally. "That's *really* the end of the world."

He had never stopped teasing me about our arrival in Bingham.

"Well, if you're sure you won't fall off, I guess we can spare the train fare."

So I packed the battered old family suitcase and started for San Francisco that June. Someone had told me it was cold there, so I went off garbed in a heavy coat, which Mother had remodeled from a friend's hand-me-down. My long, braided hair, wound around my head, was topped with a burnt-orange straw hat, with beads all over it—another contribution from a neighbor. At last, I had a chance to use my prized hatbox.

As I stepped off the train, I felt like the original country cousin, especially when the Eskelsons, beautifully groomed and poised as always, met me. But their warm greeting put me at ease at once.

Miriam and her mother had moved from Bingham a few years earlier and we had a lot of gossip to catch up on. Miriam had bobbed her hair in the new style and still radiated that certain air which I envied so much. She looked at my long hair speculatively, as I unbraided it before going to bed.

"Isn't that a lot of bother?" she said. "Why don't you get it cut like mine?"

I caught my breath at the daring idea, wondering for a

moment what Mother would say—but I made up my mind quickly.

"All right, I will."

When my long braids had been chopped off and my hair was dressed in the new Irene Castle style, I looked even more incongruous in my Bingham best. With this head start, Miriam began to tackle the clothes situation. She tactfully insisted that I share her wardrobe until we could assemble my own, and her mother offered to sew some clothes for me. Mrs. Lynch, a childless friend of hers, took me on shopping trips as if I were her own daughter. In their generous hands I felt like Cinderella being dressed for the ball.

Primping at the mirror, I could hardly believe the transformation. The gangling greenhorn had become a smart city girl—at least, in outward appearance. But, as the saying goes, fine feathers don't make fine birds. " 'Andsome is as 'andsome does," Mother would say.

I determined to emulate Miriam in deed and word. For she was the very model of a well-bred young lady. If she could manage her five-foot-eight figure gracefully, why couldn't I manage mine? We went dancing quite often and it was a relief to find that the Amazon was now matched in size by the dashing young men who squired us around.

That enchanted seventeenth summer opened an entirely new and fascinating world to me. There was so much to see and do that the golden days slipped far too quickly behind the Golden Gate.

We drove to the beach, and spent many a gay afternoon watching the seals cavort on Seal Rock and lunching at the Cliff House. There was also the lure of Chinatown, the delectable sea food on Fisherman's Wharf, and the rides on the picturesque cable cars to Nob Hill where a panoramic view of the entire Bay area unfolded. Wherever we went we seemed to become the center of an animated crowd. Were the boys attracted to us only because of Miriam's great beauty and charm—or had a little of her appeal rubbed off on me?

This world-shaking question was put to a test one night at a party given by one of Miriam's friends.

"Look at that tall, dark boy over there," she whispered. "Isn't he attractive? Wonder who he is."

He was indeed a handsome fellow, with dark, wavy hair, regular features, and a pleasant smile. I felt a pang of envy as I watched him dance with Miriam. Oh, well, I sighed—she got them all.

But a few minutes later, I was astonished to see him nodding toward me, and Miriam brought him over to make the introduction.

There are people who win one's heart without apparent effort. Gay, handsome Harry, with his Southern drawl and courtly manners, had just such a fatal charm. I hung enraptured on every word, as he explained that he came from North Carolina and had a good job in San Francisco. After he asked if he could see me again, I floated home on clouds.

When he called for me the following evening, I was so flustered that I stumbled through introductions. To my delight, even an older woman like Mrs. Eskelson was captured by his charm.

After that first date I went out with no one but Harry. No one else really mattered. If San Francisco had been captivating before, it took on an even greater enchantment when we explored it together.

The summer ended all too soon. It was a great wrench to tear myself away from San Francisco—and especially from Harry. But now I had something exciting to look forward to through the long winter in Bingham. For Harry promised to come and meet my family in the spring.

IV

IT was through misty eyes that I saw the faces of Harry, Miriam, and Mrs. Eskelson slide by the window when my train pulled out of Oakland. But my spirits soared the moment I caught sight of the family waiting at the station in Bingham the following day.

They couldn't have changed much in two short months, but I now saw them with fresh eyes. Mother, in her early forties, was getting a little stouter, and her hair, quite gray now, framed her strong, youthful face with its creamy English complexion. Fearnley and Max—grown into robust adolescence—were trying to get free samples out of the chewing gum machine. Lloyd was industriously pulling the braided pigtails of Gertrude and Lynn. Only Keith, perched on Dad's shoulder, seemed to be taking any real interest in the arrival of the train.

But when I stepped off there was a joyous whoop, as they all rushed to greet me. Fearnley shook hands—he had gotten one of those electric buzzers from a mail-order house—and roared happily when I screamed. A year before, I would have chased him, and caught him, but now I was a dignified young lady in no mood for childish pranks.

When we got back to the big old house, Mother eyed my new clothes with obvious approval. Though she had never had the opportunity to develop a sense of high style, she knew good things when she saw them.

I hesitated for a moment before taking off my hat to reveal my bobbed hair. The Irene Castle bob had not yet taken hold in Bingham and I expected her to be shocked, but to my amazement she looked pleased.

"I 'ope ye saved a lock for luck," she said.

"I did, Mother," I said with relief, opening a new gold locket which Harry had given me. "See?"

There was a lock of brown hair—and, on the other side, a picture of Harry. Mother stared at it curiously.

" 'Andsome chap . . . 'oo's 'e?" she asked at last.

"Harry."

" 'Arry 'oo?"

" 'Arry . . . I mean, Harry Howard Hicks."

" 'Arry 'Oward 'Icks? Well, therr's a name ferr ye."

"For heaven's sake, Ivy—couldn't you have found a fellow named Rralph Rroberrt Rricharrdson or something she could pronounce?" Dad said with a chuckle.

It was good to be back in the warmth of our family— joining the evening prayers, watching Mother bustle around, and marveling at the way Dad could, by a quiet word and stern look, break up indoor football games, six-day tricycle races, or blazing civil war among the boys.

When school opened, my classmates seemed to notice that the ugly duckling had sprouted some new feathers, and dates were no longer a problem. Free of many adolescent frustrations, I was able to concentrate all the better on my studies and to participate in many extracurricular activities. As assistant editor of the school paper, captain of our debating team, member of the student council, and lead in the senior play, I had the busiest and happiest year of my entire school life.

At home things had brightened, for Dad's lease was still yielding well. He celebrated our continuing prosperity by stopping by the Bingham Merc from time to time to buy a surprise for Mother. One night, he came home with a green wool coat. Mother gulped and tried her best to be gracious about it.

"Of all the colors I 'ate, it's green," she told me in private. " 'E should know 'ow I 'ate green."

A couple of weeks later, Dad came trailing home with a piece of lovely and expensive blue velvet out of which he expected her to make a shirtwaist.

"Now where woold I wearr it?" she asked me indignantly. " 'E should know with all these chillrren aboot, I can't wearr a fancy thing like that. 'E's runnin' amook."

It became my job to act as intermediary and take careful note of what Mother wanted and to pass the secret word along to Dad. The surprises began to hit the target after that.

As autumn turned into winter and the holiday season approached, we seemed destined to have the merriest Christmas of all. For once, we were all in good health and there was gift money hidden in the sugar bowl. It would be my last Christmas at home, although I did not suspect this at the time.

After our exuberant Christmas Aunt Gert and Uncle Lije joined us for the New Year's Eve celebration. Mother and Aunt Gert had a big day, engaged in their favorite indoor sport—arguing interminably about minute details out of their past life. The men sat quietly near the stove while Mother and Aunt Gert gave themselves over to a full-dress debate on whether it had been Cousin Lucy or Aunt Edith who had gotten the lucky sixpence out of the family plum pudding the Christmas of '93.

"It was Cousin Lucy," Aunt Gert said stoutly. "I remember she started cryin', she did. Thought she'd bit th' end off 'er spoon."

"Put yer 'and out and see if ye're awake, Gert," Mother said firmly. "That was the year before. Aunt Edith broke 'er new gold crown on th' coin in '93."

"Christmas in England musta been a blessin' for the dentists," Uncle Lije observed drily.

"What'd 'e say?" Aunt Gert demanded fiercely. "Is that old fool talkin' aboot me?"

New Year's Eve was Uncle Lije's night to shine. Mother and Aunt Gert had established in our household their English custom of "first-footing" on New Year's. In their encyclopedia of superstitions, one of the worst omens of ill fortune that could befall a home was to have a dark man be the first to cross the threshold in the New Year. To forestall this dire possibility, they kept Uncle Lije poised and ready to dash around to the front door as soon as the clock had tolled twelve on December 31.

He rushed out of the back door on cue that year, and appeared a few seconds later at the front door. He knocked, then stood in the doorway, his thin, dour face quite solemn, as he began the traditional chant:

"The old year out, the New Year in,
Please to let the lucky bird in.
With a pocket full of money
And a cellar full of beer,
Good luck to last you all the year."

Recalling how things had turned out in previous years, in spite of first-footings, I could not escape the impression that the lucky bird had slipped up somewhere. But this was 1924

50

and it certainly looked like a lucky year. It was to be an important year for me. But lucky? Even now, I do not know.

Since times were good, we had our traditional oyster stew on New Year's Day. There were fruit cake and wine for the other first-footers who stopped by that day. Since we were Mormons, we took no stimulants—except for Mother's cup of afternoon tea. Dad explained that she needed it for her health.

Spring came early that year. The melting snow set little freshets dancing down the hills and the fir-scented winds of the West whispered through the canyon. I felt it all in my heart—the end of the long winter of my childhood and the growing, stirring sense of adulthood.

Harry and I corresponded regularly. His letters were becoming more ardent and he kept urging me to marry him after I graduated from school in May. But I was determined to go on to college and study law.

Just the day before graduation, I was called from class to take a long-distance telephone call in Mr. Neilson's office.

"Where are you?" I asked excitedly, when Harry's voice came over the wire.

"In Salt Lake City, kid," he replied. "How do I get to Bingham?"

Hardly believing my ears, I stammered directions. The following day, I met Harry at the station and took him straight home to meet the family. My brothers and sisters stood around staring at him as if he were a man from Mars, and then went whooping out of the house while Mother and I got supper ready.

"Well, your 'Arry looks a fine young man," said Mother, whose approval filled me with joy. " 'Is intentions must be serious, if 'e's come all this way."

Meantime, Dad and Harry were having a man-to-man talk in the front parlor.

One night, shortly after graduation, Dad and I sat down to discuss my future. We had often talked about the possibility of my entering law school. It is our Mormon belief that the glory of God is intelligence, and so our church pays particular attention to education. I knew that Dad wanted me to attend college. But he had six younger children to raise and an unstable income, and the chances looked remote. He studied the matter carefully, as was his habit. Then he said gravely that we simply could not afford four years of tuition.

I could see the troubled look on his face, and knew how much he valued education. But I realized there was no use in denying the hard facts. I guess my eyes filled with tears, for he looked at me with deep sympathy, and said softly:

"As you go through this life, my girl, you'll find that you seldom get the things you'd like to have. In fact, very rarely do you get what you want. So if you would be happy as you go through life, you'll make what you *get* be what you want."

Of course, I might have attempted to put myself through school instead of accepting Dad's decision with resignation. But the prospect of marriage began to edge out thoughts of college. Harry had taken a job in Salt Lake and came out to the house on weekends. Propinquity certainly made the heart grow fonder.

In the meantime, I needed some spending money, so when I learned that Theodore Chesler, owner of the Princess Theater, needed a ticketseller, I applied for the job—which certainly had its advantages. After the box office closed, I would slip into the theater and watch my favorite silent-screen stars in the current attractions—Rudolph Valentino in *Monsieur Beaucaire*, Gloria Swanson in *Manhandled*, Norma Talmadge in *Secrets*, Harold Lloyd in *Girl Shy*.

As I sat in the little booth doling out tickets and change, I tried to follow Dad's advice and make this job be what I wanted. But I knew there was more to the world than what I could see from the glass window of the Princess Theater, and the Hollywood never-never land that unfolded on the screen confirmed this notion.

One soft June night, Harry picked me up after work. We walked home arm in arm and sat down on the porch to watch a full moon light up the mountain peaks. Perhaps the magical night made us feel more romantic than ever. Harry painted a glowing picture of the sort of life we would have together. I was deeply smitten. My head whirled with visions of the gay, adventurous time we'd have—visions far removed from the realities of marriage. Before we parted that night we set a date, and I went to bed blissfully thinking of Harry, too elated to sleep, impatiently waiting for morning so that I could break the news to Mother and Dad.

What can one say about an unfortunate early marriage? I'd like to skip it, not write about it at all, but it was a part of my life—perhaps a very educational part—and it would be dishonest to pretend it hadn't happened.

Like all young couples, we started with high hopes and many illusions. After a small wedding at home on July 31, 1924, we drove off to Yellowstone for our honeymoon. Our future seemed as bright as the moon that lighted our way through the craggy, brooding Rockies on those enchanted nights.

Our wedding trip was no sooner over than Harry confessed he had thrown up his job—without a word to me. He wavered between the urge to try his luck in California or go back home to North Carolina. I was imbued with the notion that a woman should be ready to follow her husband anywhere.

"Tell you what, kid," Harry said, with his carefree air. "I'll flip a coin. Heads, we go east—and tails we go west."

This seemed a strange way to make such an important

decision. But, as a bride of nineteen thoroughly in love, I had unbounded faith in Harry's judgment. So when the coin came up east, we blithely set forth in Harry's Ford for Rocky Mount, North Carolina. On the way we had our first spat—though you could scarcely call it one, for there were no angry words between us. For some unfathomable reason, Harry simply stopped talking to me and lapsed into a sulky mood that lasted for days. Try as I might, I couldn't seem to penetrate the wall between us. By the time we reached Rocky Mount in a scorching heat wave, I was so miserable and lonely that I would have given anything to turn back, rather than face Harry's family.

Luckily, his father possessed all the understanding and kindness that Harry lacked. A tall, snowy-haired gentleman of the old school, "Daddy" Hicks greeted us affectionately. "We're happy to have you here, Ivy," he said, clasping my hand with old-fashioned courtesy. "I must give Harry credit for making a good choice."

The deep freeze into which my heart had settled began to melt. If it hadn't been for Daddy Hicks's gentle sympathy, I would have given up then and there. For the moody spell that struck my husband on our trip east became more or less chronic. From the gay, high-spirited companion of our courtship, he was transformed into a withdrawn, brooding man who seemed completely indifferent to his home and wife. His selling job kept him on the road a good deal. I never knew when he was due back until he hung his hat in the hall. His presence did little to relieve my loneliness, and the effort to adapt myself to a new environment often left me bewildered and uncertain.

I wasn't raised in a home where people got up whistling "Dixie," and I had to get used to other customs of the South. I loved Southern cooking, but had much to learn about it. For instance, the green bean, to me, had always been a canned vegetable which we ate every now and then. That this was a total misconception became clear the first time I tried to cook fresh beans for my husband. He took one bite and gave up. Being eager to please, I undertook to investigate the local formula for preparing green beans. But it seemed too complicated for me to grasp, involving the use of black kettles, ham fat, hours of work, and some incantations in a deep Southern dialect that I could not master.

Then I came face to face with a number of items on the bill of fare which my Mother, in all compassion, had not warned me about. There were grits—which I thought were for canaries until I got to North Carolina—greens, fat back, and okra. If we hadn't been invited to eat with Harry's family quite frequently, I am sure we would both have perished from malnutrition.

Our finances didn't fare much better. Harry was one of those restless men who are always devising schemes for making their fortunes elsewhere. With frequent job changes and moves, our debts piled up menacingly.

Since Southern men prefer to keep their wives at home, I broached as tactfully as possible the subject of getting a job. Harry raised no objection—in fact, he welcomed the idea. So I found work as a sales clerk in a local department store. Our combined salaries helped pay off our outstanding debts. But my job did nothing to improve our relationship—for now Harry resented my so-called independence.

Luckily, we were then living in Petersburg, next door to a delightfully gregarious family, the Baxters, who led the kind of life I understood—exuberant, happy, and close-knit. Mrs. Baxter—Miss Molly to the neighborhood—filled the empty place left in my life by separation from my own mother; and her daughters, Nellie, Grace, and Madeline, became my closest friends.

When Harry was away, I virtually lived next door. I had

never worked out the intricacy of making corn bread, so I made a barter arrangement with Miss Molly. In exchange for the light bread I made for her family, she gave me corn bread to slip on our table when Harry was at home.

Daddy Hicks, who had developed angina pectoris, took a turn for the worse that fall. We were called to Rocky Mount, where he was in bed under the care of a nurse.

Just a short time before lunch one day I was sitting in his room, when I had one of those strange, psychic experiences I've never been able to explain. Suddenly I had an eerie sense of premonition and walked over to Daddy's bed. I asked the nurse what time it was.

"Ten of twelve," she said.

"Is anything wrong with him?" I whispered, nodding toward Mr. Hicks, who lay with his eyes closed, apparently asleep.

"He seems all right," she said reassuringly.

I went over to my sister-in-law, Kate, who was standing by the window.

"Kate, I just have a feeling he's going to die at twelve."

She gave me a shocked, disbelieving look. The nurse went back to reading a book.

At noon the whistles of the tobacco plants began to shrill. I got a sudden chilly feeling. Mr. Hicks started to gasp—and before we reached his side, he passed on.

This tragic timing may seem incredible. I cannot account for it rationally, nor can I attempt to explain the weird psychic sense I seem to have inherited from my mother, who had similar experiences. Perhaps in time experiments in extrasensory perception, like those conducted by Dr. Rhine of Duke University, will solve the riddle of these phenomena.

In any case, Daddy Hicks's death left me stricken, and I felt that it took all the meaning out of my marriage. With him gone, there was no one to turn to for comfort or advice.

56

With the coming of spring, Harry's feet began to itch again. His job bored him, he said. And again the perennial question arose: where to next?

He discarded an idea as fast as it arose. Finally, we agreed on California. It was impossible to see how any change could be for the worse. So we disposed of our house and belongings, and I went on ahead for a short visit with my family. En route to the train Harry began to wonder whether Washington might offer greener fields than California.

My patience, worn thin by his constant vacillation, finally gave out. "Harry, I'm just sick of all this uncertainty!" I exploded. "I never know what we're going to do next. Perhaps I'd better go home and stay."

"O.K., if that's the way you feel," he said, with a shrug. "Go ahead and stay. Who cares?"

"That's just it—you don't seem to."

By the time I reached home I had decided that there was no future in our marriage. Worst of all, Harry had never wanted children, so there was nothing to show for our four years together.

When I told Mother that I wasn't going back to my husband, she was deeply disturbed. "Everr' married couple 'as theirr differences," she pointed out. "They just 'ave to worrk them out. Have you done your part?"

"I've tried my best. But it just isn't any good. Besides, I want children and Harry is dead set against them."

For the first time since I had been a tiny girl and rebelled against a certain set of ribbons Mother wanted to put in my hair, I set myself firmly against her wishes. Dad listened to my story with grave eyes.

"I don't think marriage can be treated lightly," he said. "But none of us is perfect and none of us knows everything. We all have to live our own lives. Whatever you think is best, Ivy, will be all right with your mother and me."

In the weeks that followed there was ample time for self-analysis. It was tempting to absolve myself of blame. But in most cases, it's the wife who must make the greatest compromises, who yields and bends to her husband's whims and moods. Had I been too impatient with Harry? Would he outgrow his wanderlust and settle down in time?

At last, my parents urged me to see if we couldn't iron out our differences. With conflicting emotions of hope and dejection, I embarked on a long bus ride across the continent —it seemed the longest ride I have ever taken. En route, the urge to get off and turn back was overpowering.

Why was I making the trip, I kept asking myself, if I couldn't even summon a sense of anticipation or eagerness about seeing Harry again. He was one of those restless, immature men, I realized, who tired of everything the moment they achieved it. The chase was all that really mattered to him. Once he had gained what he wanted, he began to long for something else—another job, a new experience, a new sensation. I knew that neither a satisfying marriage nor a stable career could ever come of such an approach to life.

When I reached Rocky Mount, I called Harry's sister Norma, who asked me to stay with her. Harry came in reluctantly late that evening. Carefree and handsome as ever, he eyed me coolly and, without a welcoming kiss or even a handshake, he said casually, "Hello, there—surprised to see you. Why did you come back?"

My heart sank in dismay. "I don't know why I came. Perhaps it was a great mistake."

When Norma and her husband Tom had gone to bed, Harry and I sat in front of the dying fire, writing a melancholy little epitaph to it all. Each of us felt that the other had been at fault and didn't seem inclined to give an inch.

"What are we going to do?" he asked.

"I don't know. I don't see how we can patch things up and go on."

"I don't either," he said. "As a matter of fact, I've found someone else."

"That's quite natural. I guess that's about all there is to it." I sighed. "I'd better go on back."

"Is there anything I can do for you?"

"Well, since you mention it . . . yes. You can pay my way back home."

"All right, kid," he said, with apparent relief that he'd gotten out of it so easily.

With a heavy heart, I left for Utah a few days later. It was not easy to admit defeat. But, as the miles rolled away, the clouds of self-doubt and uncertainty began to lift. Come what might, I was sure of one thing. From now on I couldn't depend on anyone else to shape my life. It was sink or swim on my own.

When I reached home, Mother said simply, "Well, what is to be will be."

I never saw Harry again. Some time later I was shocked to learn that he had been killed in a plane crash. The sorrow I felt was over the untimely loss of a human being. By that time our estrangement was so complete that I could only weep for Harry as a man who had died too young and needlessly.

Having rushed into a youthful, ill-considered marriage in my eagerness to experience love and life, I now had to start afresh. My confidence was shaken by this failure, but I knew that bitterness and self-pity were futile. Besides, the demands of daily living left no time for brooding. My family was in one of its lean periods, as the mines were running at only half shift. I was determined to find a job and give them all the help I could. It wasn't ambition that drove me to seek a career, but necessity that caused a career to seek me out.

V

THE autumn of 1929 was a singularly inopportune time to make a fresh start. That October the stock market crashed and unemployment rose by leaps and bounds. Since we owned no stocks or bonds, the great crash seemed of minor significance, affecting (we thought) only the big Wall Street manipulators and having nothing to do with our small world. But when Fearnley and Max lost their jobs and Dad went on reduced pay, we began to understand what the depression meant.

Mother and Aunt Gert fought the economic crisis with the only weapon at their command: frugality. Aunt Gert insisted that the whole thing would have been prevented if people hadn't thrown their money around and gone on wild spending sprees. She became even more careful about switching off the lights and about honoring her pet superstitions, such as not walking under ladders, opening umbrellas in the house, or spilling salt. In a mighty effort to break the back of the depression, the Baker family always put its right shoes on first and kept its hats off the beds.

On New Year's Eve, 1930, Uncle Lije's impersonation of the Lucky Bird seemed a singularly brave, if futile, gesture. There he stood that cold night in the doorway, this somewhat gaunt gentleman looking as if he had just bitten into a sour pickle, asking that we admit him as the bearer of good tidings for all the year. Well, I reflected, the way things are going we should be thankful that it is Uncle Lije tapping at the door. I had half expected to find the Raven quothing "Nevermore."

Such concerted assaults upon the forces of ill as we made seemed to have little effect. We counted ourselves lucky even to have a roof over our heads, as foreclosures and evictions were commonplace in those days. During one of Dad's prosperous streaks, Mother had persuaded him to make a down payment on a pretty little bungalow in Salt Lake City. For she had never abandoned the dream of living in an attractive home like the English parsonage. They had rented the Salt Lake City house for some years, the rental covering the mortgage payments.

In a lean period, they had fallen so far behind on these payments that they were in danger of losing the house. Aunt Gert and Uncle Lije came to the rescue and paid off the mortgage, thus saving the homestead.

For many months we paid this debt back out of the rent money. But one day, Mother decided that Dad needed a new easy chair and spent the money instead at a furniture store. When Dad found out, he was furious.

"But Gert doesn't need the money," Mother insisted.

"It doesn't matter whether she needs it or not," Dad said firmly, his eyes hard as rocks. "We owe it to her, and from now on that money will go straight to her."

It did, too. And finally the place had all been paid for and my family left Bingham to live in it. In the depths of the depression, it was a great boon to have a mortgage-free home, though maintenance was quite another problem.

Dad and I were now the main breadwinners for the entire family. He was still working part time in the Bingham mine, while I found a job as a long-distance telephone operator, earning a basic salary of eighteen dollars a week. By taking the night shift and working over weekends, I was able to pick up an extra four dollars a week. I had started on the job with the notion that I could save enough money to get to college—but the dream crashed, along with the stock market.

Poor Fearnley tramped the streets every day. Though he found only an occasional odd job, he returned for dinner with some flippant wisecrack to hide his frustration and disappointment. Max and Lloyd took paper routes and caddied at the golf course, while Mother did practical nursing. With all these odd jobs and odd hours, our home life became quite disjointed. Dad was out of the house early and, since I worked in the evenings, I would see him only on a day off. His black hair was streaked with gray now and there was a worried look in his expressive gray eyes. He was troubled by a bad cough, but refused to see a doctor.

One cold gray morning in February, he set out for Bingham in a car pool with several other miners. The car broke down in a blinding snowstorm.

"There was a gas station back there," Dad said. "I'll go back and call one of my boys to pick us up in my car."

As he walked along the highway, head bent into the storm, a speeding car bore down on him, attempting to pass another auto. It struck Dad and tossed him into the air like a whirling stick.

When the call came notifying us of the accident, Mother got me out of bed and we rushed to the little suburban hospital where Dad was being treated.

"His leg is broken," the doctor said. "And he's got some

nasty cuts around his head. But it doesn't seem too serious."

I almost collapsed with relief. Mother stood firm.

"Will it be all right to take him home?" she asked.

"I don't see why not," the doctor said.

Tenderly, we moved him back to his own bed. But his head had hardly settled on the pillow when he lost consciousness. In a panic, we called our family doctor.

"I suspect a fractured skull," he said gravely. "We can't move him right now."

Day after day, Dad lay there unconscious while one or another of us kept watch at his bedside. The days grew into weeks and we tiptoed around the house, white-faced and frightened. We realized just how much we had come to depend upon his quiet strength to see us through. We found ourselves forced to make all our own decisions without his thoughtful counsel. It was almost as if the family had lost its center of gravity.

At the end of the third week, Mother asked the church elders to form a prayer circle for Dad. They stood around his bed with us and we all prayed for his recovery. But Dad just lay there, pale and seemingly unhearing, through it all.

The next day, he opened his eyes briefly and seemed to be trying to smile.

Then, about a month after he had slipped into coma, Dad opened his eyes and smiled at us wanly. The doctor felt it was safe to transfer him to the hospital, where he completed his recovery. But when we got him home again, we noticed that his cough was still bothering him. Before we could even talk to the doctor about this, Dad got violent stomach cramps —and went back to the hospital with a ruptured appendix.

Though the operation was a success, his coughing spells persisted. But he paid no attention to them. He liked nothing better than a game of whist or five hundred or checkers with one of the boys.

"Prosperity's just around the corner," Fearnley would wisecrack. "If it doesn't get here soon, these checkers'll be so thin we can spend them for dimes."

"Doesn't it seem to you that Dad's cough is worse?" I asked my brother.

"He just coughs when I've got four kings on the board to his one. He's tryin' to blow the tops off mine."

When the doctor stopped by next time, Mother talked to him about the cough and he decided to run some tests. Then we learned the worst.

Dad had silicosis.

His lungs had been permeated with tiny particles of metal dust during the years when he had worked underground. Now these tiny, sharp pieces of metal were literally cutting his lungs to pieces. There was no pain, outside the discomfort of the cough.

"I'll be back on my feet before long," Dad predicted confidently.

But we knew there was no cure for silicosis at that time.

We had received no redress from the man whose car had struck Dad. In those days few people carried car insurance and this man was supporting nine children on what he earned from a part-time job. His total assets were sub-zero. To pay Dad's medical bills, we had mortgaged the house for two thousand dollars—and that was now all spent.

After dinner, the family would gather in the living room for prayer and then Dad would get the young ones started on their homework. He would play a few games of checkers and Mother would take out her sewing basket.

When I got home from work late at night, I would often find Mother still up, putting patches on the patches on our clothes. Every cent that any of us earned went into the family kitty, but there was nothing left for new clothes, and Mother was determined to keep up appearances.

The grim, gripping feeling of poverty hung like a pall over

everything in those days. We were not strangers to poverty, but always before we had felt hope—when this spell was over, things were just bound to improve!

Somehow this was different. Poverty seemed to be everywhere around us and hope was hard to muster.

But the depression and Dad's illness brought us closer together as a family than we had ever been. In those long evenings we spent together—we had no money to go out—we tried to keep each other cheerful. When the others had gone to bed, Dad, Mother, and I would sit up late mulling over ways and means to spread the little bit of money we had to best effect.

Could we afford a new pair of shoes for Lynn this week—or should we keep her out of school until I had another payday? Could we talk the assistant cashier at the bank into letting us skip a mortgage payment? If so, we could probably get Lloyd's tonsils taken out by a doctor who would perform the operation in his office for only fifteen dollars. It was comforting just to share our burdens and sustain each other's morale. The next morning we'd smile and reassure the younger children that all was well.

But we knew we were fighting a losing battle. We needed help.

Elsewhere, I suppose it might be called by the name of charity or relief. But those were not words that we Mormons used. In good times, we tithe our incomes and use part of the tithe to maintain the church welfare program. In times of need, church members can draw from this storehouse.

The Mormon Church is so organized that there is a bishop assigned to each ward of the church. The bishop, like all our church leaders, is a volunteer, who gives gladly of his time to see to the needs of those in the ward. Our bishop, Carl C. Burton, would visit us regularly, and as he saw the family fortunes declining he would send help from the church welfare organization, or, as we called it, the Lord's storehouse. We maintain a chain of farms, storehouses, and granaries where enough food and clothing are kept to supply every Mormon for a year. Thus, the bounty of all our people is distributed to those in need. It was this source of welfare which sustained our family now.

We did not feel as though we were on relief, for we made a contribution of work in return for the things we received from the church. Mother spent hours working in the cannery and the boys did odd jobs. We were made to feel that we were earning our way, rather than being given a handout.

Every dime I earned at the telephone company went into the family till, but it was like a drop in an empty bucket. I had to find a way to earn more money. In those days it took courage to drop a job to hunt for another. Finally, several incidents occurred that actually impelled me to make an effort.

One busy morning when lights were popping all over the switchboard, a young trainee pulled out every one of her lines, cutting off all conversations. The supervisor let out an agonized screech.

"What in the world have you done?" she demanded furiously.

"Oh, I told them all to call back," the trainee said casually. "I have to go to lunch now."

"Really! So you disconnect all lines while you traipse off to lunch?" the supervisor shrieked, and gave her a dressing down that must have singed the cross-country lines.

We were all terribly sorry for the poor trainee, but none of us was immune from the supervisor's watchful eye and sharp tongue. My own turn came soon. The board was loaded with lights when I began to put through a long-distance call. I had just plugged in the circuit when the supervisor ordered me to pick up a local line. As the long-distance operator had already come in, I had to complete this call. Plugging into my board, the supervisor began to berate me for ignoring her command.

Her tirade seemed so unjust that I ripped off my earphones and cried, "Stop screaming in my ear! If I don't know how to operate the board after all the training I've had, then the company has wasted a lot of money on me."

Flabbergasted, she sputtered, "Such insolence! You go to the chief operator right now!"

After listening to my outraged story, the latter said calmly, "You must realize that the supervisor is responsible for a number of boards, while you're only operating one. So try to be more patient with her. You'll be a supervisor yourself some day, and you'll see that it's no snap."

This talk gave me pause for thought. Did I aspire to a supervisor's job—and would I too scream at some poor operator doing her best to keep her circuits clear? I just couldn't visualize a long, happy life at the switchboard. Besides, the irregular hours and confining duties made me realize that I was not by nature cut out for this line of work.

At this time I heard of an opening for a night teacher in the public schools. If I found a job with daytime hours, I could work three nights a week as a teacher. So I decided to take the plunge.

One cold January morning, when I was off duty at the phone company, I started on a job hunt. Since I enjoyed selling and had had a little experience at it in Petersburg, I headed for Auerbach's Department Store.

In the drab personnel office, job hunters were huddled on benches around the room, looking as if they were afraid of being thrown out into the cold if they uttered a sound. I assumed what seemed to be the proper pose, but I am just not made for quiet waiting. After twiddling my thumbs for a while, I decided to take steps.

Behind a desk at the top of the room sat a man reading a newspaper. From his appearance I assumed he was the personnel manager. And if anyone else were to spend so much time behind a paper, the personnel manager would probably fire him.

So I marched up to his desk and asked, "Excuse me, but are you Mr. Murphy?"

Down came the newspaper. Up went the eyebrows. He seemed completely surprised to discover anyone else in the room.

"Why, yes. Won't you sit down?" he said politely.

"Thank you. I'm Miss Baker and I came here to see you about a job. But I haven't much time. If you can't see me now, I'll go someplace else."

Months of interviewing girls during the depression must have hardened Mr. Murphy to the most pitiful kind of stories. But he was obviously taken aback by this confident approach from a young lady who implied that "someplace else" there were jobs begging for her. We looked each other over carefully. I saw a rather slight man, with a balding pate covered by a few sparse gray hairs. Suddenly, he smiled and asked where I had worked before. He did not fall out of his chair when I mentioned the name of a Petersburg store, so I dropped in the names of a couple of stores in Richmond where I had only shopped.

"What salary would you expect, Miss Baker?" he asked casually.

"Twenty-five dollars a week," I said, just as casually.

"Good heavens! Don't be ridiculous. We can get any number of clerks here for twelve or fifteen a week."

He nodded toward the people waiting around the room. Then he scowled.

68

"Well, I suppose you can get plenty of clerks, Mr. Murphy. But you can't get *salesladies* for that salary."

After eying me sharply, he said, "I tell you what I'll do with you, Miss Baker. I'll put you in ready-to-wear and I'll give you what the girls there are making—sixty-five a month and a commission on everything you sell. If you're as good as you say, you'll make your twenty-five a week."

So it was that Auerbach's acquired one slightly inexperienced, but brassy, saleslady. Evenings, she taught American history and citizenship in the public school system—but days, she was out to make at least twenty-five dollars a week selling ladies' ready-to-wear.

My colleagues on the floor weren't exactly waiting to boost me up the ladder of success. They had their own pet customers, of course, and a lot of practice in sizing up the buying potential of anyone who wandered in. When a client came in who looked as if all she wanted to spend was time, they would graciously step aside and leave her to me.

As I'd always enjoyed company, I would entertain anyone who wandered in. On my first day, a little old lady came in who looked as if she had started the depression. Surely she must have dressed before daylight inside an Indian tepee. She looked at me and wiggled the toothpick she had in the corner of her mouth. So I stepped up to ask if I could help her.

She wanted to see a dress, and naturally I started with what we called our more modest-priced lines. But she wheeled around, wiggling the toothpick with vigor, and headed for a rack where we kept the quality goods. I thought she would take one look at the price tags and bolt out of the store. Instead, she picked out an elaborate red afternoon dress and followed me to the fitting room.

"Get the fitter in here," she ordered, when she had tried it on.

I was writing up the order with a triumphant flourish, when she said suddenly, "Keep the fitter in here. I want to see some evening gowns."

She picked out several lavish evening gowns and then called for some tailored clothes. Every time I went back on the floor, the other girls watched me with their mouths open. For by the time she left, her toothpick at a jaunty angle, she had bought five hundred dollars' worth of merchandise. When she gave me her name a light dawned—for she was one of Utah's famous and eccentric "mining queens."

In those depression days, salesladies hungering after a commission were only a little more intent upon a kill than a tank full of barracuda, no matter what you may have heard. But we had our ground rules. One of the most fundamental was that you did not take credit for a sale to a customer with whom another girl had been working. When I was out to lunch one day, a sales clerk sold a fur coat to a woman with whom I had spent considerable time that morning. When I found out, I was mad.

"You made a dollar and a half on that sale," I told her. "If you need it worse than I do, you're welcome to it. But don't complain when I take one of your sales."

"Try and get one," she challenged.

Despite these untoward incidents, I managed to make enough in commissions to earn the twenty-five dollars a week I had blithely asked for. Later, I was impressed into other activities at the store. Probably because of my voice training at the phone company, I was asked to appear on a radio program sponsored by Auerbach's. When the store put on fashion shows the salesgirls acted as models—and for once my height proved to be an asset.

Of course, there is always the perennial wolf on the prowl wherever girls are at work. One of these small-time Casanovas had been pursuing me, and one night he appeared at a style show we gave at a local theater. After pirouetting across the stage in a green taffeta ball gown, I changed into my work clothes and found this man waiting at the stage door. He gushed some flowery compliments, then said silkily, "It's such a grand night. How about driving out to Cottonwood Canyon and seeing the cherry orchards in bloom?"

"Thanks so much," I said icily. "But I walked back from the last cherry orchard I went to see. Good night!"

This abrupt reply appeared to accomplish its purpose, for it sent that particular Lothario packing, never to darken our stage door again.

One day, after I had been at Auerbach's for about a year, I worked out a complicated scheme to take off work legitimately for three hours and get a permanent wave. But I forgot to explain the details of this maneuver to Mr. Latimer, the department manager. When he missed me that day, he hit the ceiling. I was under the dryer in the store beauty parlor when my boss called to rake me over the coals and give me my walking papers.

"Something important?" the beauty operator asked when I ducked back under the dryer.

"Just lost my job," I said as casually as I could. Jobs in those days were no more valuable than right arms and she looked at me with real pity.

A few minutes later the personnel manager called and asked me to stop by and see him before I left the store. As I'd already been fired, I had no intention of taking another tongue-lashing. Before I left the beauty shop, Mr. Murphy appeared in person and explained that they didn't want to let me go and had other plans for me. Then he urged me to apologize to Mr. Latimer for being absent without leave. Sighing with relief at this reprieve, I was only too glad to make my peace with the boss.

A few months later I was summoned to the head office.

What had I done this time, I wondered nervously, as I waited in Mr. Auerbach's office while he studied my employment record. He looked up and, with a sharp glance at me, asked abruptly, "Where did you say you worked before you came here?"

Oh, he's found out about my bluff, I thought bleakly. Realizing that the best defense was the truth, I told him exactly what I'd done. Scowling, he looked back at the record I'd spun out for the personnel manager.

"I had to have experience to get the job," I explained. "And I had to have the job to get experience."

Unexpectedly, he laughed, and praised me for the showing I had made in the store.

"I'm going to put you in charge of the art needlework department . . . a hundred and twenty-five dollars a month to start."

I floated back to the floor, my head in the clouds. But I soon came down with a thud, when I realized that I knew nothing at all about a buyer's job, and the sum total of my knowledge of art needlework could be stuffed through the eye of a needle and still not trip the proverbial camel. But a hundred and twenty-five dollars a month was serious money, and so I set about learning. I pored over old records to find out what to order for the department. I took a chance on ordering new goods in large quantities and put on big sales and promotion campaigns.

Within a year I had accomplished two things—almost doubled sales in the department and worked myself into a state of collapse. For I had not yet learned the importance of leaving your job behind you at the end of the day. I would lie awake nights, my mind racing with quotas and sales figures. By day I worked under such tension—mostly of my own making—that I had bouts of indigestion. I lost weight and my nerves were ragged. To avoid joining the "ulcer society," a rest was indicated.

Luckily, they were no longer holding a place in the bread line for the Baker family. Fearnley, who was twenty then, had come home one day to announce that he had a job.

"We're on Easy Street from now on!" he informed us jauntily, explaining that he'd found work in a night club.

"How much do they pay?" I asked.

"Gosh, Ive, I was so surprised when the guy hired me, I didn't ask about the dough. But I'm sure he's going to pay me."

It wasn't much, but at least it restored his belief in himself and helped with the family budget. He had been wandering around in a rosy daze for weeks, having fallen in love. It wasn't long after he had taken the new job that Fearnley came in one night with Iris, his ladylove. They were beaming like two kids who had just found a gallon of ice cream.

"Meet Mrs. Baker," Fearnley announced.

I guess I gasped louder than the rest. The family was now managing to keep its nose above water only so long as there was not a ripple on the surface. And our boy Fearnley had come home with a bride—and another mouth to feed!

"You haven't lost a brother," said the irrepressible Fearnley. "You've gained a sister, and she's got a job."

We must have brightened somewhat at this news. Iris was a charming girl who soon won our affection, and after the newlyweds moved in with us, she became a welcome addition to the family.

As a nonworking member, I felt like a drain on our resources, while recuperating from my collapse. I was champing at the bit, when a letter came from Adele Howell, an old friend who had moved to Los Angeles. Would I come out and help her market a new line of cosmetics? This seemed a heaven-sent opportunity to restore my health in the warmer California climate and to earn a living at the same time.

Those were the days when we were all being urged to "get in on the ground floor" of something big. Undaunted by the fact that I knew no more about cosmetics than I had known about needlework, I set out for Los Angeles. But we had such trouble getting the business started that, for once, I began to regard my ignorance as a distinct handicap. Even by depression standards we were doing badly; we weren't taking in enough to pay expenses. For Adele, who had money of her own, making cosmetics was a hobby, but for me, trying to sell them was a serious business.

Steady employment of some kind was essential. It was not only a question of keeping a roof over my head but of finding a line of work with a future in it. How often I regretted that I lacked a college education, which might have prepared me for a real career—although, of course, plenty of well-equipped college graduates were jobless in the depressed thirties.

But as I look back, I can't help wondering if a better education would have set me on a straighter course and avoided the hit-or-miss quality of my early career—if you could call it that. I moved from job to job like a rolling stone —and like poor Harry, whose way of life I had deplored.

I also shudder at the brashness I developed. When I want to make excuses for myself, I recall that day-to-day survival was what really mattered in those hard times. If you weren't tough in spirit and supremely confident in manner, you might as well have joined the bread lines.

When I told Adele that I planned to find a part-time job to augment my puny income from cosmetics, she was anything but encouraging.

"Ivy, they're giving all the jobs to native Californians," she pointed out. "You haven't got a tinker's chance."

"Well, someone's going to have a chance to turn me down," I replied. "Because I'm certainly going to ask."

The next morning, I appeared at Bullock's Wilshire, looking as native as was possible for me, and asked to see Mr. MacArthur, the personnel manager.

"Did you want to see him about working here?" the receptionist asked, getting ready to pull the trap door which would drop me through the floor.

"Certainly not," I replied casually. "I'm Miss Baker and he's expecting me."

I was counting on the absentmindedness of a busy man who might believe he had promised to see a Miss Baker about something. Luckily, it worked—and I was ushered into his office.

As I walked the length of that room, which seemed endless, I suddenly got panicky. But it was too late to back out now. As I approached his big desk, he came forward to greet me and cordially asked me to sit down.

"Now, Miss Baker, what was I going to see you about?"

"You weren't going to see me about anything, Mr. MacArthur," I blurted out. "I'd like to see *you* about working here."

His eyebrows shot up. Then he threw back his head and laughed.

"Oh?" he said, looking at me closely. "When do you want to begin?"

"But, Mr. MacArthur," I stammered, "you haven't asked anything about my previous experience."

With a twinkle in his eye, he said, "You got in here, didn't you? What do you want to do?"

I explained that I had done some modeling and asked if I might work as a part-time model. To my astonishment, he consented. And the next morning I was strutting around in a handsome tailored suit in the French Room. But what a comedown it was to get into my own clothes after being gowned in such luxury all day.

Shortly after I had started work at Bullock's, a distinguished-looking gentleman stopped to ask me about a suit I was modeling. I talked enthusiastically about its fine points and did everything I could to steer him to a salesgirl.

"No, I'm not going to buy this suit. But you'll be hearing from me," he said crisply. "What's your name?"

A few minutes later, I was summoned hurriedly to Mr. MacArthur's office. I went in with shaking knees, wondering what stupidity I was guilty of this time.

Seated next to Mr. MacArthur was the man who had taken my name.

"This is Mr. Lawson, Miss Baker," Mr. MacArthur said. "He's in charge of personnel for all Bullock's stores."

Mr. Lawson looked at me searchingly.

"Miss Baker, why aren't you *selling* clothes?" he asked.

"Well, I have sold clothes. But I'm modeling now because I don't have a full day to put in."

"We want you selling for Bullock's. And I don't think you can refuse. We'll pay you a hundred and thirty-five a month and a 4 per cent commission on all sales over the quota."

This sounded like big pay to me—more than I'd ever earned. It meant that I'd be able to send money home, where they were still having a hard struggle.

Adele urged me to drop the cosmetics line, which looked like a long, probably futile, haul and to accept the Bullock's job.

But fate was to take a hand in things again. One day, a cousin of ours stopped by at Bullock's to give me the family news. Mother's letters had been cheerful, but he said gravely, "Your dad looks very poorly. I don't think he'll last much longer."

Shocked by this news, I talked to Mr. Lawson and he

agreed that I had to go home. But there would be a job for me at Bullock's, he assured me, whenever I wanted to return.

When I got home, Dad's appearance dismayed me. He had gone downhill fast in the months of my absence. He was emaciated and drawn, but there were still the same warm, wise smile and the understanding light in his eyes. I knew there was little we could do—but hoped that my presence at home would comfort him somewhat.

Determined to stay with Dad as long as he lived, I looked around for a job and found one at Keith O'Brien, a Salt Lake department store. There I was delighted to find Chloe Woods, an old friend from Bingham, also working as a salesclerk. A pretty, vivacious girl, she liked dancing as much as I did, and we sometimes double-dated. Although I enjoyed going out occasionally, men did not concern me seriously. Having been burned once, I was not eager to leap into matrimony again. Besides, at the age of twenty-seven, I was not meeting many eligible bachelors.

One day, when Chloe and I were lunching together, she announced excitedly, "I've got a handsome friend coming to town this weekend. How about a double date? He's got a nice fellow traveling with him."

I hesitated, for I wasn't keen on blind dates. Then Chloe launched into a glowing description that made the unknown gentleman sound like the greatest thing since the invention of the wheel. This made me even more reluctant.

"How tall is he?" I asked.

"Oh, he's not so tall. But he's a good dancer."

"How tall?" I persisted.

"Not quite as tall as you, Ivy," she admitted.

Well, that did it. I never went out with a fellow who wasn't as tall as I and she knew it.

"It'll spoil things if you don't go, Ivy. I mean, with this extra fellow here, my friend'll . . ."

"Oh, I'll find somebody else to go along," I said.

"But suppose you don't?"

"Then I'll go myself."

Evidently, there was no manpower shortage in Salt Lake that week—because every girl I knew was dated up. I had promised to go along if I couldn't find someone else, so I had to keep my promise.

It was with no feeling of elation that I waited for the other three to call for me that Sunday afternoon. The date which they had brought for me was shorter than I, as described. But what I had not been told was that he was also much older. I started to glare at my friend, when suddenly this man smiled at me and I forgot about everything else.

His eyes crinkled at the corners, and his face burst into the kind of good-humored grin that just warmed up the room. It was the kind of smile that won a girl—this girl anyway—completely.

After visiting amiably with Mother and Dad, he held out his arm to me and we walked out, laughing happily.

Months later, Mother told me about the conversation that ensued between her and Dad after we had gone.

"Well, what d'ye think of 'im?" she asked.

"I liked him. Seemed like a nice fellow."

"Good thing ye did. 'E's going to be yer son-in-law," Mother announced.

My date's name was Roy Priest.

We were going to Heber City, a resort about sixty miles from Salt Lake, to swim in the hot springs and dine and dance at the clubhouse.

On our way Roy noticed the many gophers scampering across the fields. We might do the farmers a favor, he remarked, if we helped them get rid of some of these ratlike pests so prevalent in the West. An avid amateur sportsman,

Roy carried a hunting rifle with his fishing gear in the trunk of his car. Why not pause to shoot some gophers, he suggested.

The idea frightened me, as I had never been anywhere near a gun, and Chloe turned pale at the very thought. With trembling hands I raised the rifle, as Roy launched into the first lesson in gunmanship. I tried to sight as instructed and fired away, scaring myself more than the gophers with the noise. Of course, all my shots went completely wild.

In order to encourage me, Roy said I was doing fine—except that I shot right-handed and left-eyed. Taking careful aim, I pulled the trigger again and, much to my surprise, a gopher spun around dizzily and then scampered away, minus his tail. "Uh-uh," Roy chuckled. "You hit the north end of a southbound gopher."

The boys kept teasing me about my aim, and I hoped that by the time they got back to town I would have lived it down. But one day a large package was delivered to me at the store. The girls gathered around curiously, as I unwrapped layers of tissue, only to find another package and another until I got down to a kitchen matchbox. To my chagrin—and the great amusement of my co-workers—out fell three little gopher tails. The enclosed note read: "For my favorite marksman to add to her collection—Roy." The girls were all convulsed when I explained about shooting the north end of a southbound gopher.

This thoughtful and ingenious memento of our first date —certainly a far cry from the candy or other conventional gift most men would send—delighted me so much that I looked forward eagerly to seeing Roy again. His job as a wholesale furniture salesman for Beebe and Runyan, an Omaha distributor, kept him traveling through five Western states. Luckily, Salt Lake was his headquarters and he got into town quite often.

VI

RARELY has a romance blossomed under less favorable circumstances than Roy's and mine. At the time we first met, I was active in local politics, thanks to Mother's initiative and example, and I'd become an enthusiastic member of the Young Republican organization. After our first date Roy found himself swept along on our political rounds so frequently that he later commented, "I didn't know whether I was supposed to be winning a bride or an election."

The woes of courting a "lady politician" became an habitual joke shared with Dad by Roy whenever he called at our house. "When you've been married to one as long as I have, you get used to it," Dad would sigh, with a sly glance at Mother.

"Now, Orange, come off it!" she flashed back, with a twinkle in her eye, for no one enjoyed a good-natured joke more than Mother. "You 'aven't been so badly done by."

"No, Mr. Baker has nothing to complain of," Roy offered

gallantly. Then turning to me, he asked, "Well, Ivy, are we going dancing—or drumming up votes again?"

He had a good case, for our romance occasionally played second fiddle to politics—especially around election time. As Mother's all too willing apprentice, I was often involved in meetings, rallies, and ringing doorbells to bring out the vote. Fortunately, Roy accepted these activities with good grace— which made his stock rise even higher with Mother.

Ever since the family had moved to Salt Lake in the 1920s Mother had been knee-deep in civic and political affairs. Her good-neighbor policy was just as effective in the big city as it had been at Bingham. In a very short time her neighbors were wondering how they had ever gotten along without her.

By the time I had returned from the South, she was "Mother Baker" to everyone in our part of town. She was busy carrying homemade pies, applying poultices, and listening to troubles and triumphs all through the neighborhood. By some mysterious system of her own, she had sorted out the Republicans from the others and you could be sure that they were registered and voting for " 'Erbert 'Oover" in the 1928 election.

In the ensuing years her handsome, animated face, her white hair, bobbed and waved in the new fashion, and her stocky figure became a familiar sight at party events, where old regulars would listen attentively to her wry and penetrating observations.

In the 1932 Presidential election she not only stumped vigorously for Hoover's reelection, but also threw herself heart and soul into the campaign of Bill Seegmiller, an old friend of Dad's, who was running for governor of Utah.

Well in advance of the Republican state convention, where the candidate would be nominated, Mother and I were out working for Bill. It occurred to me that it would be exciting to go as a delegate to the convention.

"Well, why don't you?" Dad said when I broached the subject at home.

"You know how they pick the delegates from this precinct! The same little clique holds the district mass meeting and elects the same two delegates every year . . . you know that."

"Don't ye realize that everr' 'omeowner in our neighborhood can go to that meeting and vote?" Mother asked. "If ye can't take it from therr, ye don' deserve to go to th' convention."

The meeting at which delegates from our precinct were chosen was held at a neighbor's house. Generally only a handful of voters would show up and they always elected the same man and woman to represent them. The delegates would be elected shortly after the meeting opened. But, according to state law, they had to continue the meeting until 9 P.M. So, with their work done, everyone would just sit around and chat.

Prior to the meeting that year, I visited some of Mother's good friends in our district, and enlisted about thirty people in the crusade to make Ivy a delegate. They promised to gather at our house at 8:30 on the night of the meeting.

When we walked into the mass meeting, the old guard suddenly woke up and looked around. One of my friends put my name in nomination and just before the nine o'clock deadline, I was elected. It was then too late for the regulars to do anything about it—and I was off to the convention.

Like a schoolgirl selling raffle tickets at a county fair, I sailed into that convention. Hard-boiled old politicians from all parts of the state seemed to be amused by my enthusiasm and spirit, though they had little faith in my sagacity. Before I had left, Mother had given me a piece of political advice which I have never forgotten.

"Remember, Ivy, ye're going to the state convention as a

delegate for your father's friend, Bill Seegmiller. Naturally, ye're going to do everything ye can to 'elp 'im. But, remember, ye're not *against* the other man, Bill Lowe. 'E might get th' parrty's nomination and then 'e would be your candidate —and ye want to be able to work for 'im."

Perhaps our enthusiasm did help somewhat, because Bill Seegmiller won the nomination. But I don't know whether we did him a favor—for that was 1932, the year of the first Roosevelt landslide. Republicans just didn't win in Utah that year. Even our great Senator Reed Smoot, who had served for many years as one of the most influential men in the Senate, was not returned to office.

"It's the times are out of joint," Dad said sadly.

"Well, we'll 'ave to put them back in joint," Mother said firmly, her unfailing optimism refusing to accept defeat.

One night when I got home from the store, Mother announced that Mrs. Openshaw, the wife of our family doctor in Salt Lake, who was active in politics, had asked us to dinner the following night.

"But I can't go, Mother," I said. "Roy's coming to town."

"So much the better. We'll take 'im along, too."

"But, Mother, you can't drag us all along."

"Why not? Ye know she'll like Roy. If she just knew 'e was going to be 'ere, she'd 'ave invited 'im 'erself."

"Well, call her up and ask if it's all right."

"Oh, of course it'll be all right," she said airily.

To Mother's way of thinking, her friends in Salt Lake were no different from her neighbors in Bingham. Everyone was running a boardinghouse, as far as she was concerned, and there was always plenty of food for three or four extra guests. It had gotten so no one would set the table until Mother walked in the door and they could see how many she'd brought with her.

The following night, Roy wasn't surprised to find that our

plans had been switched. Instead of going out to dinner, we went with Mother to the Openshaws', where I *was* surprised to discover the reason for her insistence. Plans were afoot—initiated by Mother, of course—to make me Republican vice-chairman of our district. Once she had made up her mind, she knew how to muster the winning votes. And so I was launched into the job of getting out literature, arranging meetings, checking for nonregistered voters, and all the myriad tasks that went into organizing a district.

In 1934, the Utah Republicans decided to encourage young people to run for office and I was nominated by the state convention to run for the Legislature. I plunged into the campaign with all the fervor of Joan of Arc falling upon the British. Roy would lead the applause, when I had finished speaking, and went around shaking hands and proclaiming my qualifications to the voters.

"You're doing just great, Ivy," he would tell me. "That was your best talk yet."

It would be the third time that night perhaps that he had heard the same talk—when, all along, he had wanted to see the new movie downtown. But I needed this kind of encouragement, because my knees would be shaking every time I faced an audience. Just to see his face out front, his eyes crinkled up by that familiar friendly grin, made me feel that all was well.

Dad looked forward to Roy's visits too, for the two had become fast friends. Roy would bring the latest news and gossip and a fresh joke or two to brighten Dad's evenings.

Dad was spending most of his time in bed now and his cough was getting steadily worse. We knew it was a question of months, or perhaps weeks, before we would lose him. Even a short stay in a warmer climate had not been beneficial. Home was where he wanted to be, surrounded by the bustle and confusion of the family. Physically he'd grown weaker, but his mind was as keen as ever and he took a deep interest in all of us. He was the family confidant, and we brought our worries to him, knowing that we could depend on his wise counsel and sympathy.

One night I consulted him about the problem that was close to my heart. "Roy is twenty-one years older than I am, Dad," I began. "Do you think that's too great an age difference?"

"It is a big difference," Dad said thoughtfully. "Ordinarily, it might be a drawback. But your interests and outlook are much the same. Roy seems far younger than his years and you've always been older than yours."

"That's true, Dad. When we're together I'm never conscious of the age gap."

"Anyway, you are the ones to decide. I'm sure you've learned that you've got to make a lot of adjustments and work hard together to build a happy marriage."

His sage advice gave me the kind of reassurance I needed. For by this time I was convinced that Roy had the qualities of heart and character that would make a good husband—and I was determined to do my part.

Despite his illness, Dad also took a lively interest in the election campaign. Every night I would rush home from work to report on the latest developments. If he'd had a particularly bad day, I hated to leave him. But he would insist that I go out on my speechmaking rounds.

"Do your best to win," he would say encouragingly. "Then, win or lose, you'll have no regrets."

The printer had been late in getting my campaign cards finished and every day Dad would demand eagerly, "Have your cards come yet?"

The night in October when they were finally ready, I rushed home to show them to Dad.

"Get my glasses," he said weakly. "It's getting dark in here."

I stared at him fearfully, for the lights were on bright. Mother, who hovered over his bedside, threw me an apprehensive glance and looked toward Aunt Gert who was standing in the bedroom doorway. She had spent a restless, anxious night worrying about Dad. Sensing that Mother needed her, she had hurried over early that morning.

I picked up Dad's glasses and put them on for him. Propped up on his pillows, to make breathing easier, he stared at the campaign card for a few moments, smiling happily. Then a look of alarm crossed his pale, shrunken face.

"I can't see it," he gasped, and sank back limply.

Those were my father's last words.

Too numb with shock to realize what had happened, we stood helplessly at his bed for a moment. Then the doctor, who had been summoned earlier by Mother, came in and told us that Dad had already passed on.

I couldn't bear to let him leave us. Throwing my arms around Dad, I dropped down on the bed and began to sob. Tears streaming down her face, Mother bent over me, and Aunt Gert gathered us both into her arms. "He was such a good man," Mother sobbed. "He was such a good man."

Somehow Aunt Gert got us both out of the room so that the doctor could take over. We did our best to pull ourselves together to help the rest of the family over the shock when they arrived.

Unable to sleep that night, I kept weeping and trying to imagine life without Father.

As my mind raced back through the years, I could see him once again, holding one of the babies in the cradle of his knee

86

while Mother was getting supper ready; I could see him being carried home from work, hurt again, or could hear him as he spoke quietly to a group of friends who had asked his opinion on some subject. His had been a hard life, from the days on the farm in southern Utah to the last, racking cough. He had been beset by perils, hounded by bad luck, and never had an opportunity to fully develop his fine mind. Yet I had never heard him complain, nor had I ever known him to do anything but what seemed best for all of us.

We went through the dark hours that followed in a complete daze. When the agony of the funeral was over, we returned to a home that was emptier than it had ever been.

As the tragedy of Dad's death began to dull, the family was drawn even closer together. Alone now, we had to carry on without his wise counsel and encouragement. Roy's quiet sympathy and strength endeared him to all of us through those trying times.

Mother and Roy insisted that I must finish out my campaign for office, but my heart wasn't in it. I went through the motions, and failed to win. But apparently, I showed enough strength in that race to bring me to the attention of others in the party. Soon after, I was elected co-chairman of the Young Republican organization for the eleven Western states.

As summer approached, Roy's mind always turned to fishing. Every year he and his brother Harry spent a vacation in the beautiful Alpine-like Jackson Hole country in northwest Wyoming, where they claimed that the trout were no smaller than the average Mako shark. Since Roy was such an enthusiast about the outdoor life, it was only fair for me to listen to his fishing stories with the same rapt attention he had given to my political speeches.

I must have been a good listener, for Roy suddenly suggested that I go on vacation with them that year. His brother's wife, Merle, and daughter, Jayne, were also going along. We made all our preparations, but at the last minute the women, whom I had not yet met, changed their plans. Roy begged me to come along anyway and, with a few mental reservations, I set out into the wilds with the party.

We made our base at a pleasant lodge run by the Turner family at Turpin Meadows, opposite the majestic Teton mountains. There we came to know Dad Turner, one of those remarkable characters of the old West, and one of the greatest teasers and most entertaining storytellers I've ever known. Once, when a car pulled up with New Jersey tags and the driver wanted a bottle of milk, Dad convinced him that he had only moose milk for sale and that it was the healthiest kind of milk there was. Only the most daring cowhands could milk the moose, Dad Turner insisted, which made it very expensive, so he charged fifty cents for a quart of ice-cold cow's milk, and the customer was delighted with his rare bargain. Later, I scolded him: "Why, Dad Turner, you ought to be ashamed of yourself. Imagine charging that man fifty cents for ordinary cow's milk!"

Dad laughed and said, "Why, Ivy ... that'll make the feller's whole trip. Wait'll he gets back home and tells them about buyin' moose milk for only fifty cents a quart!"

From the lodge, Roy, Harry, and the guides would take off along the beautiful timbered trails of the Wyoming country. I liked to ride horses, but I left the fishing to them. The first time we went out on a pack trip to the remote wilds of Bridger Lake, high in the Yellowstone mountains, I felt as out of place as Roy must have at his first political rally.

The guides tactfully set up one tent for me at the edge of the clearing, then put up the others about a hundred yards away.

"Wait a minute," I said, taking a scared look at the spooky, thick forest surrounding us. "You just move my tent right over there between the Priest brothers'. If a bear comes along, he'll surely get into one of their tents first! And these husky men would make choicer morsels than I would."

During all the months that we had been seeing each other, Roy and I had never talked very seriously about marriage. Sometimes he would nostalgically mention friends he had seen on his trip who had their own homes.

"I've always wanted to put my feet under my own dinner table," he would say wistfully, but then the thought would seem to trail off.

For years Roy had been traveling through the West in blizzards, in scorching heat, and in flood. He slept in small-town hotels, ate in roadside diners, and made his friends among the salesmen and customers he met in his territory, but under his amiable, outgoing, "salesman" personality there was a rather shy, gentle man. I knew how much Roy wanted a home of his own, but he had never pressed the subject because he realized how much I was needed at home.

One night, during this trip, we were sitting around the flickering campfire. Overhead, stars sparkled in the clear Western sky. Bill Crandall, one of the guides, was plunking away softly at his guitar and singing:

> Somewhere in old Wyoming
> Lives a girl I love,
> We used to stroll in the gloaming,
> Under the stars above ... *

Roy and I sat together on a fallen tree, lazily enjoying the perfect beauty of the hour. Roy spoke up quietly, addressing his brother:

* "Somewhere in Old Wyoming" by Charles Tobias and Peter De Rose, used by permission of copyright owner, Edwin H. Morris & Co., Inc.

"Harry, Ivy and I will probably be down to see you in Oklahoma City in December."

"You know," Harry replied casually, "I've been waiting for you to tell me when it was going to be."

"You think it's a good idea?" Roy asked.

Suddenly I sat up straight and demanded, "What difference does it make whether *he* thinks it's a good idea ... as long as we do?"

"Did I say the wrong thing?" Roy asked anxiously.

Smiling happily, I patted his hand. And that was Roy's proposal and my acceptance.

Mother always loved an excuse for a party—and a wedding was all she needed to put her on her mettle. For weeks before Roy and I were married, on December 7, 1935, she and Aunt Gert were busy with plans and menus. Mother's greatest problem was to keep the guest list down, especially since she was serving an elegant wedding breakfast and wanted her legion of friends to share it. Aunt Gert was mainly concerned with serving the greatest number at the lowest cost. Every time she came to the house her shopping bag was loaded with "barge-ins" for the big event.

On my wedding day, she was on hand early to help the nervous bride into her gown and to make good and sure that none of the traditional superstitions were flouted.

"Remember, Ivy," she warned, "ye must wear something old, something new, something borrowed, and something blue. Here—I'll loan ye my necklace. It'll bring ye luck, that it will."

When I was finally dressed in my new blue crepe dress, Aunt Gert's pearls, and an old petticoat, she bustled me into the kitchen to keep me out of sight until the ceremony began.

Roy, who happened to arrive early, bounded out to the

kitchen to give me an exuberant bear hug. Aunt Gert watched him with dismay.

"Och, Roy!" she exclaimed. "Ye should neverr see the bride before the ceremony. 'Tis bad luck."

"Oh, Aunt Gert!" said Roy. "How could this be bad luck?"

All the same, she took his arm and swung him away from me toward the towering wedding cake she had baked for us. "Now, here is something to see, Roy!" she said proudly. "Have ye everr set eyes on a prettier sight than that?"

Roy allowed that it really "took the cake."

After the ceremony, performed by Bishop Carl Burton of our ward, who was always on hand for important family occasions, and Mother's delicious breakfast, we left in a shower of rice and old shoes in Roy's Chevvy, which my brothers had suitably bedecked.

Our wedding trip marked the beginning of our habit of combining business with pleasure. We were bound for Roy's annual sales meeting in Omaha, by way of Oklahoma City, where we meant to keep our promise to stop off and see Harry's family.

For a time it looked as if we would never get out of Utah. Roy had so many friends and customers along the way—and by now I knew so many people through state politics—that we were stopping to visit someone every few miles.

That evening we reached Price, where a friend of Roy's operated the local hotel. Being new to the husband role and desperately anxious to please his bride, he carefully ordered our first dinner together. He chose his favorite dish, kidneys sautéed with mushrooms, unaware that it was one of the few things that I couldn't eat. Watching me toy with my food, he said, "Oh dear, I've done the wrong thing already." I promptly assured him that if his mistakes were no more serious than this one, we would have an ideally happy life together.

Next day our route took us over Monarch Pass, Colorado, 10,000 feet up in the Rockies. As we reached the summit, late at night, the view was so breathtaking that Roy pulled to the side of the road, and we sat staring in wonder. A full moon was shining clear on the crisp, incredibly white depths below us. We could see for miles—the jagged mountain peaks reaching up, the huge pine trees casting their silent shadows over the slopes, and snow crystals shooting off light as if the place had been coated with diamond dust.

We felt as if we were alone together in a world that we had just discovered. There are little, fleeting moments like these which are filled with such beauty that they never dim in memory. I knew that this radiant moment would always cast its light for us down through the years.

After our two-week trip was over we found a four-room apartment in Salt Lake and I plunged into housekeeping with a vengeance, while Roy took up his travel routine. Though he was away from home much of the time that first year, there was never a feeling of loneliness because he was constantly in touch by phone or mail, and his homecoming was always a joyous occasion built around things we could do together.

When Roy learned that we were to have a baby, it was all I could do to keep him from wrapping me in cotton wool for nine months. The months sped by and our little girl was born one hot day late in August. Roy was so delighted that he did not seem to know whether it was dawn or high noon. Leaving Mother with me at the hospital, he went charging off to spread the good news.

His best man, Hyrum Petersen, was awakened from a sound sleep when Roy banged at his door. "Patricia Ann is here!" he crowed. "You should see her, Pete. She's the prettiest, pinkest, tiniest—"

"Naturally," said Pete drily.

Resigned to humoring the proud father, Pete awoke his wife Tracey, who made some coffee and listened patiently to Roy's effusions.

"Ivy wanted to call her Judith," he said, "because it's her favorite name, but—"

"Judith Priest!" Pete exclaimed. "Oh, no! That would never do."

Roy decided that we'd outgrown our small flat and would have to buy a house for the family we were starting. A few months later we were out for a Sunday drive on a snowy January day, when we passed through the suburban town of Bountiful, eight miles north of Salt Lake. Suddenly, I spotted a little white house with green trim and shutters, which looked like a jewel set on a thick carpet of new-fallen snow.

"Look, Roy," I cried. "That's exactly the kind of house I want."

"There's a 'For Sale' sign out front," he said, slowing down.

It was just as appealing inside as out. Though the house was small and compact, its five rooms were sunny and cheerful and its big recreation room in the basement would give us far more room than we had in our flat. The back yard would be ideal for children and I had visions of the garden I would plant come spring. It seemed so right for us that I was ready to buy it on the spot, but Roy cautiously insisted that we shop around to make sure.

"I'll be leaving tomorrow. Why don't you get an agent and look around?" he suggested.

I got an agent all right—and we went back and arranged to purchase the house in Bountiful upon Roy's return.

Amazed at my quick decision, he asked, "Are you sure this is what you want? Remember, you'll have to live in it a long time."

"I'm often wrong, but never in doubt," I replied. "And to look further would only be confusing."

Once established at Bountiful, we never regretted our choice. The town certainly lived up to its charming name. Nestled in the foothills of the Wasatch mountains, in one of the most fertile strips of the Salt Lake valley, Bountiful abounded in fruit orchards and truck gardens. Its big black Bing cherries, luscious apricots and peaches, and succulent cantaloupes were shipped—and highly prized—throughout the country.

Bountiful was such a tranquil, easygoing community that it soon became a "bedroom" for Salt Lake City commuters, and its population increased from 3,000 to about 12,000 within a few years.

The pleasant, quiet routine of our home life was short-lived, however, and I was soon drawn back into politics. During my years in the Young Republican group, I had become active in the Utah Legislative Council, which was composed of representatives of all the statewide women's organizations. The council met weekly during the legislative session in Salt Lake to discuss and endorse or oppose pending bills. Then we would present our resolutions to the legislators who were thus able to get the sentiment of a large cross-section of the state's women voters on each bill.

The older members of the council, anxious to encourage young women, offered me the honorary post of second vice-president just a few months after Pat's birth. My inclination was to decline, as I was enjoying our home and baby, and had no desire to resume political activity.

"I think you should take it," Roy said. "I'm away a lot and you ought to keep up your outside interests."

"Well, it's just an honorary job," I said, shrugging, "and it shouldn't take too much time."

94

So youth got its due and I paid the matter no great attention. The council meetings would not begin until January, when the Legislature met, and it appeared that there would be nothing for me to do before then. But in December, the newly elected president died, and I moved up a rung to first vice-president.

Roy happened to be working near Salt Lake and was home every night, when the council sessions began. One Thursday morning, as I was preparing to leave for the meeting, the phone rang. It was our baby-sitter, saying that she was ill and couldn't make it. Five minutes later, there came another call.

The acting president of the council had broken her leg— and I had to take over the meeting.

"Roy, what'll I do?" I asked in a panic.

"I'll stay home and take care of Pat," he said brightly.

It was a noble gesture—but Roy still had a bachelor's approach to babies. He liked to look at Pat, but he handled her as if he was afraid she would break apart.

"No, you've got to go to work."

"I'll take her over to your mother's. You just go ahead."

We bundled Pat into the car, and I raced away to the meeting. Scared to death, I presided over the session, hoping my inexperience didn't show too plainly. Later, when I stopped at Mother's, I found Roy waiting, slumped in a chair, with a pained expression.

"Tough day?" I asked.

He nodded mutely and then, little by little, I got his pathetic story.

On the way to Mother's, Pat had begun to cry. When she had spit up a little, he became terrified and headed for the nearest shelter, which happened to be the Petersens' house. Barging in the door, he beseeched Tracey for help. She made a quick diagnosis, changed diapers, and Pat began to burble contentedly. But Roy was still so upset that he insisted that Tracey go along to Mother's. By late afternoon, he had still not recovered.

"I'm not cut out for this kind of work," he moaned. "Perhaps you shouldn't have taken the job, Ivy."

"But it was your idea," I pointed out.

He smiled sadly. "Guess I said the wrong thing again. Your father was right. The first fifty years are the hardest."

VII

FLUFFY white clouds floated lightly in the azure-blue Western sky that spring day. Daffodils and iris, which I had planted in our new garden, were in full bloom. Pat cooed and kicked happily in her baby carriage, in a sunny spot in the yard.

I wondered if any woman could ever have been happier. After the years of struggle and privation, I had found a real sense of security. After some lonely years, I was warmly loved by a wonderful man. The close-knit family of which I had once been a part was now scattered—but Roy and I were starting one of our own. I leaned forward to look at Pat, as she laughed and crooned, and I thought that there had never, never been a baby so lovely.

With our own home, good friends, and community activities, it seemed that I had everything needed to make a full, contented life. Though I'd been thrust into the job of acting president of the legislative council, I was certainly not consumed with ambition for any higher office, nor was I restless.

97

That beautiful, calm day I was completely unaware of the forces gathering to sweep me out of this idyllic eddy to tumble me, willy-nilly, toward undreamed-of challenges and responsibilities. It seems that I was merely being allowed to rest, while other pieces on the board were being shifted into place.

My job with the council was not very demanding, except during sessions of the State Legislature when we met weekly to discuss pending bills and to propose action. At times some of the legislators regarded us as a nuisance, but for the most part they realized the value of having the feminine point of view and support. For the council members were the most influential women leaders in the state and through their club work could mold public opinion and sway the vote.

On Thursday mornings when the council met, I would leave Pat with Mother for the day. This pleased her, since there was no one left at home but Keith, who was still in high school.

One afternoon when I went over to Mother's to retrieve Pat, I found Mother and Aunt Gert deep in one of their usual arguments about the good old days. They spent a lot of time together, each convinced that she was looking after the other in her declining years. "Gert's gettin' on now," Mother would explain, forgetting that she was five years older than Aunt Gert. "And, deaf as she is, where'd there be for 'er to go visitin'? And she won't get an 'earin' aid."

When I walked in, Mother and Aunt Gert were debating the subject of whether Cousin Joe had been born on the twelfth or thirteenth of December, 1901. Aunt Gert paused in the argument to take a lemon meringue pie out of the oven.

"Now, look at that merjum," she said, proudly eying the great mound of delicately browned fluff.

"Meringue, Aunt Gert," I corrected her.

"I call it merjum," she insisted, tossing her head with finality.

"And 'ow did the meeting go along today?" asked Mother.

"Oh, fine," I said, bending down to pick up a cooky little Pat had dropped on the floor.

" 'Oo's going to be the next president after ye?" asked Mother.

"Some of them want me to run for a full term."

"Yer collegees must like ye," Aunt Gert noted, with her usual malapropism. But I decided not to argue about that one.

"That'll be nice . . . to be elected proper," said Mother.

"Oh, I'm not going to run," I said firmly. "How can I—with a baby to look after?"

"Humph," was Mother's comment. "Ye spend 'alf yer life sayin' what ye won't do and the other 'alf doin' it."

During the days that followed, friends in the council began to phone, urging me to run for election as president. I firmly discouraged the idea. It was about this time that Roy came home from his latest selling trip. He always brought me some kind of present and, remembering Dad's well-meant surprises for Mother, I tried not to wince when Roy walked in with his gifts.

This time it was a fur piece, made out of a coyote he'd shot on a hunting expedition. As coyote neckpieces go, this was a beauty—a sand-colored "poor man's fox." I burbled appropriately over it. It wasn't the sort of thing you could exchange, unless you happened to know another coyote.

I brought Roy up to date on home developments, including the drive to make me president of the council.

"I'm not going to do it," I insisted.

"Why not?" he asked.

His reaction astonished me, for I'd expected him to come up with a dozen reasons to strengthen my resolution. So I had to tell him about my plans for painting the bedrooms, planting fruit trees in the yard, and building an outdoor barbecue.

"Say, that'll be nice. I'll bring home some venison and bear next time we go hunting."

With a brave smile, I continued, "Let's tear up that old

fish pond. Pat'll be toddling around and she might fall in it."

"You do what you want to, dear," he said, heading for the kitchen to see if I had laid in a supply of ripe cheese for him.

After all, I thought, a man would be happier to see his wife working around the house, brightening it up and saving his money, than out saving the world. So I went shopping for paint brushes and paint to do our bedroom. While he was away that next week, I went to work. Unfortunately, the color on the wall was unlike the color in the can and I simply couldn't manage the ceiling. So I called in a professional to cover my mistakes. He did such a fine job in our room that I asked him to do the other bedrooms.

When Roy got home that weekend, bringing me a pair of moccasins made out of rattlesnake skin, he was mightily impressed with the paint job.

"Don't see how you did those ceilings," he commented.

"Well, I did have to hire some help," I admitted.

He choked on his Gorgonzola cheese that night, when I showed him the bill.

"Now I'm going to paper the dining room," I said. "If Mother can do it, so can I."

That proved to be somewhat expensive, too, after I'd called in a paper hanger to steam off the crooked strips and do the job over. Roy resigned himself to the inevitable. So I forged ahead bravely with my redecorating project, spending the days setting out fruit trees and calling in a contractor about the barbecue—which I thought could be used for roasting chickens when we ran out of moose steaks.

The contractor showed me some plans for the barbecue.

"The chimney will have to be higher," I decided. "I don't want these young fruit trees to get scorched."

"Yes, ma'am," he said.

Actually, that proved to be about all he said—for I kept offering helpful suggestions such as: "You'll just have to make it bigger at the base" or "Build a little table here, and use this piece of concrete from the driveway for a top." My Scottish blood would allow for no waste, so I wanted to use the rock salvaged from the fish pond.

There came a day when the contractor became downright loquacious.

"Mrs. Priest, we've used up all the rock out of the pool. And we haven't got the chimney up yet."

"Well, for heaven's sake, order some more," I said.

"Yes, ma'am," he said promptly.

The fireplace was finished when Roy came home that weekend, bringing me an absolutely description-defying perfume distilled by some Indian tribe out of the blossoms of wild cacti and other things, unnamed. I took him out to the orchard—as our back yard was now being called—to show off the fireplace.

"Didn't think you could get that much stone out of just one little fish pond," Roy said wonderingly.

"Well, I did have to buy a little more," I said sadly. "It only cost a hundred dollars extra."

"Is that all!" Roy groaned, looking up at the towering chimney, which dominated the skyline of Bountiful like an adolescent Washington Monument.

"I guess I should have stuck to politics instead of putting up this monstrosity," I said. "It really is a monument to my artistic ability with rocks."

Noting my disappointment, he tried to cheer me up. "Oh, it's not that bad. Why don't we have a barbecue and christen it Ivy's Folly?"

I wondered if I would have to spend the ensuing years explaining that it *was* a barbecue and not an outhouse.

"Those ladies still want you to be president of the council?" Roy asked, later that night. He had been writing out checks to my various tradesmen friends. "You know, I've been thinking a lot about that. Probably be more interesting than just hanging around the house, doing these odd jobs."

I couldn't help but agree that the barbecue was indeed an "odd" job. Small wonder that Roy was anxious to get me out of the building business.

Mother too had not let the subject drop. And when a group of friends dropped in later to insist that I try for the office, I was quite ready to be "reluctantly drafted."

The council was a nonpartisan organization, but its members generally followed their own party leaders when it came to voting for officers. About two-thirds of the members were Democrats and, in the circumstances, a Republican had only an outside chance of winning.

The nominating committee usually pitted one party against the other for each office. My name was put up for the presidency against that of a Democrat.

"If you can do one thing for me," I said to a friend who was chairman of the nominating committee, "I think I can win."

"What can I do?"

"Just see to it that the two who are nominated for first vice-president are Democrats."

"I'm sure we can do that, but I don't see how it would help you."

"Don't you see? My opponent, being a Democrat, will have to make a choice between the two Democrats running for first vice-president. The minute she comes out in favor of one, the other woman's friends will come over to me. Then, with the Republican votes I am sure of, I'll stand a good chance."

My friend was dubious—but luckily the plan worked. The Democrats split down the middle into two groups of angry ladies and I picked up the winning votes.

During the months I served on the council, I learned a

good deal about the important effect that women's ideas and ideals can have in the field of practical politics. I saw that politicians are anxious to enjoy the good will of women voters and that they will go to great lengths to win their approval.

"If there's anything scares me worse than a determined woman," one hard-shelled legislator admitted to me, "it's a whole roomful of them."

Women, being pleasant and firm in advancing their point of view, can be very influential in politics. But there are times, I learned that year, when you must be prepared to stand up and fight for your beliefs.

As council president, I served on the wage-hour board which was setting minimum wages for women in Utah. When the labor union representative on the board found out that I was going to vote against him on a certain issue, he started to bluster.

"I'm going to blacken you with every labor organization in the state of Utah," he threatened. "And if you ever put your head above water for anything, you'll get batted down so fast you won't know what hit you."

A threat only serves to stiffen my spine. So I boiled up and replied, "Listen, my friend, you go right ahead. But I can talk just as long, as loud, and as fast as you can. I can get around this state and tell the wives of people in the unions what you're doing for them. It's certainly not going to be too hard to convince them that they don't need you with your feet on the desk, keeping them agitated, unhappy, and out of work. So you just start batting any time."

I voted my convictions on that issue. Strangely enough, this same labor leader became one of my strongest supporters later on.

My term in office was a highly satisfactory experience, for I felt that we women were making a useful contribution to politics. When my two-year term was over, however, I was glad to be rid of the burden of work. And there was an even better reason why I looked forward to being a full-time housewife again.

Our second girl, Peggy Louise, was born just after my successor in office had been elected.

As a second-time father, Roy felt like an old pro and, instead of dashing around waking up friends at dawn, he went home to partake happily of a predawn snack of sardines and Camembert. After his nighttime vigil he deserved it.

We were too overjoyed with our new baby to notice, at the outset, that anything was wrong with her. But, as weeks went by, she seemed unable to retain her food, and we took her to the doctor, who changed the formula. But still the little girl had trouble.

On our next visit to the pediatrician, he made a thorough examination, including X rays. "There's something radically wrong with this baby," I said. "And I don't think it has a thing to do with the formula."

I was prepared to believe that she might have some intestinal constriction which could be corrected by surgery. But I was not ready for the report he gave us.

"Mrs. Priest," he said gravely, "your baby has a serious heart defect which explains the trouble she's been having keeping her food down."

"What can we do about it?" I gasped.

"There really isn't much we can do," he replied.

There are moments when we seem to recoil, almost physically, from the force of words that are spoken. I sat there, staring at him numbly, as he twirled a pencil and looked at me sympathetically across the desk.

"Well, we'll just have to make the best of it," I said, unconsciously reacting in the pattern my mother had set for me. "But I just can't sit by and do nothing. Would it help if we took her to a lower altitude?"

"Well, it helps heart patients generally. Makes it easier for them to breathe."

I called Roy, out on the territory, and he drove 250 miles through one of winter's first storms to get home that night.

"Now, it's just one opinion, Ivy," he said, trying to calm me down. "We'll take her to a heart specialist and see if there isn't something that can be done...."

But two other doctors held out no hope of a miraculous cure and both agreed that a warmer climate might help.

Christmas was upon us now. Roy faced a trip to Omaha for his annual post-Christmas sales meeting. We decided that he must go to Omaha and that I would visit my sister Lynn, now married and living in Colton, California. We had a sad little Christmas—one day early—and left on our separate routes.

The prospect of spending Christmas Eve with two small children on the train was none too cheerful. But when we went into the dining car, I found that the spirit of Christmas, like the love of children, is universal. For the steward had set up a small tree on our table and, for lack of any other decorations, had strung the tree with miniature scotties, white horses, and other bottle trinkets. This considerate gesture seemed to be contagious, and everyone in the diner entered into the spirit of the season. Rushing back to our bedroom, where I'd left seven-months-old Peggy Lou in the care of a stewardess, I gathered up Pat's gifts and went to spread them under the miniature tree. The passengers and beaming waiters watched two-year-old Pat excitedly open her presents. Then we were served a fine turkey dinner and everyone joined in singing Christmas carols, as the train rushed through the night.

In Colton, Lynn helped us get settled, and we were able to find an apartment when a friendly landlady waived the standing rule against children and pets. The California climate seemed to agree with Peggy Lou, who began to hold her food down and to gain weight. Encouraged by her rapid improvement, I sent Roy glowing letters.

By mid-April he was writing that the fruit trees were budding and the flowers were up in our back yard. Little Pat kept asking for her Daddy. I longed to be back home, and by this time the Utah climate would be balmy enough for Peggy. So Roy came down to drive us home in time for Easter.

Never had our Bountiful house seemed more inviting. The garden bloomed with early spring flowers, the soft air was scented with apricot and cherry blossoms, and the sun was like a benison of hope. Peggy Lou, a delicate child with chestnut curls and big hazel eyes, who looked like a Kate Greenaway drawing in her pinafores, brightened up in the warm sunlight. I began to believe our battle was won.

But by mid-July, during an extremely hot spell, Peggy became fretful and restless. Late one night I heard Roy moaning in his sleep. When I awoke him, he said that he'd dreamt someone was trying to take Peggy away from us. About a week later, I too awoke from a nightmare in which I'd seen Mother talking to my late father, who paid no attention to my cries for help, as I tried vainly to keep Peggy from going to them. These premonitions were no doubt caused by our anxiety as Peggy's condition worsened. When we summoned the doctor, he said, "We must take her to the hospital and put her in an oxygen tent, until it gets cooler."

Mother took little Pat, and I had a bed put in Peggy's room at the hospital so that I could stay with her. As the evening wore on, I lay down on the bed and dozed.

Suddenly, I sat up with a start. Though it was stifling hot, I felt a sudden chill in the room. In a panic, I recalled my sensation of chill before Daddy Hicks had died. Rushing to the baby's crib, I lifted the oxygen tent. She was gasping for air. I called for help and an interne and nurse rushed in to give her a hypodermic.

But it was too late. I had lost my baby.

There is no grief as great as this. I stumbled through the hours that followed, hardly knowing where I was or that Roy was beside me suffering as deeply as I.

Paralyzed emotionally, I heard words that did not seem to mean anything. "Sorry, Ivy..." "You must get some rest..." "Where shall we put the flowers?" "Ashes to ashes..." "She doesn't hear us...she must get some rest...."

Then it was all over and the voices were gone. Only Roy, sitting silently at my bedside, his head bowed, and Mother, coming in quietly from time to time to see us. Had we done everything we could? Perhaps if we had stayed on in California...perhaps if there had been an operation...perhaps ...perhaps. I could neither eat nor sleep. And, what was worse, I could not even cry.

When I thought I could stand this despair no longer, I had one of those experiences through which we come to learn the nearness of God in hours of trial.

Out of nowhere, it seemed that I heard some words once spoken by my father, "Nothing is so bad, Ivy, if you don't feel that you're alone."

Suddenly, I was no longer alone. The presence of God seemed to fill the room, as if He were a living being at my side. The tension inside me gradually relaxed and I became aware of the sounds around me.

Little Pat's sunny laughter drifted in from the garden.

A moment later she burst into my room, holding out a bouquet of flowers.

"For Peggou, Mummy," she said, using her pet name for her little sister.

Suddenly the dam burst and I began to cry. Hugging Pat to me, I sobbed until there were no tears left. Then I knelt and prayed.

VIII

PEGGY'S loss left me numb and unable to do anything but the most routine chores. The excitement and sense of usefulness which I had gotten from civic and political work were gone. All that seemed to matter now was little Pat's welfare. I couldn't let her out of my sight.

One night at dinner, she choked on a crumb. Roy and I sprang up and rushed to her side, in a panic because she was turning blue. He put his finger in her mouth, thinking to dislodge whatever might be choking her. The child bit down on his finger with her tiny teeth and couldn't let go. Our family physician, Dr. Trowbridge, lived just down the block and we started to rush Pat in that direction—Roy with his finger still trapped.

About halfway down the block, she suddenly gasped and let go of Roy's finger. We just sank down on the grass, too weak to move or speak. When we had recovered our strength, I took the baby back home—and Roy went on to the doctor to get a badly bitten finger treated.

Had this tense, unnatural atmosphere continued it could have spelled disaster for Pat, no doubt. Roy and Mother must have realized this, for they patiently tried to get me to take up some interest outside the home again.

Mother spent a good deal of time with us, and her wit, wisdom, and understanding were great sources of comfort. In an effort to strike a spark of interest in me, she often talked politics.

"Ye must use the talents God has given ye, Ivy," she said one day. "To waste them is a great sin. It's yer trust, and if ye don't use yer talents, ye fail yourself and ye fail God."

These words kept coming back to me, for I knew she was right. In pining over my loss I was forgetting my obligations to the living. Surely I had learned to face tragedy and adversity, and now it was time to pick myself up and enter active life again.

One of the first things I had done, when we moved to Bountiful, was to register as a new voter in the precinct. Since, in Utah, the local registrar is a member of the party which scored the highest vote in the district during the previous congressional election, our registrar was a Democrat.

"I thought I'd better come," I told her, "so I could cast *the* Republican vote in Davis County."

"It'll make the books look better, having you here," she admitted laughingly. "There certainly aren't too many of you."

When I told Mother that our registrar belonged to the opposition, she peered at me sharply and said:

"Ye can change that, ye know."

It was a challenge, and I soon found a willing ally in our doctor's wife, Dora Trowbridge, an energetic, outgoing woman. Dora was intensely interested in politics and was willing to start right there and ring doorbells all the way to San Francisco, if it would get the Republicans out to vote.

In time we were able to form an organization of enthusiastic women in our district. Although the party did not fare so well elsewhere, we carried our area in 1938—and got a Republican registrar.

It was Dora now who fanned my interest with various problems and intriguing tasks to get me back to work. I had been elected a Republican committeewoman from Davis County, and this made me a member of the state central committee.

"Ivy, why don't you run for state vice-chairman at the next convention?" Dora suggested one day. "You could do a lot up there to get women active in politics."

At first I wondered if I could manage it but, like a well-trained fire horse ready to take off when the bell rang, I was all set to run. Of course, Mother at once seconded the motion.

"If ye could wake up the Republican women of this state, ye could win the election," she insisted.

One day, Dora came rushing in with the news that the clubwomen we'd organized were unanimously behind me for the state office.

"You've simply got to try for it, Ivy," she cried, just bubbling with excitement.

Caught up by her enthusiasm, I discussed the matter with our state chairman a few weeks later. He listened with apparent interest to my ideas about organizing women, but made no comment about my running for office.

There is a difference between having brunch with the girls in your own neighborhood to discuss getting out the vote, and politics as it is practiced on the state level by the pros. But there are also similarities, for politics is, after all, people—and people are votes.

My mother was a real pro in this field. The reason, I can see, was quite simple. She knew and liked people—and that is one of the requisites for success in politics.

In my first attempt to run for a state office, the lessons learned at my mother's knee served me well.

Having decided to take the plunge, I immediately went to work to line up support. But at the state convention I discovered that none of the delegates who had promised to back me was willing to put my name in nomination. Then it was I came face to face with the realities of state politics. This was a "closed" convention and the leaders were doing the usual trading for various offices.

It was from a strange quarter that help came now. Bill Lowe—who had run against our friend, Bill Seegmiller, at the first convention I had attended—offered to see that I was nominated. I remembered Mother's advice of years before— "You're for Seegmiller, not *against* Lowe."

When my name was placed in nomination, a rebellion seemed to break out against dictates from the top brass. As we came down to the finish, I had a slight lead on the roll-call vote. But a last-minute trade occurred, and my opponent squeezed through with a lead of twenty-five votes out of eleven hundred cast.

When the campaign got under way that autumn, I found myself in the doghouse with the state leaders. Nevertheless, I wanted to work for our candidate and said so. Before it was over, the state chairman sent for me and gave me work to do. For, no matter how much power party leaders have in convention or in "smoke-filled rooms," they need the party faithful when it is time to reach the voters.

But I was convinced that we might have made a better showing if the campaign had not been directed primarily toward men, on the theory that their wives would vote as they did. The potent and independent political force of women had not yet been understood. Women have energy and tremendous enthusiasm, once it is sparked, and they are able to tackle any cause they espouse with optimism and spirit.

The old-fashioned notion that a woman's place is in the home—that she is too emotional and impulsive to hold public office—was fast being disproved. Her high standards of integrity, practical judgment, balance, and humanitarianism are invaluable assets to government office on any level.

Another prevalent myth held that women would not support feminine candidates for office. But more and more women were being elected as delegates to party conventions, were running local offices in cities and counties, and were serving in national government. With some thirty million potential women voters in the country, they represented a tremendous source of still untapped strength.

But the idea of unifying this force was not to see the light of day at that time. The election was over and I was to be occupied otherwise for some time.

"You're going to have a baby," Dr. Trowbridge said. "It's a good thing there's no election this year, Ivy."

We were delighted when another little girl was born in June, 1941. Since I had chosen the names for the first two girls, it was only fair that Roy should select this one. I suggested Nancy Ellen, Mary Ellen, or Joe Ellen. Enlisting the help of all our friends on this tremendous decision, he finally came up with Nancy Ellen.

She was just a toddler when the 1942 campaign got under way and it did very nicely without any particular help from me. Early in October, the national committeewoman, Margaret Marr, stopped by the house. I was making jelly from the grapes off the vines in our yard, and was glad to pause for a chat.

"We've got a lot of work to do in our congressional district this year," she said. "Would you take over the work in three or four counties?"

"Oh, I just couldn't," I replied. "You see how it is with me."

She seemed quite perplexed that none of her entreaties

would budge me. Puzzled, and a little hurt, she stopped to see Dora Trowbridge.

"It's the first time Ivy's let me down," she said. "Is she unhappy or upset over anything?"

"No. Couldn't you tell? She's expecting a baby."

"Oh, for heaven's sake! Is that what she meant when she said, 'You can see how it is with me.' But those slacks she wore fooled me."

Our son Roy arrived ahead of schedule on October 22, 1942, thus spoiling my chance of voting that year. The congressional election came less than two weeks later. There was a blinding snowstorm and Dr. Trowbridge, stout Republican though he was, would not let me out of bed to go to the polls. It was the first time I'd missed voting since I had become old enough.

World War II had cast its pall over the 1942 election, and the tragedy of the previous December 7 was still fresh in our minds. I suppose everyone has his own Pearl Harbor story. For me the date has a particular poignancy—for personal as well as patriotic reasons.

December 7 was our wedding anniversary, but Roy had been unable to get home to celebrate. So Mother and Keith came to have dinner with me that quiet Sunday afternoon. Keith was trying to listen to the radio while five-year-old Pat plied him with questions, and Mother and I were cooking in the kitchen. Suddenly Keith appeared in the doorway with Pat perched on his shoulders. White-faced and shaken, he said:

"The Japs have bombed Pearl Harbor."

Like many another American family that heard the news, we refused to believe it—and told Keith it must be "another Orson Welles gag, like the Martians." But then, as we listened in stunned silence to the tragic bulletins pouring in, we got an inkling of the disaster. We could only imagine what it would mean in our lives, and we kept looking apprehensively at Keith, just eighteen, knowing that it would be his war.

Keith soon enlisted in the Marine Corps as a private and was selected for officer training. Before going out to the Pacific as a flying officer, he had a short furlough. A Catholic girl friend of his had sent him a St. Christopher's medal. When he got home he showed me her letter.

"Where's the medal?" I asked. "Why aren't you wearing it?"

"But, I'm not Catholic," he said.

"Keith, you know it's the degree of faith that counts and not the brand. Why should you question the degree of faith in this medal? Now please put it on and don't take it off."

Keith should have felt well protected, for Mother had insisted that he have a patriarchal blessing from one of our Mormon leaders. Fortunately, Keith came through some of the worst battles in the Pacific without a mishap.

In our home, the war brought us close to financial disaster. Because of war shortages, furniture manufacturing had virtually ceased. Gas rationing made it impossible for Roy to get around his territory by car. What little business there was could be handled by phone.

Those were the days when, with a certain feeling of nobility, we put up with anything and we all tried to do our bit. My long-standing friendship with hard times stood us in good stead when they came knocking at our door, after Roy's business evaporated. Even he was impressed with the distance I could get out of a dollar—and I kept telling him he should have been around during the depression when Mother and I had established the course records.

The fruit trees which I had planted, thick as the forest primeval, in our back yard were yielding dividends now and our cellar shelves were loaded with jars of home-grown fruit and preserves.

"If you could just learn how to make blue cheese," Roy said jokingly, "we'd be all set for a long siege."

We had a victory garden, which we shared with the insect world. Utah being an arid state, our small but busy corner of the agricultural empire was entitled to water from the nearby irrigation ditch. Each farmer was allotted a certain amount of time to tap the water supply. It didn't sound like a very hard job, but how were we to know that we would be assigned to draw water between the hours of 1:30 and 2:15 —in the morning?

We would sleepily struggle out to the garden in our bath-robes every night to take our turn at the ditch. Then we would scramble back to bed, bracing ourselves against the hour just after dawn when little Roy would start yelling for sustenance. Sitting sleepily by the window, feeding him his bottle, I would see our neighbor groping out to the garden in his bath-robe to divert the water into his patch. This went on for a few weeks before either of us woke up sufficiently to make a deal. He turned the water on for us when he came home from work—and I switched it on for him when I got up to feed the baby.

Our fellow gardeners advised us sternly against planting squash.

"Bugs'll eat it up," everyone declared flatly.

We were supporting potato bugs, tomato bugs, bean beetles, cucumber worms, and a number of species which didn't seem to care what they ate, so I was not impressed by the prospect of squash bugs. Why discriminate, I asked. So I planted squash.

However fecund other types of insects may be, I soon discovered that squash bugs could outbreed them all. I was willing to go share and share alike with insects, but these bugs were having none of this arrangement. Furthermore, they were eating up and growing fat on the insecticide I used to discourage the others.

When, some years later, I told a fellow Utahan in the Department of Agriculture the solution I found for this insect problem, he blanched and looked around to see if we had been overheard. Since the Department was struggling with surpluses, my claim of victory over the squash bugs pointed the way to doubling our national output. I just ran an extension cord from the house, picked up my vacuum cleaner, swept the bugs off every morning, and burned them.

"Too bad squash doesn't go very well with cheese," Roy said, admitting that I had scored a triumph.

It's entirely possible that this line of research might have led us somewhere but, with an election coming up, I was soon back in politics. The top echelon of the state Republican organization was being overhauled, I heard. There would be new officers—and the party was going to start winning elections. This sounded exciting enough to me.

When Margaret Marr called me to say that she was not going to run for reelection as national committeewoman from Utah and urged me to enter the race, I was intrigued with the idea. For this would mean branching out into the field of national politics. But with three children, ranging from two to eight, I feared that I couldn't do the job justice.

"Ye'll only have to go to two-thrree meetings a yearr," Mother assured me. "I'll come over 'ere and look after Roy and the children. It'll be good for ye to get away sometimes."

With this generous offer my remaining qualms evaporated, and I was jubilant when I was elected to represent Utah on the Republican National Committee. My colleague, George T. Hansen, was chosen at the same time, and we served together for the next ten years. Ultimately, George Hansen became known as "Mr. Republican" of Utah, and he played an important role in my future.

Among the 104 members of the national committee—a man and a woman representing every state and territory— there were prominent people from the world of finance, business, industry, and various professions. Some were dyed-in-the-wool conservatives, others had more liberal leanings. There were men of great wealth, and some in modest circumstances. But, whatever their incomes and interests, they were all elected because they had distinguished themselves in politics in their own states.

The feminine contingent included women of unusual background. For instance, there was Gladys Knowles, a feminine, soft-spoken woman, who operated one of the biggest cattle ranches in eastern Montana; Olene Stewart of Nevada, a shy, peaceable woman who, surprisingly enough, manufactured explosives; and Pearl Pace of Kentucky, the very embodiment of a beautiful Southern belle, who was sheriff of her county. To her friends on the committee this charming Southern lady was known as "Two-Pistol Pearl." Mrs. Pace has since been appointed a war claims commissioner—perhaps her experience as sheriff now serves her in good stead in this important job.

At the advanced age of thirty-nine, I found myself the "baby" on the committee. My first trip to a meeting occurred at the time of the 1944 convention which nominated Tom Dewey to oppose Roosevelt for a fourth term. Newly elected members of the committee do not take their places until the postconvention meeting, so I had time to enjoy the convention and meet the delegates.

For years, as a small-fry Republican living in a little Western town, I had heard of the party's leaders; and now, meeting them on a presumably equal basis, I felt like a girl being presented to royalty.

At first, I was inclined to follow Confucius's advice and "save face by keeping lower half shut" in this distinguished company. But I've always had an impulsive tendency to speak my mind when the opportunity arises. This trait has given me a few embarrassing moments.

One night, at a special meeting of committeewomen, we seemed to be getting nowhere after hours of debate on a minor issue. So I mustered the courage to get up and say:

"Madam Chairman, it's after 1 A.M. and most of us would like to get out of here and get some sleep. I'm sure we've made up our minds about this.... Could someone put it in the form of a motion so we can vote and go to bed?"

Realizing this was a pretty daring speech for a freshman member of this august committee, I sat down, blushing with embarrassment. But, to my relief, there was a burst of applause and one of the committee veterans, sitting next to me, patted my hand and said, "Thank you, young lady. That's what should have been said two hours ago."

No more than I could help being outspoken could the committeemen help being politicians. Many old-timers still regarded women in this field as a necessary nuisance, but looked askance at the distaff side in important office.

One piece of business which came before the committee was the election of a new secretary. We women felt that one of our sex should get the job, while the men picked a candidate of their own. Their strategy was to split our vote by putting a second woman in the race. This move created such a furor among the fifty-two women members that the men got cold feet—and none would allow his name to be put in nomination. So, with quiet smiles of satisfaction, we sat back and made our decision between the two candidates—both of them women.

With the 1944 debacle behind us and forgotten, we turned our attention to the next time at bat. The prospects were fairly bleak. Utah was almost solidly Democratic, from the governor's mansion down to the courthouse benches. The opposition had been winning elections for so long that we were just working to keep the minority vote from looking too bad. Our party, by and large, seemed to go into each campaign like lemmings headed for the cliff.

My new job gave me the opportunity at last to try a plan for organizing women voters at the precinct level, where elections are won. Edith Garner, state vice-chairman, Mrs. Alex Jex, president of the state Republican clubs, and I began a grass roots organization to prepare for the 1946 election.

We traveled across the state, working with county vice-chairmen to establish Republican women's study clubs in every voting district, and conducting workshops to instruct women in campaign techniques. We stressed particularly the need to canvass the district for new or unregistered voters, to organize a corps of workers to staff mail rooms and distribute literature, set up telephone committees, arrange meetings for candidates—and, last but not least, to form fund-raising committees.

The response we received exceeded our expectations. Given an objective and a specific job to achieve it, women were willing to devote untold time and energy to the cause. They soon discovered that all a volunteer worker in politics had to do was to volunteer—and she'd have practically a full-time job.

As we intensified our program, I was away from home so much that Mother just moved in to look after my family. But she kept an eagle eye on me to make sure that the country was being saved.

Our candidate for the Senate was Judge Arthur V. Watkins of Utah County, a onetime country lawyer who had risen to prominence by dint of his integrity, wisdom, and courage. His foresight and untiring efforts had been instrumental in securing an expanded program of irrigation and reclamation for Utah—an important service, for water was the life blood of Utah, as well as of other Western states.

Despite these achievements, there were probably no more

than three people in the state who thought Watkins could win. They were, left to right, Judge Watkins, Mrs. Watkins, and myself. We went into every nook and corner of the state and found that the groundwork laid by our grass-roots drive now began to pay off. Wherever we went there was a corps of trained volunteers to assist county chairmen in getting the campaign rolling. Mr. Watkins spoke before every type and size of audience, from meetings of business, labor, and forum groups to informal teas and special lunches. Frequently, I would pinch-hit for him so that he could get from one meeting to the next. Between meetings Mrs. Watkins and I would poke into stores and offices in the business districts, gathering up an audience. There was nothing too menial or insignificant for us to undertake, if it meant getting our candidate's message across.

While the Watkins campaign was vitally important, it was only part of the job. For I had been elected vice-chairman of the Western Conference organized by party leaders of the eleven Western states. Our main objective was to reactivate the party organization and campaign for the election of senators, congressmen, and governors in these states. My chief assignment was to work with the women's groups on the same grass-roots plan we had used in Utah and to set up women's clubs, staff committees, and conduct workshops wherever we went.

As election day approached, we became more and more encouraged by the enthusiastic ground-swell we felt everywhere.

With two other Republican women, I paid a call on a Roman Catholic priest in southern Nevada. He was familiar with the political picture in the state and said that he felt there was a swing toward the Republicans that year. As we left, he looked at our trim black suits curiously. "I say there, Mrs. Priest," said the Irish priest with a twinkle in his eye, "is it customary for Republican ladies always to wear black?"

"No, Father, it isn't customary—it's just become a habit in the last fourteen years," I replied.

"Well, come November the fifth, you can put on color," he predicted.

His forecast proved quite accurate. In Utah, we elected Arthur Watkins to the Senate and Bill Dawson, a Republican from my own district, won one of our state's two congressional seats; Nevada came through with a Republican governor and Senator George Malone; the state of Washington sent Republican Harry Cain to the Senate; Montana elected Republican Senator Zales Eckton; Idaho elected Senator Herman Welker; and California sent Richard Nixon to Congress. It was our biggest string of victories in over a decade. I promptly sent a jubilant wire to Father Moran in Nevada:

"Hooray, Father . . . I'm wearing red today."

IX

IN politics, as in the theater, it is axiomatic that the show must go on. Like other troupers, I was often on the road when I longed to be at home—especially on holidays and important family occasions. On Mother's Day in 1947, I'd hoped to be with my own mother, but instead I was on a train bound for Utah, after attending a national committee meeting in Washington.

When I changed trains in Chicago I was startled to hear my name called over the station loudspeaker. I hurried to the passenger agent's phone with dread, for no one would go to such trouble to reach me unless it was urgent.

My brother Keith's voice came over the wire. "Mother's in the hospital," he blurted out. "I thought I'd better warn you."

"What's happened to her, Keith?" I practically shouted.

"She's had a stroke."

"Oh, no! How serious is it? I'll get on a plane right away."

A few hours later I was at her bedside. With her usual

courage, she tried to smile, though she was paralyzed except for limited use of her right hand. But she made some improvement and within two weeks the doctors gave me permission to take her home.

Her sharp blue eyes lit up with determination when I told her that I was going to teach her to walk again. We started in the morning, when I would help her out of bed. Standing behind her, I would put my arms around her waist. Then, with my legs pressed closed behind hers, I would push one leg forward and then the other. In this way, I would walk her to breakfast. If her appetite was good, she would feed herself with her good hand. Then I would walk her into the living room, sitting her in a chair against one wall. Every hour, on the hour, I would march her from one chair to another.

Active as her life had been, this invalidism was hard on her, and I was confident she would not submit to it for long. Her valiant efforts to help herself gave me a couple of bad frights. Once, I heard her crash to the floor, trying to get out of bed without me. Another time, she fell in the bathroom—her body blocking the door so that I could not get in without pushing her out of the way first.

During those months, I had no time for anything but Mother and my home. Pat was now a pert, blond, freckled-faced miss who groaned over going to school. Nancy and Roy still needed a lot of care, so any political chores which could not be handled over the telephone were out of the question for me. But it was amazing how much could be accomplished on the phone.

Aunt Gert was a regular visitor those days. She had finally broken down and bought a hearing aid, but she really didn't need it to carry on a conversation with Mother, who had difficulty talking since the stroke. Aunt Gert would sit down across the room from Mother, prudently turn off the hearing aid to save the battery, and launch into a discussion laden with countless errors that I had heard Mother correct a dozen times. Poor Mother would sit there speechless, her eyes cracking sparks, as Aunt Gert rambled on, murdering the truth, as Mother knew it, with every sentence.

"Well, I'll stop by in a day er two, Clare," Aunt Gert would say cheerfully as she swept out. "Take care of yer *paralellis* now," she added.

But Aunt Gert's savings on the battery could not last forever. From the kitchen, one morning, I heard her delve into a bit of family history that sounded exciting and provocative. It was a reminiscence about the marriage of an elderly cousin back in England. Immediately after the ceremony, so the story went, the cousin's young bride had quietly vanished with the groom's life savings, the table silver, and a fur wrap belonging to the parson's wife.

"I never trusted a woman as put on them kind of airs," Aunt Gert said vehemently.

Mother's eyes blazed with indignation. She had always insisted that the bride was too good to be true—and that's why *she* hadn't trusted her. They'd argued this point so often down through the years that Aunt Gert automatically began to reject the argument Mother was not able to make.

"If ye'd not lost yer scarrf at the weddin', and spent the 'ole day searching for it, ye'd 'ave seen what she was really like," Aunt Gert said.

Suddenly, there was an interruption.

"Put yer 'and out and see if ye're awake," came a familiar voice. "I didn't lose me scarrf. It was me purrse. And I saw plainer than you what she was like. Butter wouldn't melt in 'er mouth, it wouldn't."

It was one of the clearest remarks Mother had made since

her stroke. I listened with amazement and joy. Aunt Gert, seeing Mother's lips move, cried, "Eh, look, Ivy, yer mother's talkin'," and hurriedly turned up her hearing aid.

"What'd ye say, Clare? I 'ad my 'earring aid off."

Mother repeated the statement as calmly as if she had been talking all day.

Her recovery now became rapid. She seemed to eat more, building up her strength to straighten Aunt Gert out on a number of points, and soon was able to move around by herself.

While she had been in the hospital, the doctors had discovered that Mother had diabetes. So sugar was now strictly forbidden. But she could move around now and reach the sugar bowl. At times, I found lumps of sugar in her purse.

"It's for the little ones," she would explain, when I scolded her.

When summer came, she would call one of the children in and pass out some change.

"It's a terrible 'ot day," she'd say. "Run down to the corner and get us all a Popsicle."

The child would start out eagerly.

"Better get us each two," Mother would say. "It's really a terrible 'ot day."

In spite of all this, she was back on her feet and ready to take up her struggle against the Democrats again that fall. She went back to her own house—leaving quite an empty place in ours.

One Saturday morning, when the children were home from school, Pat wandered into the house and said, "Gee, it's dead around here without Aunt Gert and Grandma! Nothing to do."

At that moment piercing shrieks from the back yard sent

me racing to the window. There were young Roy and Nancy decked out in Indian feathers, neatly tied to the apple tree with the lariat their father had brought home, along with moccasins and cowboy hats from his last trip. This gear had provoked a regular game of cowboys and Indians, and Pat was inclined to be absent-minded after tying up the pesky redskins.

"I'll give you something to do," I snapped. "You march right out and untie your brother and sister."

"Oh, they like to be tied up," Pat protested above their shrieks.

"It certainly sounds like it, doesn't it? Hurry up, now."

Nancy had started school that fall and with just little Roy at home with me all day, the place seemed empty—if a house with a husky five-year-old boy can be called that. I still had my national committee post and, with Mother well again, I felt free to resume activities.

One night that winter, Roy wandered into the living room just before bedtime. I was finishing up a basket of mending.

"I can't find those sardines," he said.

"Oh, Roy, were they something special? I'm afraid I used them for sandwich fillings for the tea this afternoon."

"Well, they were the first Norwegian sardines I'd seen since the war. But I can get some more. You didn't use up my Liederkranz, too, did you?"

"At a ladies' tea? I should say not!"

He was back a few minutes later, with cheese and crackers.

"Well, how's politics?" he asked. "And who's running this year? 'Arold Stassen against Rroberrt Tawft?"

We had fallen into the habit of imitating Mother's accent on candidates' names and I sometimes had to check myself outside the family circle, particularly with certain names.

"No, I think it will be between Tom Dewey and Senator Tawft," I said.

"You for Dewey?"

"I always have been. But I'm on the national committee, Roy, and that makes a difference. I must stay neutral until the state convention. We're in charge of the party machinery and it wouldn't be fair to take sides until the delegates are picked. But then I'll come out for Dewey."

My colleague, George Hansen, a man of profound integrity, agreed that we had to maintain neutrality in the maneuvering that preceded the state convention. I must have done a good job, for one of Dewey's backers in Utah took me out to lunch and berated me for not declaring myself.

"We mean business, young lady. We're going to get this nomination for Tom Dewey. We won't stand for fence-sitters. People have got to say where they are, or we're going to get rid of them."

My reaction to a threat is automatic—I get mad.

"Oh, you are?" I shot back. "Well, let me tell you something. As long as I am a committeewoman, I am supposed to stay neutral. And I shall stay neutral until the time comes to declare myself. As for getting rid of me on the national committee, you go right ahead and try. But make sure you don't need a lot of help yourself."

His high-pressure tactics alienated many Dewey supporters and, instead of having a delegation solidly pledged to Dewey, we were split down the middle. We shepherded the remnants of our forces to Philadelphia for the 1948 convention, where I could now work for my candidate.

After Mother's illness, it was Aunt Gert and Uncle Lije who looked after the family while I went to what Aunt Gert insisted upon calling the "confection." As I was making final arrangements, Pat appeared in my room looking quietly worried. This caused me some concern, as normally Pat was a noisy worrier.

"What's the matter? Don't you want to stay with Aunt Gert?"

"Oh, sure. I'm just worried about you."

"Worried about me? What for?"

"You might get lost in that big crowd and not get back to us."

No mother can resist a pitch of that kind. So it was that my solicitous daughter went along to the convention with me. At the age of eleven, she was the youngest, and probably the most active, page on the floor.

The convention hall, gaily decorated with bunting and flags, was jampacked with thousands of delegates and their alternates, waving their banners and flags, exuberantly shouting and staging demonstrations for favorite sons. Excitement ran to fever pitch because Dewey, Taft, and Stassen, the three strong contenders in the ring, each had a hard core of supporters determined to fight it out to the end.

The main job of national committee members at a convention is to look after their state delegations—to see that they have tickets, badges, transportation, and all pertinent information. George Hansen and I set up our Utah headquarters in a suite at the Bellevue Stratford Hotel, and it soon became a madhouse. Convention headquarters were also at our hotel and its facilities were taxed to the utmost. The crush was so great that it was all you could do to fight your way through the lobby or into an elevator. There was constant visiting back and forth between state delegations and candidates' quarters, and behind-the-scenes maneuvering for delegates' support.

The pro-Dewey faction of our Utah delegation was doing its utmost to remain intact. Despite its efforts, one of the

Dewey supporters slipped over to Taft on the first ballot—"just to make it look a little more even," as he later explained.

While Taft had fervent adherents and Stassen had great appeal for the younger delegates, Dewey led the roll call from the start, and was nominated on the second ballot. Pandemonium then broke loose. The band blared out "The Sidewalks of New York," and the New York delegates, ninety-six strong, led the snake dance, joined by state after state, as it wound wildly through the hall.

In the midst of all this excitement my young Pat distinguished herself by getting lost and scaring the life out of me. A group of us were bound for a band concert and Pat had gone on ahead in another car with one of her fellow pages, whose mother was also a committee member. When we arrived at the hall, we could find no trace of the girls and we were frantic.

"They couldn't be inside—we've got their tickets," I said.

"Let's just make sure before we get the police," said Dane Hansen, a Kansas delegate who was the brother of my colleague, George. He suggested that we divide forces and each comb a section of the arena.

When we finally reached our seats, we found the two young ladies calmly ensconced in them.

"Mother, you got lost!" Pat said accusingly.

They had gotten into the hall without tickets, simply by explaining that their mothers were committee members.

A few days later, I had to go to the convention hall without my little guardian. I left her at the hotel with instructions to wait until she was called for by our cousin Carter Helton, an Ohio delegate. Later he showed up without her, and worriedly told me she was not at the hotel. Frantically, I made my way to a phone booth to call the police—when I spotted her out on the floor, happily prancing around in a demonstration.

"Nobody came for me, Mother," she explained. "So I got in a cab and came over myself. I was afraid you'd gotten lost again."

When the entire proceedings were over, Pat managed to get me back to Utah safely.

This was 1948—the year when my party hypnotized itself into believing that it just couldn't lose. It didn't occur to me to buck this belief until just before the Dewey train arrived in Idaho. In Pocatello, while waiting to board the campaign train and ride back to Utah, I mingled with the crowds at the station. The negative comments I overheard about our candidate came as a shock.

"Why so blue, Ivy?" asked one of Dewey's aides.

"I think we're losing an election," I replied. "That's why I'm blue."

"Oh, don't be silly. Many people say they don't even see why we're wasting money running this train around the country. We should be home cutting our wood for winter."

"Well, if the adverse criticism I heard out in the railroad yards was any indication of how people feel, you'll have plenty of time to cut your wood," I replied.

Dewey made an outstanding speech in the Mormon Tabernacle in Salt Lake City. The church permitted use of the Tabernacle for political meetings only for presidential candidates of both parties. The enthusiastic response of the huge crowd made my fears seem groundless. A few days later I was even more encouraged, when I met my very good friend Mrs. Stewart, Democratic state vice-chairman, in the hotel lobby.

"How are things going for you people?" I asked.

She nodded toward a prominent visiting member of her party who was chatting with a group across the lobby.

"If we don't get that woman out of here soon, you're going to win the state," Mrs. Stewart confided.

"What's she done?"

"Just about everything. Yesterday, while making a speech in a railroad town, she told her audience that Dewey should not be sent to the White House because his wife wasn't up to the social responsibilities; after all, she was just the daughter of a railroad man!"

"Maybe we could get her to make that talk up in Pocatello," I suggested brightly.

As we continued to read the good news in the straw polls, our dream of returning from the political wilderness grew stronger. George and Priscilla Hansen asked Roy and me to join them for a "victory dinner" at the Hotel Utah on election night.

They had ordered a very special cut of beef prepared for the occasion and we sat down in gay spirits to tackle the first course. We pooh-poohed the discouraging early returns coming in over the radio but, just as the roast beef reached the table, we got the first results from Iowa. Never did a state so "safely Republican" go so surely Democratic—and never did roast beef lose its appeal so quickly.

By the time we left the hotel, the "victory" party had fallen completely apart. The only bright spot we could find was the election of J. Bracken Lee as governor of Utah—the first Republican to win this post in almost a quarter of a century.

In my own Congressional district, we had even lost our Republican representative, Bill Dawson, who had been beaten by a 30,000 vote margin by a woman lawyer named Reva Beck Bosone.

Well, there's nothing to do after a losing campaign but to pick up the pieces. So we went back over our state to see where we had made our mistakes. There were certain places where the party needed strengthening. The fact that a Democratic woman candidate had won in my own district was food for thought. For, after our success in 1946, we thought we had patented the idea of building up the women's vote for the Republicans. But the obvious over-all fault was overconfidence.

When the national committee met in Omaha in January after the election, feelings ran high. In the post-mortem over our failure there were bitterness and fault-finding. A movement was started to oust Hugh Scott, national chairman. But his supporters rallied round and the battle was on. Naturally, I had to speak my mind, and finally was able to get the floor.

"Ladies and gentlemen, this is the biggest display of poor sportsmanship I have ever witnessed," I declared. "And I've witnessed some big displays.

"You are blaming one man for every mistake that was made in this campaign. And every man and woman in this room knows deep down in his heart that he failed to do his job back in his own state.

"Too many of us read the polls and expected victory to fall into our laps. If Tom Dewey had been elected, every one of us would be in Washington today assuring him of how much we had done for him and hoping he wouldn't find out how little."

Hugh won a vote of confidence, by a slim margin. But the handwriting was on the wall and, the following August, he resigned and Guy Gabrielson was elected.

"Ye better quit wringin' yer 'ands over what 'appened last time and get ready for the next time," Mother said pointedly.

Roy came home from his sales trip one weekend early in 1950 to find the sink full of teacups and sandwich plates.

"Well," he observed good-naturedly, "I see the campaign is getting started."

"We're eating water-cress sandwiches this year," I said. "Trying to get down to fighting weight."

133

"Better try raw meat. What the Republicans need is more good red blood."

"I guess we have too many chiefs and not enough Indians."

The planning and plotting was under way and we were poring over lists of possible candidates for state offices. We had a Republican governor and one senator in office. In 1950, another Senate and both Congressional seats would be up for grabs.

We were most directly concerned by the fact that a Democratic woman, Mrs. Bosone, had won the Congressional post in our district. She had mobilized the women to win the election by an overwhelming majority and, during two years in Congress, had kept them pretty well behind her. There was no doubt that the women of our district, including some Republicans, were proud that one of our own sex was representing us.

While we found many capable people to run for other offices, few were willing to take on the battle against the redoubtable Mrs. Bosone. Some men turned pale at the mere mention of the idea. One day, a delegation of party men, headed by Franklin Riter, an attorney in Salt Lake, called on me.

"Ivy, we've been talking it over and we think we've come up with the candidate who can beat Mrs. Bosone."

"Wonderful!" I exclaimed. "Who is it?"

"You."

"Me! Now wait a minute, Frank," I said, hoisting the signal of distress which I had seen on other faces when this idea was broached. "What made you pick on me?"

"Well, you're a woman and this should be a woman's race. Besides, you're a good campaigner and we think you can win."

"Thanks for the compliment. It's not that I'm afraid to try. But we can't afford it and—"

"We'll raise the money for your campaign."

"And I've got a husband and three small children."

"All the more reason. You owe it to them."

"No," I said flatly.

He smiled and said no more. But wherever I went in the state, at county meetings prior to the state nominating convention, the same suggestion was made and each time I tossed it off.

As the winter wore on and spring came, we still hadn't found a candidate. In April, when the filing date was close at hand, a party of state leaders called on me.

"Everyone wants you to run, Ivy," they said. "No one else is coming in—there won't even be a primary. So it's up to you."

"The party has been pretty nice to me," I said. "I owe it a lot. And I'd hate to think this seat would go to a Democrat just by default." I hesitated, feeling myself weaken, and added, "Well, let me talk it over with Roy and Mother."

The truth is I was excited and deeply flattered that the party had chosen me—even if no one else wanted the honor. By this time, I suppose, I was ready to have my arm twisted.

Of course, Mother was delighted with the idea. She had the campaign strategy all plotted out and I had won by a landslide before we even stopped talking.

"If ye keep yer 'ead on yer shoulders and go in therr fightin' 'ard," said Mother vehemently, "ye'll give them a rrace they'll neverr ferget!"

"Sure, Ivy," my husband chimed in. "You're just the girl that can do it."

Their supreme confidence and faith in me were like shots of Adrenalin. So, when the delegation came back for my decision, I agreed to run. "But I'm not going into this just to fill out the ticket," I added. "I am going in to win!"

"Mother's going to run for Congress," I heard Pat say to

young Roy. "You'd better keep your face clean and quit catching frogs."

I could only wish it would be that simple. As a lonely five-to-one shot, I wondered how I was ever going to overcome a deficit of 30,000 votes in a district that was predominantly Democratic.

X

NO matter how carefully you plan it, there are times when you suddenly find yourself a committee of one, in charge of lifting the entire world with a lever. The delegation that had gotten me into this race had gone off blithely, its mission accomplished, and I was on my own, with a tremendous job to do and very little to do it with.

Friends began to offer congratulations and support, down to the last twig on each family tree. The children shouted with delight, Roy beamed with quiet pride, and Mother wore her look of determination. Then the family began to rib me, as my family is apt to do.

Pat would march Nancy and young Roy in after school every day and shake hands quite formally with me.

"What's this all about?" I asked.

"Got to build up your handshaking muscles," she explained.

Young Roy dragged out all of Nancy's thirty-five dolls one

day so that I could practice baby-kissing. And his father came home from a sales trip with a bear trap.

"It's just great for catching voters," he explained. "I can get them for you wholesale."

But, after a time, the novelty of Mother's running for Congress began to wear off. The family's attention once again was directed toward such normal problems as where are all the clean socks; you still owe me twenty-five cents from my week-before-last's allowance; and what happened to that hunk of salami I left in the icebox behind the head of lettuce, Ivy?

As the hot, enervating days of summer wore on, I came to have the feeling that the campaign was a mountain I was carrying on my shoulders. To some extent, I suppose this must be true at the start of any political campaign. There is a candidate, with ideas and enthusiasm, to begin with. As he is able to fire others with his own convictions, he ceases to be alone and gathers adherents.

But it was up to me to make a start and if I sat at home, doing nothing, surely nothing would be done for me. It wasn't difficult to find things to do; it was just a question of what to tackle first.

The Democrats seemed to be rolling in money, and they had a striking candidate in Reva Bosone, a handsome redhead with penetrating blue eyes and a keen mind—and she was an excellent speaker. She had served in the State Legislature and had been a municipal judge for a number of years. By cracking down hard on reckless drivers and by working for rehabilitation facilities for alcoholics, she had made a name for herself before going to Congress.

Looking over the returns of the last election, I saw that Mrs. Bosone had piled up her greatest majorities in the industrial areas, where the labor vote was big, and in the precincts where a large number of women registered. To beat her, I would have to cut into her strength, while holding the Republican vote in the district.

I knew that the women of the district would give us both a cordial reception. The working people would probably listen to me because I was a working girl, my father had been a miner, and I realized the importance of a full lunch bucket. I knew what I believed, and hoped I could convince others enough to win.

The Republican campaign opened officially with a big rally at Saltair in September. Political workers from all over the state assembled and as I saw them, waving "Priest for Congress" banners, my confidence soared. I don't believe people like to listen to long political harangues. So, with my knees shaking a little, I stood up that day and tried to make it snappy. I just told them how necessary it was for all of us to work for the whole ticket, from the senator down to the local officials.

In downtown Salt Lake, George Hansen located an empty store, with a big window on the street, and rented it for headquarters. When we moved in, I sat down in the dusty, dimly lighted office and suddenly felt terribly alone again.

"Now, what do I do?" I asked myself.

As if in answer to a prayer, Tommy Wheelright appeared in the deserted room at that moment. A young Salt Lake newspaperman, Tommy was just checking in to find out what was going on. A nice-looking, tall, slim young fellow, he sat there chewing thoughtfully on his thick copy pencil, as I talked on about the issues.

Tommy, it turned out, was a Republican who had never been associated with any faction of the party. Before he left he volunteered to handle my publicity. I was like a prospector who had tripped over a rock—and found that it was pure gold.

George Hansen decided this office would be ideal for the entire Republican ticket, and the place was soon bustling with activity. When it came to allocating campaign funds for advertising, radio, television, office staff, and so forth, the leaders were anxious to use the money where it would get the best results. In Wallace F. Bennett, our candidate for the Senate, they had a real winner and naturally most of the outlay went into his race. Although I could hardly blame them, I couldn't help recalling their glib assurances about expense money when they persuaded me to run.

It was George Hansen's beautiful and dynamic wife, Priscilla, who took the bull by the horns.

"Look here," she told the finance committee. "You got Ivy into this. She didn't want to run . . . but you insisted. And she's got to have some money and some help. If you don't get busy and raise it, I'm going to."

Good as her word, Priscilla took over as my campaign manager and things began to hum. We were able to get an old friend, Leona Knudsen, to act as office director, and Mrs. Jex staffed our mailing room with volunteers from her women's Republican clubs. Priscilla hustled me down to see an advertising man, Dave Evans, who took on our account. So now we had a team and, as long as our credit was good, we would be in the fight.

Estimates of my chances of victory—which could be summed up as "anything's possible"—were just slightly higher than the odds quoted at Democratic headquarters, where they were saying, "Don't be ridiculous." For this latter, at least, I was thankful. I had been through the Dewey campaign, and complacency was something I would always be glad to see on the other fellow's platform.

Since ours was the only race in the country that year between two women seeking a Congressional seat, it attracted newspaper attention, locally and nationally. At the outset, the papers predicted that voters would be treated to a "cat fight." If so, it started on a strange note. A reporter interviewed both of us and came out with a story which quoted me:

"Reva Bosone is a very smart woman, well-educated, well-groomed, good-looking and a good sport. I like and respect her very much. But get me started on her voting record and I can and will attack down the line."

And what did Reva have to say to the same interviewer?

"Ivy Priest is a gracious, charming woman, who is almost universally well-liked. She and I differ, and differ sharply, on politics, but so far as a person is concerned, Ivy is a swell gal."

At least in energy and endurance I thought I had the edge on her. And I set out to prove it by seeing as many people as I could.

Early every morning, I started out in the family car, a 1947 Chevvy, packed with campaign literature, to make my rounds of coffee *klatsches*, cottage meetings, lunches, and teas. My old friend, Tracey Petersen, often came along to pick up audience reaction.

At first, I tried to keep up with the housework, with Pat's help. But we got to the point where no two socks matched and one could hardly get through the door for the galoshes, coats, baseball bats, and dolls that were scattered in the hall. So again I sent out an S O S for Aunt Gert.

Things got back to normal very quickly, with her in the house. She had the children dashing off in all directions to buy a can of peas that was on sale here and fruit juice that was on special somewhere else. Lights, which had blazed for hours as the youngsters traipsed from room to room, got turned off and the menu began to feature such Aunt Gert specials as "dough-gots," a fried bread that the children loved.

"Now ye get on with th' 'lectioneerin'," Aunt Gert said. "And I'll look after these young imps."

Both Reva Bosone and I were often invited to appear on

the same platform. She was always given the "clean-up" spot, since she was the incumbent. On one occasion, at a legislative council meeting, I was given the last time at bat, as a past president of the council, and I made the most of it. Reva talked about her record in Congress and I tore into it when my turn came.

We bowed out of the meeting together and walked to the elevator side by side.

"I've got Clarence's car today," she said. "May I give you a lift?"

"I'd appreciate it, Reva, if you would."

"Ivy, you were really rough on me in there today."

"Why, Reva, no one was more surprised than I when you led with your chin!"

We rode on downtown together, chatting amiably about the rigors of campaigning.

I was reminded of my grandfather's remark that politicians could be friendly enemies. By becoming bitterly partisan, he said, they often forgot the greater good, and destroyed unity. He would illustrate this comment with his favorite story about the time when Utah was to be admitted as a state in 1896. Brigham Young, realizing the value of two strong political parties, called the Mormons together and announced that one half of the church would be Republican and the other half Democratic. My grandfather and some of his family wound up on the Republican side, while other members of his clan were in the Democratic faction. How authentic this story is I can't say, but Grandfather Baker told it with gusto. To this day the Bakers of Utah seem about evenly divided. My father's cousin, Judge Clarence Baker, was elected to the municipal bench in Salt Lake on the Democratic ticket.

As time went by, the opposition began to take me a little more seriously and I could sense that I was making some gains. The crowds at rallies began to get bigger and there was more enthusiasm among my supporters. But we still had to counter the recurrent taunt of the Democrats: "What is there about a Bountiful housewife that qualifies her for Congress?"

"Some of our best voters are housewives," Tommy Wheelright, our publicity man, observed. "Why don't we make that work for us?"

And so, whenever I appeared at a women's meeting, I would try to use the opposition's taunt to good advantage.

"I'll bet there are many housewives in this room who have sound ideas and would make excellent congresswomen." This gambit usually got a big hand.

There was an air of elation and confidence around our headquarters now. We were going down the stretch—and we felt that we were closing the gap. If the ground swell continued we would surely win.

When Roy came home for weekends, he had to join the campaign caravan in order to see me.

"This is like the days when we were courting," he said wryly. "Tell me, if I vote for you will you lower the tariff on Norwegian sardines?"

"Your daughter Nancy said she'd get the third-grade mothers to vote Democratic if I didn't promise to pass a law against Limburger cheese," I said. "You didn't wrap it up when you put it back in the icebox last week."

"Let's go home, Ivy. My feet are killing me."

"Just one more meeting, Roy. And then I promised Priscilla and George we'd stop by. They've got some people they want us to meet."

Young Roy and Nancy spent their spare time around the neighborhood tacking up posters and passing out campaign cards. Pat organized a bicycle brigade, the duties of which were rather nebulous, but its members all had my posters affixed to their bikes.

Aunt Gert, ever alert to keep the children on their best

behavior, would admonish young Roy, "Ye better wash yer face, ye young imp. Ye'll lose yer mother more votes than ye'll get, lookin' that way."

Dave Evans, at the advertising agency, suggested the idea of running a daily slogan in the papers with my picture. We started this simple little scheme because we couldn't afford big ads and television time—and, to our amazement, it caught on. People began to watch for the slogans which we varied from day to day.

"Tell her to keep it up," said one man who came into our headquarters with a scrapbook full of the ads. "That's the stuff!"

He left a twenty-five-dollar check as a contribution. The mail was bringing in many small contributions of this kind. Occasionally, more affluent friends would send in fifty or a hundred dollars to help out. We received some aid from the national committee, and Priscilla Hansen was finding it easier to raise money for me locally. But insufficient funds were still one of our main headaches.

"Roy, if I just had enough time and a few more dollars, I could win this campaign," I told him when he got home one weekend.

"I can't do anything about the time," he said. "But go ahead and spend the money, if it'll help. We'll dip into our savings."

About ten days before election day, Reva and I met again on the same platform, reinforced by the state leaders of both parties. The occasion was the Junior Chamber of Commerce luncheon in Salt Lake.

The chairman announced that he would pick questions at random from a prepared list and that we would each have two minutes to answer them.

I tried to reply to my first query briefly and to the point.

When the Democratic national committeeman followed, he said, "Before I answer my question, I would just like to tell our friend Mrs. Priest that was a canned speech, if I ever heard one."

When my turn came round again, I took up his challenge.

"Mr. Chairman, may I suggest to your friend on the Democratic side that he take a few lessons in canning from a housewife—and he'll learn that you must have quality merchandise to put in cans!"

The audience responded with laughter and applause. Heartened by this response, I answered my question. After that, the clash between the Bountiful housewife and the Democratic committeeman took the spotlight.

When it was over, the Republican chairman rushed over to shake my hand with elation. "That's great, Ivy," he said. "I bet you picked up two hundred votes in here today."

"I only hope you're right," I said. "But you know votes are not counted by applause."

Several days later, I came swinging home before lunch to pick up some extra campaign literature and a little powder for my nose before speaking to a ladies' club. My next door neighbor came in excitedly.

"A woman came to the house yesterday, Ivy, with some Democratic literature and she started telling me that your children weren't getting the proper care.

" 'Do you know Mrs. Priest?' I asked her.

" 'No, I don't know her,' she said.

" 'Then, how do you know she's neglecting her children?'

" 'Well, anyone knows that a mother of young children can't spend so much time campaigning and still give them the proper care.' "

"I looked out in her car," my neighbor added, "and saw two children sitting in the back seat, eating cupcakes. So I asked her, 'Are those your children?'

" 'Why, yes,' she said. 'I don't have anyone to leave them with, so I bring them along with me.'

" 'Well,' I told her, 'Mrs. Priest doesn't have to do that.

At this moment her aunt is giving them a nourishing meal. They don't have to have cakes for lunch in a car.'

"Was her face red! Without a word she got back in that car and drove off. I thought you'd want to know about this."

"I wish she had stopped at our door and told Aunt Gert about my neglected children," I said, laughing. "If Aunt Gert had had her hearing aid turned on, there would have been a riot."

In politics, you get used to all sorts of tactics, and I resolved not to let them get me down. As I drove along, though, little memories began to come back to me. In the past ten days I'd been asked more and more questions about my husband and children. Innocent remarks, they had seemed at the time—but now I wondered what was back of them.

There was the usual question period after the luncheon speech that day. After a series of exchanges on the political issues, a woman, evidently embarrassed, stood up and asked, "Mrs. Priest, do you think that a mother with small children at home can be in politics—I mean, without neglecting her children?"

There it was again. Was it just a routine question? Or was a subtle suggestion being planted in the voters' minds?

"I certainly do," I said, facing her squarely. "I happen to have two wonderful women in my family—my mother and my aunt. One of them is now looking after my children, who have never yet come home to an empty house—and they never lack love and attention."

They were perhaps just a little startled at my vehemence. By this time I was getting annoyed. Back at the office, Leona Knudsen, my secretary, saw that something was amiss.

"Anything go wrong at the meeting?" she asked. "You look like you're upset."

As I blurted out the story, Tommy Wheelright appeared in the doorway and, thoughtfully chewing the end of his big pencil, he said, "The only way to meet a whispering campaign like this is head on. I didn't want to worry you, but we've been picking up a few crank letters along this line."

"Tommy, you should have told me."

"Well, I didn't think it was serious . . . but if this goes on, I think we better do something."

"But what can we do? I can't take those three healthy youngsters around with me and show them off! I can't send Aunt Gert out ringing doorbells."

"I remember something you said the first day I came in," he went on. "It made such an impression on me. You said you were running for Congress because you believed our children should have as good a country as we can make it."

"That's right—I think it's part of my job as a mother to take part in politics."

"O.K., then we'll toss this one back at them, too," said Tommy with determination. "Just let me figure something out."

And he did. At his suggestion we sat for a family portrait. Later the papers carried our ad, featuring this picture and individual ones of Pat, Nancy, and Roy, Jr., smiling over the caption:

Three Reasons Why I'm Running For Congress

The text of the ad set forth briefly the sentiments I had expressed to Tommy about a mother's responsibilities as a good citizen—with all that this implies.

This tactic appeared to have some effect, for the letters and queries about my poor, neglected children ceased—and I could only hope that the lady who had been ringing doorbells was now home looking after her own family.

We closed the campaign in an absolute fury of activity. We could almost feel victory in the air, so we redoubled our efforts for the final push.

On election day, Roy and I turned out to vote early.

"Let's go around and pay all our bills," Roy suggested. "Then, win or lose, we'll start off all square with the world."

I turned pale when I saw the pile of bills we'd collected—for, no matter what they tell you, it costs money out of your own pocket to run a political campaign.

This chore done, we spent the day stopping at polling places in the district to thank those who were working to bring out the vote.

Then Roy and I went back to Bountiful to get the early returns at home with the family. The first scattered reports on the radio were encouraging. But the really electrifying news came when the chairman of Utah County phoned to announce that I'd carried the county by 2,000 votes. This area, the second largest in our district, was partly industrial and partly agricultural—a good sign. As soon as I put down the receiver there was another piercing ring. This time it was the chairman of my own Davis County who said excitedly, "Ivy, you've carried the south end of Davis County." The family was jubilant over this good news. "Ye're winnin'!" said Aunt Gert, as she whirled into a Highland fling. And the small fry took up a chant, "Mom's going to Congress!"

Mother, seasoned politician that she was, asked quietly, "'Ave ye 'eard from Bingham yet?"

"No, but I'll find out right away."

So I called my lifelong friend, John Creedon, in Bingham, and asked, "Did I carry the old home town, John?"

"Afraid not, Ivy," he replied. "The old-timers were for you but the town has changed, you know. Not many Republicans left."

This was disappointing, but the continuing reports still had me in the lead.

Later that night, Roy and I went to Salt Lake headquarters where we got the returns from Tooele County. Wallace

Bennett was well ahead in the race for the Senate seat, but I had dropped behind.

"Looks like I've had it," I said sadly to Roy.

"There you go jumping the gun," he said, patting my hand. "This is a race—and what a race!"

About midnight, the seesaw began to swing up again. I took the lead and well-wishers started to crowd in.

"We're proud of you," they said. "You didn't seem to have a chance—and you're winning!"

"Hold everything. The returns aren't all in yet," I'd say, trying to keep from getting overconfident.

By 2 A.M. I was still ahead by 400 votes. Then the ax fell. The late returns from the north end of my county came filtering in and my small lead began to melt.

The newsmen gathered around to watch the figures go up on the board, and my heart sank as I saw Reva take an insurmountable lead. There was nothing to do but concede defeat.

When I picked up the phone to congratulate Reva, a confused secretary said, "She went home, Mrs. Priest. When she saw you'd won, she went on home. She'll call you in the morning."

"Oh, I'll call her . . . I've got *news* for her," I said.

XI

THE impetus of the campaign, with its people and problems and constant round of activities, carried me along on a wave of excitement. When it was over I felt like a deep-sea diver coming up for air, and it took me a while to get back to normal.

"What if ye didn't win?" Mother said, the following morning. "Ye made a good race, didn't ye?"

"But not good enough," I replied dejectedly.

Mother looked at me with all her compact majesty. "Let me tell ye something, young lady. Sometimes ye win when ye lose."

About this, she was to be proved right—but I had no way of knowing it at the time. All I knew was that, by popular mandate, I had been reelected to my post as a Bountiful housewife.

Aunt Gert had left her mark on the family. The place was spick-and-span, the cooky jar was full, the shelves were lined with canned goods she'd picked up at "barge-in" prices, and the children, when they wanted to communicate with me, shouted at the top of their lungs. It took me a week to convince them that I had my battery turned on.

There was a blunt forthrightness about Aunt Gert which was quite disarming, after one became accustomed to it, and I think a little of it had worn off on the children. When Aunt Gert put a pie down on the dinner table and watched us taste it, she'd look around and say, "Isn't that the best pie you ever ate?"

We'd all agree, and she would lean back, looking content, and announce with complete lack of modesty, "Oh, I'm a very good cook. That's one thing I can say for myself."

One day Aunt Gert asked Katie Priest, a visiting cousin of Roy's and me to lunch. We happened to arrive a little early and Aunt Gert came to the door in a house dress, with her hair still tightly wound in kid curlers. However, she greeted us with the aplomb of a hostess dressed in her very best, served us a delicious lunch, and completely won Katie with her naturalness and charm. When she served one of her specialties, lemon meringue pie, for dessert, she said unblushingly, "Katie, isn't this the best pie you ever ate in your life?" And Katie admitted that it was.

While we cleared the dishes, Aunt Gert dressed to go downtown with us. When she appeared in her stylish suit and furs and her feather-trimmed hat, Katie gasped, "Why, Aunt Gert, you don't look like the same woman. You look— like a grand duchess."

Preening herself, Aunt Gert tossed her head imperiously and said, "Yes, I'm not a bad-looking woman for my age, am I, Katie?"

Walking downtown, we chanced to meet an old friend of Uncle Lije's whom she hadn't seen for many years.

"Well, well, Gertie," he said, staring at her admiringly.

"I'd have known you anywhere. You look just like you did twenty-five years ago!"

Aunt Gert gave him a withering look and exploded, "Well, I must have looked *damned* old twenty-five years ago!"

Kentucky-bred Katie was completely taken aback by Aunt Gert's swearing but, like the rest of us, she soon realized that it was typically Aunt Gert and became one of her greatest fans before her visit was over.

Usually, we had a little family Christmas celebration a day or two in advance, so that Roy could get off to his annual sales meeting. He always seemed to catch cold just before the Omaha meeting. Even Gorgonzola at its ripest would lose its appeal for him, and it would wring my heart to see him sniffling throughout the long drive east in the dead of winter.

One year we decided to postpone our usual Christmas celebration and let Santa Claus catch up with the children in Omaha. We started on the long drive in fine fettle, for Roy had managed to avoid his usual cold. Just a few days before Christmas we had dinner with Roy's boss, Joe Clarkson, and his wife, and got back to our hotel fairly early. In the middle of the night Roy awoke with abdominal cramps which got so intense that I hastily summoned a doctor.

Roy was immediately taken to the hospital in an ambulance. We were distressed to learn that he would have to undergo a prostatectomy, a fairly serious operation.

"Well, at least you didn't catch cold, dear," I said in a feeble effort to be gay.

The youngsters were quite disturbed, not only about their father but also about their own uncertain fate at this critical time of the year.

"How's Santa ever going to find us in this hotel?" young Roy asked.

"Oh, Santa always goes to the hotels," I assured him.

First portrait. At the age of
3 months, I sat for an itinerant
photographer in Kimberley,
Utah, where I was born.

Family tintype. My parents; Fearnley, 6; Max, 2; Ivy, 9. Mother made
my dress from her lace wedding gown. We thought we looked elegant.

Second grade. My class at Bingham Canyon elementary school posed
for traditional picture, an important event. I'm fifth from left, back row.

Amateur model. (I am second from left.) Salesladies at Auerbach Company, Salt Lake City, sometimes doubled as models. Flapper styles of 1920s look familiar today.

Bingham Canyon in its infancy, circa 1910. Our house climbed up right side of mountain below Kennecott Copper Mine, where Father worked.

Robert Phillips—Black Star

Inaugural ballgown. Clad in champagne satin, I attended
President Eisenhower's first inaugural ball, an exciting occasion (*upper left*).

In office I sign documents before catching plane for a speaking
engagement on Treasury Bond drive (*upper right*).

Swearing in. Secretary of the Treasury George M. Humphrey administered oath of office as Asst. Secretary H. Chapman Rose
(right) and Administrative Asst. William Parsons looked on.

Treasury Department Photo

Photo by Peter Berkeley—Brown Palace Hotel, D

Award address at ceremony honoring me as the "Most Successful Home-maker of 1954." An unmerited tribute, I thought (*lower left*).

Easter Seal campaign. As chairman of National Society of Crippled Children campaign in 1957 I received first seals from Ruthie Frischer, aged 9 (*lower right*).

Associated Release Service, Inc. National Society for Crippled Children & Adult

Campaign lunch. General and Mrs. Eisenhower at a Republican meeting in Denver. He looked incredulous as we outlined ambitious plans for 1952 campaign (*left*).

Easter bonnet photographed at a Washington benefit tea. Though I'm a public official, I'm also a woman and I love hats. This rose turban is one of my favorites (*right*).

Photo by Larry Gordon Studios

Treasury Award for the Savings Bond Program went to Robert J. Kiesling of the Camden Trust Company, Camden, New Jersey.

Official USAF Photo

Peggy Louise, aged 15 months, photographed just two weeks before we lost her (*above*).

Family reunion. Home from a speaking trip and delighted to be back with Roy, Nancy, and Roy, Jr. (*left*).

Homework. My method for shelling peas for the freezer is to use the wringer of an old washing machine (*bottom left*).

Azalea Queen. Daughter Pat with Admiral Lynde D. McCormick, who crowned her queen of Norfolk Azalea Festival (*right*).

Entrepreneur. Young Roy (seated, left) brought streams of friends to have bills autographed (*below*).

Photo Craftsmen, Inc., Norfolk

McCall's—Peter Martin

Cash room. In Treasury vaults I am surrounded by packages of currency and bags of silver, a mere $30 million. This cave of riches seems like an Arabian nights' tale come true (*left*).

Vice President Richard M. Nixon and I confer in his quarters in the Senate Office Building. A good likeness of pretty Pat Nixon is in the background.

"But how'll he know which number room we're in?" asked Nancy.

"He can read, can't he?" Pat demanded, moving in to support the adult side of the Santa Claus question.

Nancy, who was so earnest and judicial in her approach to life that she always reminded me of my father, decided to check all of this with her devoted friend Sam, the elevator man.

"Sam said that Santa comes to hotels first, before he even goes to houses," she reported to young Roy.

"Aw, they just tell that to hotel kids to get 'em to bed early," her brother said.

We had brought their Christmas presents along in the trunk of the car and I did a little plotting with the hotel staff who were delighted to have a hand in a real family Christmas. The bellboys smuggled presents up and hid them in a linen closet on our floor. Our old friends, Bob and Mary Swann, brought over a big fir tree, and another friend, a local furniture dealer, Bill Bergstadt, gave the decorations.

On Christmas Eve we started out for the hospital to see Roy. As the elevator arrived at our floor, I suddenly remembered I had to go back to our room to "make a phone call." Giving me a knowing wink, Sam, the elevator man, took the youngsters on downstairs.

The hall maid brought the presents out of the linen closet and helped me spread them under the tree. Then I rushed downstairs to take the children to the hospital—leaving a bellboy and the maid busily trimming the tree.

"You know, Dad, Santa might even come while we're up here," young Roy told his father.

"You left the key for him, didn't you, Mummy?" asked Nancy anxiously.

Santa had, indeed, arrived early—and the children were enraptured. The Swanns came, laden with Christmas goodies, and the Bergstadts brought their two little girls to celebrate with our children. Since the hotel dining room was closed, Mrs. George Papineau, the manager's wife, sent up refreshments, and we invited the few stranded hotel guests to join our party, while a beaming Sam, the maid, and the bellboys joined in the festivities.

But this gaiety was tinged with anxiety because of our uncertainty over Roy's condition. On Christmas Day we took his presents to him and learned that the operation was imminent. Luckily, it proved successful and he rallied quickly, but we had to leave him in the hospital so that the youngsters could get back to school on time. When he was strong enough, Roy came home by train—and promptly caught a cold.

These days, I found myself studying Pat with fascination. She had left off wearing long brown stockings and the cowboy boots her Dad had brought home from a trip. She was a bobby-soxer now—and in silk stockings for weekend dates. Blond, blue-eyed, and vivacious, she had suddenly become very much the young lady. But she was having no wallflower problem, I reflected, recalling my own adolescence. The only problem here was to convince her that books were of equal importance with boys—well, almost, anyway.

Nancy was approaching her tenth birthday and Roy had celebrated his eighth. Nancy was largely absorbed in dolls, a hobby I found much more becoming than her brother's. He liked to collect snakes or, in a pinch, earthworms.

My father had always said that there are four things a child needs—plenty of love, nourishing food, regular sleep, and lots of soap and water—and after those, what he needs most is some intelligent neglect. "After all, people, even little people, are responsible individuals," he would say. "So you must give them a chance to be independent and dependable."

Dad certainly practiced what he preached, for he and

Mother worked too hard to be able to give all seven of us constant attention. But we never doubted that we were deeply, personally loved.

Roy and I tried to follow this homely child-raising pattern. If I hadn't felt the children were dependable, I couldn't have carried on a busy life outside my home. But intelligent neglect does not rule out discipline, and there are times when keen watchfulness is called for.

Just before school was out that year, I had to attend a meeting in Salt Lake, and announced that I would not be home until dinnertime. I got the children off to school in the morning and, as I was about to leave, I noticed that Pat had left her books behind. So I stopped by the school to give them to her. When the secretary sent for her, we learned that she was at home "sick" that day.

Then I remembered overhearing Pat on the phone the night before, talking to a friend about a swimming party at Saratoga, on Utah Lake. I then asked the secretary if Pat's friend was at school and discovered that the spring epidemic was infectious, for she too was out "sick."

This called for quick action. Getting into the car, I drove fifty miles to Saratoga. When I stepped up to the pool, two embarrassed young ladies and their boy friends stopped their splashing and stared at me in dismay.

"Pat, get out of that pool and get dressed at once." Then, turning to Pat's girl friend, I said, "You, too, young lady. Your father would expect me to take you home."

Meekly, the girls crawled out of the pool and went to the locker room. While they were dressing, I turned to the boys. "I assume you have a way to get back," I said matter-of-factly.

"Oh, yes, ma'am," they said, and quickly swam away.

Looking quite sheepish, the girls slunk into the car, and the lecture they got on our homeward drive must have taken all the glamour out of hooky-playing. But I felt a little sheepish myself as I recalled my Bingham school days, when I was guilty of a similar offense.

One balmy spring day, two classmates and I cut class to go to a Rudolph Valentino movie. To our great dismay, we saw Principal Neilson coming toward us on the street. In a panic, my companions turned and fled. Feeling trapped, I faced the stern principal. "What are you doing out of school?" he demanded.

"I—I don't feel well," I stammered. "I'm going home." And before he could call my bluff, I raced away.

When I got home, Mother was waiting to put me straight to bed, for the principal had called to check on me. And so I was obliged to waste a lovely spring day being "sick."

I had to concede that Pat's attempt to go A.W.O.L had been carried off better than mine.

From time to time, when I had to attend distant meetings, the children were glad to have Aunt Gert back. The cooky jar would get filled, there would be "dough-gots" and scones on the menu, and, when the hearing aid was turned off, I suspect a few plots were hatched against adult society. Once the neighbors informed me that Miss Pat had figured out how to start the family auto and drive away quietly, and again the long arm of parental law pulled on the brake.

In 1951, we had only a local election and, since my friend Dora Trowbridge, the doctor's wife, was running for the city council, I did most of my politicking in our neighborhood, keeping busy enough ringing doorbells and rounding up voters to neglect a bad cold. The day before election, Dr. Trowbridge ordered me to bed.

"You've got pneumonia," he announced.

"That's silly—people don't walk around with pneumonia."

"Most people don't."

"Well, you'll let me get up and vote for Dora tomorrow."

"I will not."

"If your wife loses this election by one vote, I'll never forgive you, Doctor."

But Dora won easily without my vote and I recovered from pneumonia in time to attend the next national committee meeting in San Francisco, in January.

At this session the talk swung to prospects for the presidential election of 1952. It became clear that Senator Taft, whose bid for the nomination at the two previous conventions had failed, would have plenty of support this time.

My colleague, George Hansen, was heartily in favor of Taft, but I had no hesitancy in saying that Taft, whom I greatly admired, could not win a national election. I shared the general feeling that, though Taft was a brilliant senator and was deeply respected in his home state of Ohio, his personal magnetism was not great enough to make him a popular candidate. While George and I discussed candidates privately, we were committed to public neutrality until after Utah's delegates to the national convention were chosen that spring.

Vernon Romney, who had been one of the "new faces" to assume leadership of our state party in 1944, had resigned as state chairman in 1950, in order to work for Senator Taft's nomination. He was busy corralling delegates, not only in Utah but in other Western states as well.

Once again, I found myself in an uncomfortable position as the state convention approached. Sentiment for Taft was very strong, with most state leaders declaring for him, and I was asked to pledge my support. But I remained committed to neutrality.

Late in 1951, I was invited to a luncheon in Salt Lake which turned out to be a Taft rally for local leaders. Everyone stood up and pledged support. When my turn came, I voiced my great admiration for Senator Taft and added, "It is not the prerogative of national committee members to select candidates. It is our business to help elect them. And, with that in mind, I will not express any preferences. However, if Senator Taft becomes the party's candidate for President, he will have my wholehearted support."

My personal situation was somewhat complicated—as was that of many other Republicans—because I did not know precisely whom to be for, if not for Senator Taft. At that time, General Eisenhower was being mentioned as a candidate—but he had not stated that he would run. It was only a short time before Utah's convention, where delegates to the national convention were chosen, that Ike's hat was tossed officially into the ring.

By that time, Utah's delegation had been pretty well buttoned up by Vern Romney, who was in full charge when our state convention opened and, I'm afraid, had occasion to become pretty annoyed with me.

At any rate, our delegation was fully instructed for Taft— and I found myself operating as a committee of one. For all the state officials, including the governor, the senators, and all but two county chairmen, were Taft supporters. I felt like the stranger in the crowd, the only one out of step.

By this time, General Eisenhower had set up his pre-convention campaign offices in Denver. One day, Nick Morgan, chairman of the Utah Citizens for Ike, called to suggest that the Utah delegation might like to come to Denver to meet the general.

"I know they're all pledged to Taft," he said. "But I've arranged for train tickets and we'll pay all expenses, if you think they'll go."

"Why, certainly," I replied. "I think they would be delighted to meet a great American leader. In fact, I would be a little embarrassed if we didn't pay this call on the general."

And so it was that all our delegates, except Vern Romney,

made the trip. It was my first meeting with Ike, and I was tremendously impressed by his warm, outgoing personality, his buoyancy, and complete naturalness. When he smiled and firmly gripped my hand, I felt as if I'd known him all my life, and a sense of confidence and optimism swept through me. His background as commander of the world forces which he had led to victory, his knowledge of world affairs, and his administrative ability were assets, it seemed to me, that our country badly needed.

After the meeting, our state chairman, Pratt Kesler, told newspapermen that six of the delegates had indicated they would switch to Ike after the first ballot.

This story hit the front pages all over the country—for it was the first indication that the solid Taft forces were beginning to crumble. Our state Taft leaders were furious at this turn of events and I was completely in the doghouse.

The national convention in Chicago that July altered our family plans for the usual vacation at Turpin Meadows, Wyoming. Roy decided to take our boy with him for fishing at Jackson Hole, while the girls and my friend Tracey Petersen went along to the convention with me.

The national committee was scheduled to meet several days prior to the convention. The night before we left, I stopped to see Mother to say good-by. She was full of political advice and enthusiasm for our candidate.

"Ike's the man we need, Ivy!" she said with a determined snap of her head. "If 'e could unite all those countries in Europe into a winnin' army, 'e can sure pull us together 'ere at 'ome. 'E's got the same courage and fightin' spirit Churchill 'ad when 'e saved England."

"Mother, you don't have to give me a sales talk. I'm completely sold."

"Well, then, my girl, get on to Chicago and see that 'e gets the nomination."

Feeling well briefed and delighted that Mother still had her old resolute spirit, I went out to the car. Her supreme confidence that it was up to me to assure Ike's nomination made me smile to myself.

As I started the car, I looked up and saw her standing under the porch light which threw a halo around her white head, and bathed her face in a radiant glow. I thought I had never seen her looking so regal and beautiful.

"Rememberr—the countrry needs Eisenhowerr," were her parting words, as she waved good-by.

We arrived in Chicago to find one of those situations where everything was Fraught with Significance. A member of the national committee could hardly sneeze without someone else's pausing to wonder how it would affect the delegate totals.

Chicago was jammed with thousands of delegates, alternates, and spectators who poured in from every corner of the country. Streets and shops were bedecked with bunting and flags. Convention headquarters at the Hilton Hotel on the Lake front were ablaze with placards and banners. Throngs surged constantly between Taft's suite at the Hilton and Ike's quarters at the Blackstone across the street. Our Utah base was again at the headquarters hotel and it soon became the usual bedlam, with delegates milling around to collect their tickets, badges, and credentials, and to exchange the latest gossip. My enterprising daughters managed to stock up on enough badges, flags, and gadgets like elephant banks, Ike caps, and bicycle horns to supply all their friends back home.

It was easy to see that the race would be nip and tuck. The ceaseless gossip flying around the corridors indicated that Taft even had an edge over Ike. The outcome seemed to depend on the decisions the national committee would make on contested delegations from three states—Georgia, Louisiana, and

Texas. These states had each produced dual delegations, each pledged to a different candidate—one to Ike, one to Taft.

Therefore, the first important order of business for the national committee before the opening of the full convention was to determine which delegation should be seated. The convention would later decide whether to uphold us.

There were complex legalities involved which had to be taken into consideration. The Georgia case was the first to come up, and the Southern drawl had hardly been heard before a member protested the presence of television cameras in the committee room. Things were so tense that all one had to do was say "boo" and it would draw a rebuttal. So naturally the protest over television started a big debate. We adjourned to another room to discuss and vote on whether these preliminary proceedings should be on the air. For this skirmish, like everything else, had become a test of strength between the candidates. Taft's people wanted the TV cameras barred, so naturally Ike's adherents wished them to stay.

George Hansen, my fellow Utahan, who was chairman of the contests committee, appeared to regard television as a brash invasion of the privacy of our sessions. He is one of those rare gentlemen of the old school—the soul of honor, always courteous and generous—and basically very conservative. His instinctive reaction against the impertinence of broadcasting our discussions coincided with that of the Taft leaders.

My own feeling was just the opposite.

"How can we say to the people in July that this contest is none of your business, and then in November say, 'Come right in with the party you can trust,'" I told George. "And don't forget, Salt Lake City is right on the coaxial cable—they'll be watching this back home."

George and I had served together for eight years without

ever differing in our voting. But this time we split. The Taft people won, and the television cameras were left outside the hearing room.

A hue and cry then arose over the outcome. Charges were leveled at the national committee, whose business is to elect and not select candidates, that it was pro-Taft and unfair to Ike. The recriminations reached such proportions that the press carried banner headlines and cartoons on the issue.

At this point a wire reached us from the governors' conference in Texas, urging the committee to be impartial and fair. This telegram was the result of a resolution unanimously adopted by all forty-eight governors. Among the signatories was J. Bracken Lee, governor of Utah, and a strong Taft supporter.

This message, which came to be known as the "fair-play wire," probably produced the first break in the solid Taft forces and impressed the committee with the importance of carefully considering the evidence presented by the contesting delegations.

The Georgia hearing was then resumed, and the roll-call vote was in favor of seating the pro-Eisenhower delegation. As on the television issue, I again voted in opposition to George Hansen. "I guess this leaves no doubt where you stand," he said, with a pained expression.

"It's a difficult situation, George," I said, "and I'm not happy about it."

"Oh, I know, you have to vote as you believe," he assured me.

Later, Pratt Kesler, our state chairman, came up to me and said, "Ivy, I'm getting all kinds of wires from home saying that they want you in line with the rest of the delegation."

"For every wire you show me," I replied, "I'll show you five that say, 'Stand by your guns—don't let them stampede you. We want Ike.'"

162

George and I split again on the Louisiana case, which was also decided in favor of the pro-Ike delegation.

The day we started the crucial Texas hearings an influential Western politician, whom I had known for years, said, "Ivy, I see you're still voting against your state."

"I'm voting my convictions," I said.

"Oh, that's all right for the newspapers. It reads good. But let's get to being practical. You're a smart girl. You've come a long way in politics. We fellows would hate to see you get hurt."

I was flabbergasted.

"Well, that's right handsome of you, partner," I said. "But you're forgetting two things. I don't have to be national committeewoman from Utah. If the state committee wants my resignation, they can have it, as soon as I get home. But, no matter which candidate gets this nomination, he needs women like me in every state in order to win an election. So I won't consider this a threat at all."

"Oh, no. I didn't mean it as a threat."

"I didn't think you did," I said sweetly.

We were in the midst of the Texas hearing when I received an urgent long-distance call from my brother, Keith.

"Ivy, I'm afraid it's bad news," he said. "Mother's had another stroke."

A cold fear gripped me and, for a fleeting instant, I felt an inexplicable sense of loss—a desolate foreboding.

"How bad is it?"

"She's unconscious. We've taken her to the hospital."

"I'll get a plane home tonight."

"What about your girls?"

"Tracey will bring them home later."

Dazed with shock, I went to our suite and picked up the phone to make a plane reservation for Salt Lake. Sensing that something was wrong, George Hansen came upstairs to investigate. All my pent-up emotion broke and I burst into tears.

"She isn't going to get better, George. I know this is it!"

He tried to console me by reminding me that Mother had recovered from her last stroke. Then Tracey came in from a shopping trip with the girls, who were dismayed to hear about their grandmother's illness.

Friends on the committee began to call and to come by to offer help and consolation. Elizabeth Heffelfinger, committeewoman from Minnesota, an Eisenhower supporter, asked for my proxy so that she could vote it.

"I wouldn't think of giving my proxy to anyone but my national committeeman," I said.

"But he's for Taft!"

"That's beside the point—he represents my state."

As I was leaving, I handed my proxy to George Hansen.

"Hadn't you better give it to one of the people who would be voting the way you are?"

"I'm going to leave it with you. After all, you are representing the people of Utah."

I later learned that during the roll call on the Texas case, George cast his own vote for the pro-Taft delegation. But when he was called upon to vote my proxy, he just shook his head—for he refused to take advantage of an extra vote for his own side.

Tense with anxiety, I boarded the plane that night. Mother's illness blotted out all thought of the remaining contest or of the convention which was to open the next day.

Mother was still unconscious when I reached the hospital. My brothers and sisters had all gathered at her bedside and we took turns staying with her. In the painful days that followed, one of us was always beside her.

Lloyd and his wife Margaret drove down forty miles from Ogden every night. Lynn and her husband Mack closed their upholstery shop and came up from Richfield. Gertrude was at the hospital almost as much as I. Fearnley, Iris, Max, and Mary Lou were in and out every day.

Keith, practicing law in Salt Lake City, and his wife Jessie took over the practical details of the lives of all of us during this dread period of suspense. And Aunt Gert, unusually subdued, sat quietly holding Mother's hand.

Days went by in a blur. Sometimes, I left the room for a few mintues to watch the convention proceedings on television. When General Eisenhower was nominated on the first ballot, I rushed back to the room and told Mother, again and again.

I do not know whether she ever heard me.

For, without ever regaining consciousness, Mother died, just three and a half weeks after her stroke.

During all those days and nights at her bedside, with my brothers and sisters, Roy, and Aunt Gert drifting in and out, I had time to think back over our lives together.

I could remember Mother as the most truly giving person I had ever known. I could see her late at night, getting everything ready for the next day's holiday—cooking and sewing until the small hours for us. I could see her getting us all dressed up to go to Salt Lake City, braiding our hair so carefully and scrubbing the boys until they shone. There was the time when Fearnley and Lloyd, dressed to go, had crawled through a sooty pipe on all fours while Mother was cleaning the rest of us up and the time when, reaching over to pull one of the boys back from the open train window, she had watched her own new hat blow out into the fields.

I remembered Mother, bowing her head during the family prayer hour, smiling happily as she looked down at the face of my baby brother. I could see her bustling about Bingham, helping the foreign-born when they were in trouble. I remembered how her face would pale when Dad was brought home injured—and how she would turn to face the problem. I recalled the hours we sat up during the depression, trying to stave off disaster.

Then, in Salt Lake, she was Mother—and later Grandmother—Baker to an entire generation. I saw her, white-haired and regal, marching down the aisle at our family weddings— then at state conventions, this quiet-spoken housewife who held no post higher than precinct committeewoman, being sought out eagerly by governors and aspirants for the presidential nomination.

In a steady stream the memories poured back, bringing pictures that swam before my eyes until they were drowned for a time in my tears.

And then it was Roy, quiet, bowed with sorrow, but efficiently making the funeral arrangements and guiding me through them. Faithful Tracey, shepherding and comforting the children through the sad hours. Finally it was all over and we sat down together, the family, just for a quiet hour of remembrance.

As I looked around at my brothers and sisters, and the good people they had married, I realized that here was the monument to my mother and father. And then, two by two, they returned to their homes, and Roy and I were left to look back on the day.

Hundreds of people from all parts of the state had come to say good-by to Mother—who was known as Mrs. Republican. She had regarded her job as the most important in the party—a worker in the precinct. It kept her in touch with people. She had become an important figure in the state not by dint of holding office or power—but just by being where she was needed, believing, being a good neighbor, and doing a good job.

Without her there was a great void in all our lives.

Just a week after the funeral, I was still dazed and grief-

166

stricken, when the phone rang. It was with a dull and lifeless voice that I answered.

"This is Art Summerfield, Ivy, in Denver. I want you to know how sorry we all were to hear about your loss."

I thanked him for calling and we exchanged a few general remarks. I had known Art for a long time as a Republican committeeman from Michigan and I congratulated him on his election as national chairman and director of the Eisenhower campaign.

"Ivy, I want you to serve as assistant chairman of the committee . . . in charge of the women's division," he said.

"Art, I just couldn't do it. After all, I've just buried my mother."

"You simply must do it. I've talked to people in every part of the country . . . and everyone says that you are the woman we need. You'd be amazed at the friends you have."

"I'm very flattered . . . but I simply couldn't consider it."

"I know your mother would want you to do it."

I paused and recalled the last words that Mother had said to me. . . . "Rememberr—the countrry needs Eisenhowerr." I knew Art was right. This is what she would want me to do.

"I'll talk it over with Roy," I promised. "I'll let you know."

When I discussed it with Roy, his response was immediate.

"Why, certainly, you should do it," he said. "If Aunt Gert will come down and look after the children, we'll get along."

Young Roy was even more emphatic.

"You mean you'd be in charge of getting all the women to vote for General Eisenhower?"

"That's the idea, son."

He put aside the alarm clock he was reconstructing and looked thoughtful for a moment.

"That's great! Get everyone to vote for him. He's gotta be elected."

When I went to see Aunt Gert and explained the situ-

167

ation, she commented, "I'll be glad to 'elp you out. We've all got to do what we can for Ike. I carn't make speeches . . . but, then, ye carn't cook."

Conceding that she was right, I hurried home to pack a bag, pausing long enough to phone Art in Denver that I was on my way.

I won't need to pack much, I told myself, it's just an overnight trip. . . . But I didn't know then that I was starting a long journey away from Bountiful.

XII

TEN days after Mother's funeral, I arrived at campaign head-quarters in Denver, feeling heavy-hearted and full of doubts about my ability to do the job I'd undertaken. But there was no time for introspection, as I was immediately ushered in to confer with General Eisenhower.

With his warm, friendly smile, he stood up and came around his desk to greet me. He hardly looked like a man who had just come through the tension of winning the Republican nomination and was immersed in plans for an arduous campaign. Everything about him reflected determination, confidence, and buoyancy. I felt a lift myself, the minute we shook hands.

"I've heard wonderful things about you, Mrs. Priest," he said. "I'm glad we could get you on the team."

"I'm flattered—and just a little scared," I said.

"The feeling is mutual!" he said, and the grin broadened.

Art Summerfield then joined us and we plunged into a discussion of campaign strategy. Before the meeting ended we agreed on a definite first step and sent telegrams to twenty-five top Republican women leaders, asking them to meet with General Eisenhower in Denver on August 18.

When I returned to Bountiful the next day, Aunt Gert was in masterful control of the home front. Cookies were baking in the kitchen stove, and Roy and Nancy were off on a tour of neighborhood groceries—the morning ads in their hands—buying the specials in soap powder, pears, and canned beans which Aunt Gert had circled. Uncle Lije, now retired, was sitting silently in a corner of the kitchen, snapping green beans which—oh, glorious sight—my daughter Pat was blanching and putting into freezer bags.

"Brought ye a few beans for the freezer out of the garden," Aunt Gert explained.

"Mother, there are simply tons of them," Pat wailed. "And I've got a date to go swimming this afternoon."

There was order in the house, obviously, and I went about my final preparations to leave with an easy mind. We celebrated Pat's sixteenth birthday a few days early, I kissed the children good-by, and returned to Denver for the meeting with the women leaders.

General and Mrs. Eisenhower were guests at our luncheon meeting. We had an opportunity for a few moments' chat with the general's lady, and she won us as completely as he had. Her feminine charm and friendliness put us at our ease at once. As she talked, her blue eyes sparkled and her engaging smile lighted up her face. I couldn't help but think that Mrs. Eisenhower would be a real asset on Ike's campaign tour and that she would make a captivating first lady.

After lunch we developed plans to organize women on a broad national scale reaching into various professions and every phase of our economic life. This would be a greatly expanded program using the techniques we had tried out in the Western Conference back in 1946, when we had trained a corps of active Republican women in Western states. What we now needed was a large group of volunteers all over the country to augment regular party workers in the presidential campaign.

The general sat at the speaker's table, listening with an air of disbelief, and pulling on his ear from time to time. I'm sure he must have wondered how we could accomplish our ambitious objectives in two short months.

At one o'clock the following morning I caught a plane for Washington, where Art Summerfield had established our national campaign headquarters.

I bought a one-way ticket. Anything less, it seemed to me, would have reflected a lack of confidence in my own durability. Weary from the all-night flight, I arrived next morning to make a discovery that many have made before me. The airline flight to Washington may be short. But the mental transition from wherever you start to Washington is not made quite so speedily. They ought to establish some kind of decompression chamber outside the Capital for newcomers —because Washington takes a little getting used to.

There was a press conference waiting at Republican head-quarters. Slightly wilted from the midsummer heat, I stood up to a barrage of questions from reporters without suffering too many mortal wounds. Then I faced the photographers— the founders of the "just one more" club. They flashed away from every angle and then one of them innocently suggested that I sit down atop a filing cabinet. I was about to walk into this trap when Anne Wheaton, our publicity woman, quickly interceded.

"No cheesecake!" she told the photographer firmly.

Not until then did I realize that I was being maneuvered into posing like an arriving actress. That would have rattled the rafters!

But all booby traps in the nation's Capital do not explode

like a flash bulb, as I was to discover. When you got right down to it, I was a housewife from Bountiful, Utah, who had been plucked up suddenly and plunked down behind a desk in Washington to help run a national campaign. I had done some electioneering out in the West and had watched grand strategy being developed at the national committee level. But none of this had exactly prepared me for the situations I found myself facing in the nation's Capital.

It was at once apparent that Washington and I were not going to change each other. For better or worse, we'd have to live with each other for a time. So I hung my hat up at headquarters in the Washington Hotel, settled down at my desk, and, looking out the window at the historic Treasury Building across the way, wondered just where to begin my small job of organizing the women of America for Ike.

Almost immediately after my arrival, I was asked to be guest of honor at a luncheon given by the Republican women. It was to be my introduction to the influential party regulars and I was especially eager to make a good impression. We had just come out of a tense convention which had left many unhealed wounds—and it was essential to concentrate now on the main event.

After luncheon, there were a long skit and an even longer series of reports from district leaders. I sat and fidgeted as time went by and wondered if I was getting the "treatment" —to show me that I was, after all, just another woman from the sticks. It was nearly 3:30 before I was at last called upon to speak—and I tossed aside the talk that I had taken great pains to prepare.

The anger boiling up inside me must have been channeled into a fighting speech—as in a pressure cooker, the pent-up steam just boiled out. I told them that, if we were ever going to win an election, we had to bury our preconvention differences and rid ourselves of petty jealousies and bickerings.

Elections were not won by cliques or factions but by united effort. Most of all, we had to shake off the apathy and indifference that had settled over the party as a result of five straight defeats.

When I sat down, there was a burst of enthusiastic applause, and the women answered the rallying call with eager pledges of support. But the next few weeks would determine how effective this beginning had really been.

That was my baptism of fire with my own party in Washington, but I had yet to face the Democrats. Left on my own, I would have picked a time and place carefully—but someone jumped the gun. One day I was handed a note from our TV division, asking me to appear in a television debate with Mrs. India Edwards, the experienced and able director of the Democratic women's division. I was just leaving on a flying trip to New York, but paused long enough to voice an objection.

"Why didn't you consult me before you made this arrangement?" I demanded of our radio director. "This is really not a smart thing to do."

"Why not?"

"India Edwards is a professional in politics. I'm a rank amateur. She'll make mincemeat out of me—and it'll hurt our cause."

Having said my piece, I dropped the subject and flew on to New York for a Republican women's tea. Later, I was talking with friends when we were joined by a woman whom I hadn't met.

"I may have to go down to Washington tomorrow afternoon," she said to a friend.

"Why?"

"Oh, they've scheduled a debate on TV between India Edwards and the new woman chairman of the Republicans. But she won't do it and I may have to take her place."

173

My eyebrows shot up. "I happen to be that woman and it's news to me that anyone's going on in my place," I said.

"Oh—are you the new chairman?" she asked in astonishment.

"Yes, I am."

"Well, there must be some mistake," she said, somewhat flustered, "or I must have been misinformed."

"Somebody has been misinformed—for I intend to go on."

Back in Washington the next day I lost no time in phoning our TV division. "What made you think I wouldn't keep that commitment?" I asked. "There are many things I don't like to do, but that doesn't mean I'm not willing to try."

Feeling quite nervous and ill at ease, I went on the air with India, but a small case of nerves can sometimes put you on your mettle. Mrs. Edwards, a veteran at political debate, got the best of it, of course. She knew exactly how to cut off my arguments, how to make her own points sharply and leave me dangling at loose ends. I realized that I'd been concentrating too much on organization and that it was high time I boned up on the campaign issues.

The experience left me somewhat shaken but ready to come back for more. As Mother used to say, "Ye've got to be like a good rubber ball. The 'arder ye throw it, the 'igher it bounces."

Mrs. Edwards and I left in a cab together after the show. She was kind enough to offer warm words of encouragement.

"I know how you felt," she said. "I remember the first time I went on against a woman of experience. But you did very well. I don't dislike people for disagreeing with me."

I assured her that I shared her sentiments, and we have remained good friends ever since.

The opening speech of the campaign was slated for early September in Philadelphia. Expecting to be back that night, I left the office without even an overnight bag. Wearing a gray flannel suit with rhinestone buttons, I got on a plane for Philadelphia. When we landed I was handed a typewritten sheet of instructions for those traveling "on the campaign plane."

"What's this?" I asked Katie Howard, a member of Eisenhower's policy committee.

"The general wants you to make this swing out to the Midwest with us," she explained.

"Well, I suppose I can buy a toothbrush and sleep in my slip until we get to a place where I can buy some clothes," I said, rather taken aback.

At five o'clock next morning we sleepily boarded the plane bound for Kasson, Minnesota, where the general was to speak at the annual plowing contest. Ike sat up front with his chief advisers, working on his speech, his brows knitted in concentration. The party included Sherman Adams, Fred Seaton, Bob Cutler, Gabriel Hauge, Jim Hagerty, Dr. Snyder, and a score of reporters and staff. We took seats where we found them, and when Ike wanted to consult one of us, he would walk back and drop into the next seat for a chat. He laughed heartily when I told him about my precipitate departure from Washington without so much as a toothbrush.

When we reached Minneapolis, I expected to have at least an hour for shopping—but they whipped us out to Kasson without waiting a minute. Turning to Katie Howard, I asked, "What do you think I should wear to the plowing contest?"

"If you don't have a pair of overalls," she said drily, "I think a gray flannel suit would be just the thing."

The huge throngs and the cheering reception Ike got for his speech that day left us all in high spirits. Looking very happy, he sat down with the rest of us for a fried chicken dinner in a farmhouse. Then we were rushed on to Chicago, where I expected at last to get time for some shopping. No sooner had we arrived than I learned that Katie and I were to be guests of honor at a tea, beginning in about ten minutes.

"What'll I wear, Katie?" I demanded.

She considered the problem carefully, then said brightly, "Why not that gray suit—the one with the rhinestone buttons?"

Just the thing, I agreed, and with a final tug at my hat, departed for the tea. As it turned out, I lived in that gray suit until we got back to Washington. This experience certainly taught me how to travel light.

From Mother I had learned the basic political law that elections are won in the precinct. The first essential was to develop a strong enthusiastic group of local workers who were willing to go from house to house, ringing doorbells, seeking out voters who leaned toward the party, and making sure that they registered and voted—for if the vote didn't get into the ballot box, it couldn't be counted. At Washington we were far removed from the precinct level, but what we aimed to do was to build a channel of communication that would reach right down to where the voters lived. In Bertha Adkins, the able director of the women's division, I had a quiet, hard-working executive assistant. Together we were sometimes hard put to it to sift the workable ideas from the wildly impractical ones that were flung at us.

One bright suggestion came from a woman who urged us to inaugurate a cross-country torchlight parade, starting on each coast and culminating in a giant rally for Ike in Chicago. Such unimportant details as food and shelter for this monster "walkathon" she would leave to the "master minds of the campaign."

Having reached out into all fields to find women leaders who would work for Eisenhower, we now had to keep their enthusiasm high and supply them with materials. My job, as I saw it, was not to sit at a desk in Washington and worry about operational details, but to get out into the field and rally the support of women. I had a gray flannel suit, would travel—and I did. It seemed that the only sleep I got was on a plane roaring 20,000 feet above the country.

Often my itinerary would undergo a last-minute change. One day, as I was preparing to leave for a talk in North Carolina, the committee received an S O S from Pennsylvania. Governor Goodwin Knight of California had been on his way to speak at a big rally in Norristown, when his wife suffered a serious heart attack. I was assigned to fill his speaking engagement—and, at the same time, had to find someone else to take my place in North Carolina. I arrived without so much as a note on which to base my speech. But then I glanced at a song sheet that had been handed me, carrying pictures of Washington, Lincoln, and Eisenhower, with a quotation under each. The quotes were Washington's "Put only Americans on guard tonight," Lincoln's "If our freedoms are ever threatened, it will be from within," and Eisenhower's "The strength of unity lies in united action." From these rousing but disparate elements I improvised the opening, body, and closing theme of my speech—and prayed that it made sense.

Pressure of this kind was always with me, and occasionally it led to minor disaster. When the Nixon campaign train was scheduled to stop at Salt Lake, I happened to be aboard and was asked to introduce Mrs. Nixon to my home-state audience. I was delighted by the chance—and happy too that the trip meant a reunion with my family for the first time since my departure for Washington.

At the rally I improvised what I thought was a pleasant enough little speech and wound up with this peroration, "And now I present to you the *next* wife of the Vice-President of the United States, Mrs. Dick Nixon."

This slip of the tongue got a big laugh in Utah because of the early Mormon history of plural marriage. I was covered with blushes, and Senator Arthur Watkins, on the speakers' platform, laughed heartily at my discomfiture. But I had the last laugh, a few minutes later, when he stood up to introduce Mr. Nixon and came out with two spoonerisms, "I present my good friend and esteemed colleague in the United States Senate, the next Price-Vesident of the United States, Nick Dixon."

That night, I was at home in Bountiful with the family. Aunt Gert and Uncle Lije had somehow turned the kitchen into the family meeting place, and our parlor—usually strewn with flotsam and jetsam from the day's activities—was now pristine. When I announced that the Nixon caravan would be coming through Bountiful the next morning and that I was going to join it, the children were beside themselves with excitement.

"You mean they're going to stop here for you, Mother?" asked Roy, his eyes round with disbelief. "The motorcycles and all?"

I told him that was the case, and he was looking duly impressed when Nancy said, "Oh, we'll miss it, Roy. We'll be in school."

"They'll probably let us out for that," Pat said hopefully.

And their father put in, "Why, this is an event for our town. It isn't every day that a vice-presidential candidate comes to Bountiful."

So it was the next morning that the blaring campaign caravan carrying the next Vice-President of the United States stopped in front of the school and, while hundreds cheered, the three Priest children stepped out solemnly, thanked Mr. Nixon for the lift, kissed their mother good-by, and went on to their classes.

Young Roy was proud of the fact that his birthday fell in the same month as that of his hero, General Eisenhower. Aunt Gert promised to bake him a special layer cake. I asked for the recipe, because I knew it would please her, put it in my purse, and promptly forgot it.

When I got back to Washington I found the headquarters staff buzzing with plans to make Eisenhower's birthday, October 14, a special occasion. With sudden inspiration, I remembered Aunt Gert's recipe tucked away in my purse. We proceeded to send out letters to all women's page editors and radio program directors, reminding them of the date and suggesting that they feature an Eisenhower birthday cake. In case they wanted one, I sent along Aunt Gert's recipe. The response was overwhelming—and I wondered how many million Americans sat down that night to celebrate our candidate's birthday with a cake made from the prized recipe of a little old lady who'd come to America from the Midlands of England.

As I dashed around the country from speech to speech, I would join the campaign train or plane wherever possible. The general was always anxious to hear about women's reactions to the campaign. We kept him briefed on our activities through Katie Howard, who sat in on all the strategy councils.

When things were going well and he had delivered a speech that pleased him, we would find Ike in high spirits, smiling exuberantly and radiating confidence. When, occasionally, he was dissatisfied with his own performance, a worried frown creased his brow and his mood became introspective. But, either way, we were carried along by his sheer drive and enthusiasm.

The reports coming in from the field were so good that we feared they might constitute a real danger to our cause. Remembering 1948, we tried to avoid overconfidence, and redoubled our efforts to keep our people on their toes. I talked politics so much that I welcomed any little quiet moment when I could get my weary mind off it.

Flying into Cleveland one night from San Antonio, I

faced a long ride from the airport through the cold, drizzly night. I asked the taxi driver if I could sit up front, near the heater.

Weary from an all-night trip, I welcomed a chance to cat-nap. But the driver wanted to talk.

"Hey, lady," he asked after a mile or two of silence, "ain't you goin' to ask me how I'm goin' to vote?"

"No. Why should I?"

"You're the first person's got in this cab today who ain't."

"Well, I just hope you do vote. That's your duty."

"You ain't asked me, but I'm going to tell you how I'm going to vote," he persisted. "I'm going to vote for General Ike."

He went on to sum up his reasons, delivering quite a political speech. When he had finished, I said, "You know, I'm going to vote for Eisenhower, too."

"Gee, did I convert you, lady?" he asked happily.

This conversation reminded me, however, that I hadn't gotten around to casting my own absentee ballot. I picked it up the next time I was in Washington, full of good intentions about getting it notarized, but a mountain of other small problems popped up out of the "in" basket and I forgot all about it. My next trip was taking me west, so I tucked the ballot in my purse, resolving to get it notarized at a hotel.

In Chicago I stopped off to make a speech at the National Safety Congress—a welcome change of pace. It would be a nonpolitical meeting where I could see old friends like Blanche and Ralph Robinson, Earl Campbell, Alice Mills and many others with whom I'd worked for years in developing safety programs.

I'd no sooner checked into a hotel, when politics caught up with me again, via a call from Bertha Adkins. Before leaving Washington we'd agreed to get out an important radio recording to the state committees. Now Bertha said, "We can't get our recordings. We've used up our money."

Shades of 1950! Even in a national campaign we were plagued by a money shortage!

"But they must be sent out," I told her.

"The radio division says we don't have the money," Bertha insisted in her matter-of-fact way.

"Find out how much it will cost to get that recording out to thirty-six states," I said. "And call me back."

I could just see Bertha, putting down the phone and trying to figure out a way to humor this wild woman from the West. A little later she called back and quoted the cost. I began naming the states to which the recording was to be sent.

"But, Ivy, they won't do it without the money," she said flatly.

"Tell them the money will be there Monday morning without fail—but the recordings must be in the mail to-morrow."

I put down the phone, not even bothering to conjure up a picture of the expression on Bertha's face. Instead, I looked in the mirror and asked myself, "What have you done now, Ivy? Where will you get that money?"

After pacing the floor for some anxious minutes, it occurred to me that the measure of a good executive was how well he could delegate responsibility. And here I was, trying to take on the extra burden of fund-raising. Why not hand over this chore to someone who had the experience to tackle it? So I immediately called an old friend, an astute business-man, who responded with reassuring alacrity. "You can stop worrying," he said. "The money will be in Washington Monday morning."

Saved by the bell, I put on my hat and sallied forth to the Safety Congress. There's something to this delegating business, I thought on the way there; I must try it more often.

But this wasn't always possible. Small crises kept cropping up that seemed to demand personal attention. There were feelings to be smoothed out between embattled factions, and importunate requests such as the one from a lady candidate who wanted Mrs. Eisenhower, or at least Mrs. Nixon, to come and stump her district. There were hundreds of speeches to deliver and thousands of people to see. When I finally got back to Washington, I opened my purse and there was my absentee ballot—still unmarked.

I would have taken care of it at once, but the memorable television broadcast by Dick Nixon, in which he answered the charges of improper fund-raising leveled against him, came at this time. We were inundated with thousands of wires and phone calls overwhelmingly endorsing Nixon as vice-presidential candidate. We stayed up all night at headquarters, opening telegrams, and, for a time, my old experience as a phone operator came in handy on the flooded switchboard. When this crisis was over, I boarded a plane for Minneapolis. As I opened my purse to get my baggage check, I came upon my absentee ballot. It was the Sunday before election and there was no time to lose.

Rushing to a hotel, I started looking for a notary even before I unpacked. But not on Sunday, ma'am. Leafing through the classified phone book, I began calling notaries until at last I found one—at home in the suburbs. So I hopped into a cab and, with a great feeling of relief, set out to mark my ballot. When I asked the notary how much I owed him, he tipped back his chair and looked at me wonderingly.

"Lady, anybody who'd come five miles out here just to cast a vote don't owe me a dime."

"Well, it was a pretty important vote to me."

"Musta been. Mind tellin' me who you voted for?"

"Why, no. I voted for Eisenhower."

"You know something—he's my man, too."

That out of the way, I could face the last few days of the campaign with an easier mind. On the Eisenhower train headed back east we had a party to mark the end of the crusade. The general thanked his staff warmly for all their work. He had always shown great concern for the welfare of the people working with him and was never at ease until he was sure that the stenographers, clerks, and others who did important behind-the-scene jobs had been looked after. Now, at this farewell party, just before disbanding what had become a traveling family, his thoughtfulness was reflected in their warm response.

On election day we gathered at headquarters at the Commodore Hotel in New York. In the women's division we had set up our own offices and we gathered there early. You could have cut the tension with a knife. Our optimism remained, but there was nothing further to be done. We could only wait and hope.

Sitting around would gain us nothing but ruined manicures, so I took off and went shopping. When I came back that afternoon, my secretary, Grayce McKenna, shrieked, "Look, Mrs. Priest is wearing red shoes!"

"That's right—we're winning an election," I assured her. "And red is my victory color."

The first returns to come in were from a small town (population: 12) where every last citizen had voted for Ike. We whooped with delight as other favorable returns began to trickle in.

The trend accelerated early in the evening and the hotel became one happy madhouse. There was no roast beef to grow cold and tasteless this year—as there had been in 1948. We ate with good appetite.

Upstairs in their suite, General and Mrs. Eisenhower stayed in seclusion. Our repeated entreaties to them to come down and help cut the victory cake in the women's division met with a firm, polite refusal from Mamie—who insisted that the results had to be absolutely certain. But the rest of us were circulating about from floor to floor, exchanging handshakes, kisses, and bear hugs. The place was a pandemonium. It had been a long time since we'd had anything like this to celebrate, politically.

Then, late in the evening, Governor Adlai Stevenson gracefully conceded defeat—and into the women's division came President and Mrs. Eisenhower, their faces wreathed with smiles. They cut our cake, and victory never tasted quite so sweet.

It was some time before I saw the total figures on the election—but they brought joy to my heart. For the number of women who voted in 1952 had increased by almost 40 per cent over 1948. Women had cast a total of 52 per cent of the vote that had elected the new President.

XIII

THE hills of home were beckoning me.

November, now, and the first snow would be flying soon in Utah. I was tired of hotel rooms and hurried snacks, tired of living out of a suitcase, tired of that sensation of awakening to wonder, with a start, what city I was in. I longed for the warmth of my own hearth, for the sound of the children rushing in after school trying to see if, on the hundredth try, they could get by with dumping their books in a heap on the dining room table.

Had Roy remembered to get the furnace checked and would Uncle Lije see that the storm windows were in place? And my poor flower beds, neglected this fall—I wouldn't stand a chance in the garden club show in the spring. I simply had to get home. It became a fever.

And every day, the "in" basket on my desk was full. There were hundreds of inquiries.... "Dear Mrs. Priest, do you remember meeting me at the tea in Tulsa?" ... and thousands of thank-you letters to write. There was money to account for, there were bills to pay, contracts to scan.

Every morning my secretary, Grayce McKenna, would bounce in cheerfully, almost staggering under a new load of correspondence. I'd hired Grayce first thing on reaching Washington on the basis of a purely social luncheon we'd had together—and I had been proud of my choice. A tall blonde, with cornflower-blue eyes, she always looked freshly scrubbed, even at the end of an eighteen-hour day. It was her cheerful enthusiasm that kept me going through those long November days.

By the end of the month, we had polished off the most urgent work. "Dear Mrs. Jones ... Thank you so much for your help and I know the new administration will be glad to consider your plan for ..." and "It is good to hear from you again and indeed I do remember ..." But my mind was wandering. Oh, dear, I hoped Aunt Gert wouldn't try to insist that Nancy wear long underwear to her ballet class. Then Pat had written that young Roy was keeping a pet porcupine in the back yard, just to tease her.... I would have to straighten a few things out with those children when I got home.

We finally got to the last big job—writing a report to General Eisenhower on the women's campaign activities, and compiling a list of Federal positions that could be filled by capable Republican women. On this, I could focus sharply— but for some reason or other Grayce's mind was not on her work now. She seemed dreamily wrapped up in a secret of her own. Well, it had been a hard campaign and I supposed that she was as tired as I was.

We finished the report and made an appointment to see the President-elect at his headquarters in the Commodore Hotel. After attending a tea given for me by the Republican women at the Sulgrave Club, I left immediately for New

York and my final chore as assistant chairman. That would be my report to Ike—and then, the hills of home.

When I walked into the general's office the next day, he clasped my hand, smiled warmly, and waved me to a seat.

"How are you, Mrs. Priest?" he said. "I hope you enjoyed it."

"That I did," I assured him. "Especially the ending."

"Mrs. Priest," he said, becoming suddenly businesslike. "I want you to be Treasurer of the United States."

I think that I nearly fainted on the spot. For a few seconds, all I could do was to stare at Ike speechlessly—an unusual condition for me.

Taking a deep breath, I finally stammered, "Why, I'd be honored, of course."

A little later, I walked out of his office in a complete daze. It had never occurred to me to wonder what the Treasurer of the United States did—or what I knew about filling such a formidable post. If Ike wanted me to do the job and thought I could handle it, I would certainly give my all.

Somehow, home suddenly seemed far away. I never paused to think what all this would entail—I just assumed it had to be done, and that was that. From my hotel room I called Roy, but could not locate him out on his territory. I called the house, but there was no answer. I simply had to talk to someone close to me, so I started calling my brothers and sisters. There were six of them—but I could not reach a single one. I had the most exciting news of my life—and no one in my family with whom to share it.

Roy was selling furniture that day in a small Idaho city. When his customers began to congratulate him on the momentous event, he thought that he was being made the butt of some elaborate Western joke. His friends had heard the news of my appointment on the radio, and it wasn't until he

187

straddled a luncheon stool for breakfast the next morning that he saw the news story.

"That's my wife!" he told the waitress excitedly, pointing to my picture.

"Oh?" she remarked, cocking a skeptical eyebrow, and pointed at a picture of Errol Flynn on the same page. "That's my husband. You want your coffee now, sir?"

When I got back to my office in Washington, Grayce fell into my arms, her eyes shining.

"And I've got good news for you," she said a moment later. "I'm going to be married . . . very soon."

So that was why Grayce's mind had been wandering. And good reason, too! We fell into each other's arms again. I delayed my trip home in order to attend Grayce's wedding to Albert Abajian, a United States Foreign Service officer, at the Little Church Around the Corner, in New York.

Then, on December 1, we closed up our shop and I finally headed back to Bountiful. During the past three months I had scarcely seen my family, and we had a noisy reunion. The youngsters were talking at the top of the sound range again, and if I told them to pipe down Aunt Gert would ask them to speak up so that she could hear them.

Christmas was close at hand and Roy's selling season was over. So, before the children started their holiday, he and I flew back to Washington to look for a house.

We had little time for shopping around, and were fortunate enough to find a substantial red brick colonial on a quiet street in suburban Arlington, Virginia. On the first floor there were a living room, dining room, den, kitchen and breakfast room, with a back sun porch. The basement had a big recreation room. Each of the girls could have a bedroom on the second floor. There were a master bedroom and a guest room—and on the third floor was a finished room big enough for Roy, Jr. to sleep in and carry out the vast electronic, radio, zoological, and chemical experiments in which he was engrossed. It suited us to a T, so we promptly signed the papers.

Back home again, we plunged into the twin activities of getting ready for Christmas and cleaning out the accumulation of fifteen years of active family living. There was no time to pause and think of the momentous move we were about to make, and for that I am now thankful. It's not easy to tear up roots and, as I rummaged through the attic and basement, I am glad I could not spend time shedding a tear over every souvenir—little Roy's outgrown cowboy chaps—Peggy's baby clothes, put away against the day when it would not be too painful to look upon them—the necklace made out of elks' teeth which Roy, Sr. had brought home from a trip when we were newlyweds—Pat's grammar-school homework (before the discovery of boys) with the gold stars for perfection—Nancy's homemade Valentine card from her sixth year: "I love you, Mommy."

Then there were the patented cheese cutters we'd given Dad one year, which had disappeared mysteriously after Christmas and now turned up behind the furnace, where he'd tucked them tactfully. There were old tennis shoes, old ski boots, the hats I'd intended to remodel, and the clothes I'd forgotten to send to the charity bazaar five years ago.

Out it all went, while the youngsters wailed that this object or that was still good, and their father surreptitiously sneaked out to the trash barrel to retrieve a disreputable sweater or a worn-out pair of slippers. The string and paper and cardboard boxes that Aunt Gert had so carefully hoarded in my absence came in handy now.

But there was no time for a backward glance—just decide on the next step and do it—dash to the phone to accept congratulations from another well-wisher—or run downtown to buy young Roy's Christmas present and some lamb's wool for

Nancy's ballet slippers. Then it was time for dinner, or to shower and head for the farewell tea in Salt Lake. And finally, the cartons and barrels were all lined up like soldiers, our life in Bountiful neatly tucked away. We could only hope that it would ship, without breakage, to the strange new Eastern city.

In the midst of all this excitement, I received a letter from the Bureau of Engraving and Printing, asking me to submit some specimen signatures to be printed on the currency after I assumed office. The entire family gathered in solemn conclave as I sat down at the dining-room table to pen the signature that would launch a few million bills.

"Don't anybody move," young Roy warned. "You might shake the table."

"Don't even breathe," Pat said. "The atmosphere has to be just right."

"Shall I turn the furnace up?" Father asked brightly. "The ink should dry fast."

"I've got a blotter that says 'Vote for Stevenson,'" Nancy announced. "You want that, Mother?"

"All I want is peace and quiet," I replied ominously.

"Don't disturb the next Treasurer of the United States at her work," Pat commanded. "One blot and your money won't be worth anything."

In spite of their solicitude, I managed to get a signature on paper. It didn't please me, so I tried another. Then another, this time a little fancier. And another, not quite so fancy. Before it was over, I had signed my name at least a hundred times.

"Which one do you like best?" I asked the family.

Everyone, of course, had a different choice.

"I've got an idea," said practical little Nancy. "Just send them all in and let Washington decide which is best."

"Yeah, let Ike decide," said young Roy seriously.

I followed Nancy's advice and sent them all to the Director of the Bureau of Engraving and Printing. When I asked him some time later which he'd chosen, he replied, "The first one, of course."

The round of farewell parties in the neighborhood was reaching its height now. We planned to leave just before Christmas, spend the holiday in Omaha, and continue on to Washington.

My husband's eyes shone with pride whenever our friends discussed my new assignment, but I knew how hard it must be for him to see us leaving our old home. He planned to continue with his job in the West and to come to Washington during slack business seasons.

Nancy and young Roy, now eleven and ten years old, seemed to be swept along by the excitement which I felt over going to Washington. But, with Pat, it was another matter. Now she was sixteen, a junior in high school, and very popular with the opposite sex. With that strange conservatism of habit characteristic of teen-agers, she had no desire to make a change. To make matters worse, she fancied herself in love with "the most popular boy" in her school. He was a senior and, I was informed tearfully, they expected to get married some day.

Poor Pat, I felt sorry for her—because the agonies of adolescence and young love were still fresh in my memory. In the hope of making her departure a little easier, I promised that she could come back to spend the summer in Salt Lake City. Perhaps I should not have held out the promise, but it dried up the tears in those pretty blue eyes. The anguish she suffered over parting from her own true love now was replaced with an attitude of patient, bittersweet resignation. She came along with a sigh, instead of a sob, humming, "I'll See You Again."

Late in December, the moving vans lumbered up and removed our worldly possessions. We set off for Omaha—quite a little caravan. Roy drove one car, I drove another, and we were trailed by Rosa, our new housekeeper, and her son Henry, who was going to a new job in the East.

We had done our best to persuade Aunt Gert and Uncle Lije to move to Washington with us, but she had firmly vetoed the suggestion. "Ye carn't teach an old dog new tricks," she said. "There's no place like Utah for Lije and me."

On our last day she came over to give us a proper send-off. She fussed around the house, checking crates and packages, hugging one youngster and then another, bravely trying to conceal her emotion, laughing one moment and close to tears the next.

As we packed ourselves bag and baggage into the cars, she gave us some pungent parting advice—as only Aunt Gert could.

"Now ye'll 'ave a great opportunity in Washington," she said. "See that ye make the most of it. Yer father and mother would be proud of ye, me girl—and so am I."

I couldn't talk for the lump in my throat. Handing me her handkerchief, she went on, "Now pull yerself together, Ivy. Ye've got a big job to do. Ike will keep the country straightened out. And it's up to you to keep the money straight."

As we drove off, she waved good-by, her head held bravely high, the feathers on her hat fluttering in the cold wind—a touchingly gallant figure standing alone in front of the empty house.

Our caravan made its way slowly through the winter snows to Omaha, where we celebrated Christmas together. Then, since my job demanded my presence in Washington earlier, I flew ahead with young Roy and Nancy, leaving Roy, Sr. to lead the caravan when his sales meeting was over. They sandwiched Pat in as driver of my car, Roy leading the way and the housekeeper's son bringing up the rear.

Going through the Blue Ridge mountains of West Virginia, they ran into snow. Roy looked in his rear-view mirror, saw that Pat was having trouble with her windshield wipers, pulled off the road, and went back to help her. As he reached her car, Pat cried out:

"Dad, your car is rolling!"

There it went, coasting slowly downhill—laden with furs and other items too precious to be entrusted to mere moving men. Roy made a dash—but the car had a head start. Then, suddenly, it stopped its plunge toward a precipice and came to rest abruptly against a boulder, undamaged.

When the furniture arrived at Arlington, I went to our house to supervise the delicate task of putting it in the right places. Roy called in the evening from Romney, West Virginia, and said they could make it to Arlington, if I was ready.

"Come on in—the water's fine," I cried, cheered by their safe arrival that far.

I had hot chocolate and cookies waiting for them, a fire on the hearth, and that night the Priest family was at home —2,300 miles away from home.

The next morning, young Roy was up early and rummaging through the cartons and barrels. He found his autographed picture of Ike and his chemistry set and, by the time the rest of us were awake, he had the house reeking with a rotten-egg smell, as it usually did when he experimented with sulphur dioxide.

"Phew, it smells like George Washington's horse slept here," Pat said, as she groped her way to the breakfast table.

"Mother, you've just got to make him quit using sulphur in those experiments," Nancy said. "How am I supposed to make friends here if he's going to stink up the place?"

"Watch your language, young lady, or you won't have any friends," I said. "Roy, you talk to him about that chemistry, will you?"

"Where are you going?" he asked.

"I've got to meet my new boss today."

"The Secretary of the Treasury?"

"Yes."

"Say, Ivy, if you see a delicatessen . . ."

"Oh, no!" Pat cried out in pain. "It's not bad enough that my brother's upstairs brewing up dragon's breath or something, but now Dad is going to start cramming that smelly cheese in the icebox. Honestly—men!"

"All right, young lady, you just get dressed and start helping Rosa unpack those barrels full of china. Wash it all and put it where it should go."

"What's Roy going to do?" Nancy demanded.

"We're going to wash the cars," his father announced. "And rake up the yard and then—say, what am I telling *you* this for? Ivy, you've got to do something about these girls. They're getting as bossy as their mo—as women."

"Good-by!" I said sweetly, giving my hat a pat and heading out the door for my first meeting with the man who had been designated as Secretary of the Treasury in the incoming administration.

When I reached the Treasury Building, I walked a little uncertainly into the conference room. Suddenly a man of medium height, with thinning hair and broad shoulders, bounded up, grinning broadly, and shook my hand.

"Mrs. Priest, I'm George Humphrey," he said, and proceeded to introduce me to the other men in the room—the new undersecretary and assistant secretaries.

"Just trying to get acquainted," he explained. "We're all going to be in the Treasury together and I thought we might go over a few things."

Within three minutes, I was convinced that I had been smuggled into the place under false pretenses. They were talking about debentures, "Feds," debt management—just for a moment, I thought I could understand that one—and assorted fiscal subjects. From time to time, I made a note on my scratch pad—but I'm glad no one saw it, for they would have guessed that banking had not been part of my background. It was a scrawl of questions I intended to ask later.

Doing my best to look earnest and knowing, I kept my mouth shut and survived the meeting with nothing worse than severe misgivings. Could I really do the job when I had so much to learn? But the die was cast and I was not going to resign before I had even started. After all, the job had been done under the Democrats by a woman—Georgia Neese Clark, of Kansas—who had been among the first to congratulate me and offer assistance. At least, I reasoned, I could sign my name as well as she could—or could I?

The inauguration was upon us before we managed to get the excelsior swept out of our new house, it seemed. The combination of inaugural preparations, shopping for ball gowns, winding up national committee business, getting the house in running order, learning something about my new job, plus a constant round of social activities, made this the most harassing period I'd ever known.

We had asked guests to join us in our box at the gala Inaugural Ball, and the girls fussed over their gowns until the last moment. Nancy had persuaded her father to let her have her first real party dress. Pat already had an escort, a tall, blond University of Virginia student named Larry Toombs, whom she'd met at our Republican headquarters. She seemed to be recovering from her heartbreak with customary haste.

My husband had shopped for white tie and tails in Salt Lake City. When they quoted the price, he said that his wife was only going to work in the Treasury Department, not own it.

By now everyone had been outfitted but our son and heir, who insisted that he was going to the ball dressed like his idol, General Ike. We searched the costume stores and located full-dress clothes in his size, but couldn't find a high silk hat. Then the news came out that the President would wear a black Homburg instead.

"That's all right, Mother," said young Roy. "The President can wear what he likes. But I want a high silk hat."

And so he was decked out, looking somewhat like a Singer midget perhaps, but very proud of himself. We were a happy and excited family at the ball that night. The Cinderella fairy tale had come true—only this time Cinderella had a husband and three children.

Before I could take office, it was necessary for the Senate to confirm my appointment. So I appeared before the Senate Finance Committee which inquired into my fitness. There had been some political sport made over a few new appointees, who happened to have large stock holdings which, it was charged, created a conflict of interest with their government work.

Senator Millikan, of Colorado, chairman of the finance committee, looked at me sternly and asked whether I had any holdings of stocks that would create a conflict of interest.

"I'm afraid I don't," I said, and I sounded just wistful enough so that the committee burst into laughter.

It was reassuring to have Senators Watkins and Bennett of my home state there to support and endorse my appointment.

Then courtly, white-maned Senator Hooey, of North Carolina, impeccably dressed in his dark frock coat and striped trousers, got up, pulled a bill out of his pocket, and examined it carefully.

"Gentlemen," he said in sonorous tones, "I am very pleased that this committee is confirming the appointment of such a charming and gracious lady. I think, also, as I look over this currency, that it might be a nice improvement in our money if we could have her picture on it."

Depend on a Southerner, I thought, to be gallant.

Roy had been waiting around Washington to see me safely inducted into office—while his business out West was waiting for him. Finally he had to leave before he could see me take the oath of office. The morning after he left, I was summoned to the Treasury Department to be sworn in.

Tracey Petersen, who had come east with us to serve in my new office, hurriedly rounded up the children from school, and I went to the Treasury to await the appointed hour. Tracey puffed in with the youngsters, dressed in their plain school clothes, just in time to see Secretary Humphrey swear me in as the thirtieth Treasurer of the United States. Then he presented me with the second sheet of bills printed with our signatures.

Down the white marble halls of the Treasury I marched now, with the three youngsters escorting me, to my new office. The staff was lined up to greet me and I heaved a sigh of relief—for I realized that, while Presidential appointees come and go, there is always the dependable civil service which carries on. There were flowers on my desk and everyone appeared not only competent, but happy. I shook hands all around and spent a little time becoming acquainted with each staff member.

Later I found myself alone with the children in the big, dignified office, which seemed to be haunted with history. Hanging on the wall was a huge pendulum clock, topped with the original seal of the Office of the Treasurer of the United States, made official in 1789. Behind my desk was a large walnut-framed mirror, in the Federal style. As I sat down in the big chair at the desk, I couldn't help thinking that this was a long way from Bingham Canyon.

Young Roy must have been as awed as I was.

"Gee!" he said, looking around. "Gee, Mom! How does it feel to be Treasurer of the United States?"

"I don't know, son. I'm not used to it yet."

After the children went back to school, I was alone in this great room and I realized suddenly that I *was* the Treasurer. I felt overwhelmed. My thoughts went back to Mother and to the debt I owed her. She had brought me up in politics. I had been elevated to a high office by circumstances outside myself. I had just happened to be in the right place at the right time. I only wished that she could be here now to see how it had all turned out.

The first thing I did behind that great walnut desk was to cry a little. Then I said a prayer.

XIV

A WAN January sun shone through the high windows of my first-floor office in the Treasury Building, one of the vintage structures in Washington. On Pennsylvania Avenue, the streetcars gave a peculiar, moaning shriek as they made the sharp turn at Fifteenth Street. Oblivious to the passage of time, I had been poring over figures that morning trying to prepare myself for another strange new ordeal—an appearance before a congressional budget committee which would hear our request for operating funds for the next year.

Suddenly, I looked up and saw Fred Church, the deputy treasurer, standing in front of my desk. A quiet man, whose manner was that of an erudite professor, Mr. Church was a career civil service man who knew every detail of the operation of our Bureau.

The combination of our names always seemed to amuse everyone. When I visited Federal Reserve banks and the officers brought some detail to my attention, it usually evoked a ripple of laughter if I said, "Please give me a memo and I'll take it to Church in the morning."

Now Mr. Church said gravely, "Sorry to bother you, Mrs. Priest. But I wanted to get your signature on this receipt."

Still half-absorbed in the work on my desk, I reached for the piece of paper he held out to me. As I looked at it my eyes popped. For it was a receipt for the money turned over to my custody by the previous Treasurer—a mere $32,410,-260,668.69⅔.

When I was able to catch my breath, I asked, "What does the two-thirds of a cent represent?"

"After the Civil War the state of Tennessee left two bonds on deposit with the Federal government," Fred Church explained. "Each bond was for so many dollars and a third of a cent—and they're both in your custody."

"I don't suppose we'll every find another third of a cent to round out the figure," I said, picking up my pen to sign the receipt.

"It's been there for years, Mrs. Priest," he said with a smile. "It would be difficult to find a third of a cent these days."

As I settled into the new nine-to-five routine of an office job, Mr. Church spent some time with me each day, explaining the work of our office and escorting me around to the various divisions. On my desk was a direct phone from the Secretary's office and he would summon me for luncheon meetings and conferences when I was needed.

One of the first jobs he had given us was to make a complete inventory of all of the nation's monetary resources—right down to counting every bar of gold or silver in the vaults and opening the sealed envelopes in which we kept securities that were in our custody. It was a long, arduous job, but one day Mr. Church and the Department legal adviser appeared in my office. They presented me with an official-looking paper, setting forth the total amount in the till.

It was, I'll admit, a complex array of figures to set before a novice. Neither Mr. Church nor the lawyer suggested that I study the ledger, but merely indicated the place where I was to sign. But, apprentice Treasurer or not, I wasn't going to sign anything before I read it.

"Just be seated, gentlemen," I said. "I'll look this over."

They gave me a patient glance, as if to indicate that they would humor the little lady. My eyes raced down the long columns of figures and suddenly I spotted what scemed a discrepancy.

"Shouldn't this figure," I asked, pointing to the page, "be the same as the one up at the top?"

"Why, of course," Mr. Church assured me.

"Then why isn't it?" I asked.

The men came out of those chairs as if they were shot from launching pads. Leaning over my desk, they quickly spotted the error. Covered with confusion, they retreated from my office and were gone for three hours. Then Mr. Church came back and explained, "That was just a clerical error, Mrs. Priest. Just technical."

"Well, let's try not to have even technical mistakes," I said. "With so many billions involved, we can't afford them."

How I happened to spot an error that the experts had missed, I'll never know. Perhaps it was the result of years of watching adding machines whirl up totals in the supermarkets. But it was propitious for me at this time, for it boosted my confidence. Apparently the story spread around the Department like wildfire.

The next day, the chauffeur assigned to me by the Department was driving me across town.

"Mrs. Priest, ma'am," he confided, "they sure 'nough talkin' 'bout you roun' th' Treasury Buildin' today."

"They are? What are they saying?"

"They sayin', this new lady Treasurer, she ain't nobody's fool."

Those were cheering words, which I very much needed.

My new job was, in some ways, comparable to that of the treasurer of any club or corporation—but with a number of important and confusing differences. Broadly speaking, I was responsible for receiving all money paid to the United States government by individuals, states, or foreign governments, and was responsible for payment of approximately 400 million checks annually drawn on the government Treasurer.

We are the only government in the world that puts out a daily statement of its debits and credits, which tells how much we have "in the bank." And I discovered that this government account has at least one similarity to my household account. For no matter how much comes in, it seems that at least that much goes out—usually a little more.

The Treasurer, in addition, issues a large part of our paper currency and shares with the Director of the Mint a responsibility for handling coins. There are three classes of paper money. The first is the silver certificate, which must be backed up dollar for dollar with silver which is in my custody. The second is the United States note, which is issued only in $2 and $5 denominations, and is partially backed by gold. By law, we must keep approximately $346,000,000 worth of these in circulation. The third class is Federal Reserve notes, which are issued by the twelve Federal Reserve banks and are secured by not less than 25 per cent gold with other backing for the difference.

The actual printing of the money is done by the Bureau of Engraving and Printing, which is outside of my department. They print it and we put it into circulation. It costs about one cent to print a bill—whether it has a face value of $1 or $1,000.

The Bureau turns out about one and a half billion bills in a year—one billion of which are $1 bills. The $5 note is next in popularity and some 250 million of them are issued in a year. We need only about 10 million $2 bills, presumably because of various superstitions about them. The life of a dollar bill is only about one year, and the government spends in the neighborhood of $12,000,000 annually to replace paper money.

Not unnaturally, citizens take a great interest in money and my mail is heavy with letters from people who have helpful suggestions in this field. Someone is always discovering a process for laundering money, to "make it look like new," or some method of reducing the cost of issuing currency. My favorite suggestion came from a man who proposed that we sell advertising space on the backs of bills.

Perhaps inspired by the do-it-yourself fad, one man started making his own silver coins. It was discovered that he was actually putting more silver into the homemade product than the mint uses. Much as we hate to discourage the sort of private industry that would show a profit for the government, we had to put him out of business.

Another case of misguided private enterprise was uncovered in the Treasury's check payments department. One day, a canceled check was thrown off by a machine because its punches didn't fit those on the check. Investigation revealed that this check had originally been issued to a member of our armed forces in Japan for a small additional payment of $2.54—and the figure had been raised to $2,540. Within thirty-six hours our vigilant secret service uncovered and cracked down on a gray market in checks operating in Japan.

That greed can drive men to cunning devices was further proved when the first counterfeit bill bearing the signatures of Secretary Humphreys and myself turned up at—of all places—a dog track near Boston. The $10 note had been manufactured by an ingenious printer who had read in a trade magazine that the Treasury was printing bonds by the lithographic process. So he lithographed a batch of Federal Reserve notes and passed off twelve of them in bars and at the dog track before he was apprehended at a pari-mutuel window. Treasury agents seized sheets of $10 bills valued at $50,300 in this man's Cadillac and print shop, plus an $8,000 press and a $2,000 camera. Evidently, he was a fairly good craftsman, for the notes could be considered passable when soiled and crumpled—but to the eagle eyes of T-men they were not deceptive.

Actually, in examining millions of notes that pass through our Department each year, we discover only a few counterfeits. Due to a very alert and efficient secret service, counterfeiting is kept at a minimum. In a recent year, it was reported that only one thousandth of one per cent of the $20 billion bills in circulation was spurious.

Vastly more money disappears from circulation, due to human error, than is introduced into the market by human cupidity. We have no way of knowing how much is destroyed or lost irretrievably each year. But we do know that, although all gold certificates were called in years ago, there are still $32,000,000 worth of these bills missing. Presumably, most have been lost or destroyed. That would indicate that millions of dollars' worth of bills today are likewise vanishing like the bison.

The Treasurer's office designates how much can be paid out on mutilated currency. The ruling on currency redemption states that between two-fifths and three-fifths of a bill is redeemed at fifty per cent of its value; three-fifths and over is redeemed at full value.

In a government bureau which concerns itself largely with figures I was surprised to find that this job involved more heartaches and humor than you'd find in a night court.

Shortly after I took office, a package came in from a farmer, who explained that he had dropped his wallet in the pasture. A calf had gulped it down and, since there was a considerable sum of money in the wallet, he had promptly butchered the calf.

"Enclosed, find calf's stomach, with wallet in it," he wrote.

Actually, the money had been damaged only slightly and we were able to issue new bills to him for the entire amount.

I told this story to comedian Bob Hope, when we met on a show he was doing for hospitalized veterans. "This man certainly learned a lesson," I concluded. "So did the calf," Bob responded.

Our morning mail includes any number of monuments to human carelessness with money. We may receive an old brass bed knob, stuffed full of mildewed money, or a glass fruit jar, which has been buried for fifteen years and in which we can discern a wet glob of what was once paper money. Always, there's a note explaining the injustice of it all. There was the man who tucked a few hundred dollars between the inner tube and casing of his spare tire as he set off on vacation. Of course, he had a flat, and, forgetting about his "mad money," put the spare on the wheel. He sent us a package of green confetti for redemption.

The Burned and Mutilated Money Section of the Treasury's Division of Currency Redemption handles about 42,000 cases annually—most of them attributed to poor safekeeping places.

Fire is probably the greatest mutilator of currency—as one cautious housewife discovered when she hid her $800 life savings in the ashbox of her cook stove—and lit the stove the next day. She distrusted banks and kept changing hiding places at home to prevent her spendthrift son from finding the money. But she outsmarted herself when she found nothing but charred remains.

Next to fire, Mother Nature takes the biggest toll. Though our currency is the finest in the world, it cannot withstand the ravages of dampness and decay. A Minnesota farmer once sent us a strongbox he had buried in a wheat field. In a few years the $20,000 he thought he'd deposited was in a petrified condition. After it was packed in moist cotton to soften it, his cache yielded $27,000—apparently his bookkeeping here had been faulty. But few cases turn out so felicitously. Hasty, careless safekeeping usually causes needless losses and heart-aches.

While I was only the second woman to serve as Treasurer, my office had been one of the first to hire women in the government. It was during the Civil War that women were brought in to cut and trim the currency by hand. And most men think women still do a good job of trimming the currency. Of course, today the Bureau of Engraving and Printing has the most up-to-date machinery for this operation. But the delicate work of redeeming mutilated currency is still done by hand. Working with the hatpin as a basic tool, women perform real miracles in prying apart wads of wet, burned, or mutilated bills.

Before I had the chance to learn all the details about the agency I was directing, requests began to come in for me to appear on radio and television, and at public gatherings. With the "little knowledge" that can be such a dangerous thing, I set off blithely to appear as a guest on a national network show, a short time after I took office.

"Mrs. Priest, I notice you used to be in merchandising," my host said. "A good merchant should know his product, so I want to see how much you know about the product you are handling. I'm sure you know what's on the front of a $10 bill —but what's on the back?"

The portrait of Alexander Hamilton, first Secretary of the Treasury, was on the front, and since there was a picture of the Treasury Building on one of the bills, I guessed that it was the ten.

"Right," he said. "Now, Mrs. Priest, I want to know what's on the back of a $2 bill."

"Oh, you mean the betting-window bill?" I asked, stalling for time to think.

I couldn't remember who was on the front of the $2 bill —much less on the back. Finally, as the announcer chatted on, I settled on Jefferson and concluded that Monticello must be on the back.

"Right," he said, and then with a flourish he announced, "I'm really going to stump you this time. What's on the back of a $100,000 bill?"

"Strange as it might seem, that doesn't stump me. I was so amazed to find that we made a bill of this size, I looked it over carefully. It has Woodrow Wilson on the front, which is green, and on the back—which is yellow—it has simply the figure $100,000. And you won't have to look in your wallet to verify that, because it is used only by Federal Reserve banks."

He gave up at that point, much to my relief, for my luck couldn't have held out much longer. When I got back to the office, I proceeded to memorize the design of each denomination of bill—front and back.

My handsome office had not been redecorated for some time and, being a woman, I decided it was time for a change. So I had it repainted from a sandy color to a pastel green, and wangled a domestic Oriental rug to brighten the room. Adjoining the main office was a private sitting room, equipped with a long table and a couch of cracked black leather. This room was painted in the same soft shade of green and I had the couch covered with gay flowered chintz.

The little room, traditionally part of the Treasurer's suite, had an interesting history. During the Civil War period, the Treasurer, Gen. F. E. Spinner, awoke one night from a disquieting dream. Unable to get back to sleep, he tossed fretfully, prey to an uneasy feeling that something was wrong at the office. Dressing hurriedly, he went to the Treasury, where he found that indeed something was amiss—the door to the basement vault, where $400,000,000 was stored, had been left open.

Nothing was missing, but the general never fully recovered from the shock. He made it a rule to check personally every night to see that the door to the vault was locked. And after that, he slept in the little room off his office, directly above the vault—the same room which now serves as my retreat, when things get frantic.

Government officials are not highly paid, as everyone knows. But Uncle Sam does manage to surround these jobs with a certain aura of dignity and prestige which are extra dividends not subject to taxes.

As a woman who had been appointed to a high post, I had received a great deal of publicity. Almost immediately, I was inundated with invitations to the private and official functions which dot the Washington day like the chimes of a grandfather clock.

During my first weeks in Washington, I would dash home from the office, exchange gossip with the youngsters on the day's events, shower, dress, and get into my car to return to town for whatever social function was indicated.

The modest little car which had been presentable enough back home did look a bit shabby among the limousines outside Washington embassies. Sometimes there would be a parking problem, and I would have to tramp a few blocks in my party dress and flimsy shoes. But—with what party dresses were costing me—I couldn't afford cabs, so I walked blithely on.

But one night, the old buggy quit in the midst of a downpour on Constitution Avenue. I was stalled in the middle of a busy street, wearing an evening dress and gold slippers. The motorists got tired of honking at me and finally one pulled up to see if he could help. I asked him to call a cab and then had the cab summon a tow truck. Naturally, I was late getting to the party, where I encountered Secretary Humphrey. When I told him my tale of woe, he looked surprised.

"Why, Ivy, didn't anyone tell you? You're supposed to have a chauffeur and a Department car to take you to official functions like this."

You can be sure that Mrs. Priest arrived looking more like the Treasurer of the United States from then on.

In the spring, I was asked to a dinner party at the home of one of Washington's leading hostesses—and received another lesson in the social mores of the Capital. I approached the butler in the foyer of her mansion and gave him my name. He looked the guest list over and said icily, "I'm sorry, madam, but there's no Mrs. Priest."

"This is Thursday, May twenty-first?"

"Yes, madam."

"And there is no Mrs. Priest on the list?"

"No, madam."

"Then I must have made a mistake," I said, turning to leave.

At the door, I ran into Assistant Secretary of State Don Lowrie and his wife Mary.

"Where are you going?" Mary asked.

"It seems that I've made a mistake. I wasn't invited."

"Why, of course you're expected for dinner."

"The butler says no."

"You just stay here and I'll get the whole thing straightened out," Don said.

"You'll do no such thing," I said. "I'm embarrassed enough already."

Mary Lowrie, meantime, had slipped around and was studying the guest list. She let out a triumphant cry.

"Ivy Priest! You are the Treasurer of the United States, aren't you?"

"Yes, so I'm told."

She beckoned me over to the chart which showed the seating arrangement. There was my title to the left of the host. I just hadn't been in protocol-conscious Washington long enough to learn that if you had an official title, you announced it to the butler. He just wasn't interested in your name.

"Please don't say anything about this to our hostess," I said to Don.

"Oh, she'll love it," he said.

But I was thinking about the poor butler, who was covered with mortification.

"Not a word," I cautioned. The butler's face broke into a beam, and I was probably the most carefully served guest at that dinner.

As the weeks went by, I became accustomed to Washington protocol—so much so that even out of town I assumed that I would have the same place in the batting order. It was in New York, naturally, that I got my comeuppance.

I had rushed into a store to do some shopping before returning home. Having made my purchases, I discovered that I had left my wallet back at the hotel.

"We'll take your check, lady," said the salesman.

I wrote a small check and he asked:

"Any identification? Something with your signature on it?"

"That's in my wallet, too," I replied. "Wait a minute—have you got a dollar bill?"

He looked at me as if I had lost my mind. But he pulled out a dollar bill and I pointed to the bottom of it.

"There's my signature."

If I had introduced myself as Helen of Troy, he couldn't have been more flabbergasted. But he took the check over to the buyer and they held a conference. Then she came over, studied me curiously, and said, "Lady, don't you have something other than a dollar bill with your signature on it?"

They had to take it on up through channels before the check was finally accepted.

I was just a little worried about what the steady stream of publicity and the sight of Mother being swept off to dinner in a chauffeured limousine might do to the children. After all, we had lived a pleasant middle-class existence in a small Western city and this Queen-for-a-Day role was not the stuff out of which a real life could be made.

I tried to accentuate the positive by keeping our home life as simple and natural as possible. The children entered public schools in Arlington, just as they had done in Utah. We went shopping together on Saturdays. And in spare moments—such as they were—I did the darning, worked with my flowers, or cleaned out the basement. Sunday, after church, was still very much a family day.

Young Roy's interests in life included not only science but also an active career in the field of finance. He was engaged always in buying and selling, and the small pile of cash which he kept in his room kept growing. He changed its hiding place from day to day, but I would come across it when I dusted behind a picture or straightened up a dresser drawer in his room. I considered this acquisitive instinct commendable—up to a point.

One day, I became curious about the droves of boys he

was bringing in over the weekends to have dollar bills auto-graphed by the Treasurer. I discovered that he was "selling" this privilege for ten cents per head, or bartering it for some kickback. We had a little talk and I explained that this was the sort of thing which, in adult life, a Senate committee would regard with disfavor. He wound up by using his ill-gotten coins to give a back-yard hot-dog roast for his buddies and concentrated on more ethical money-making schemes, such as selling snowballs in July. He'd packed them away in our freezer and his out-of-season prices ranged pretty high.

Nancy had reached the age where the drive to dress and behave exactly like other girls was the guiding principle of her life. Because she was a quiet, rather retiring child by nature, I think she disliked finding herself in the limelight in Washington and she did everything possible to minimize it. One day, when she was practicing ballet steps with a friend at our house, I heard the young visitor ask, "Nancy, does your mother really sign all the money?"

"Yeah," Nancy replied, disinterestedly. "Look, fourth position! I can do it!"

Mrs. Eisenhower's secretary called me at the office one day and asked if the youngsters would like to visit the White House. Overcome by her thoughtfulness, I assured her that they would be thrilled.

Mrs. Eisenhower was at the front door to greet them when they arrived, and started showing them through the residential part of the Executive Mansion, which few people are ever privileged to see. Instead of turning them over to her secretary, she conducted the tour personally, getting out the President's trophies for them to see and explaining the history of every room. She spent so much time with them that she was in danger of being late for another appointment—and it wasn't until her secretary brought her hat and gloves upstairs where she and the children were chatting that she tore herself away. The children walked away in a dream, of course.

"Better not say anything about this at school," Nancy warned Roy. "They'll think we're stuck up."

"Yeah," he agreed. "But maybe it would be all right just to tell Glen about it." Glen Spitler was his special pal.

Vivacious, ebullient Pat—on her own merits—had hardly gone unnoticed at the big high school where she was enrolled. She was having as many dates as usual and wailing as loudly as the normal teen-ager about the load of homework. She was also exchanging letters regularly with the boy back home, and I could see no diminution in the rate of exchange as the months went by. She constantly reminded me of my promise to let her spend the summer in Utah.

I was not particularly disturbed by what seemed to be puppy love. As a firm believer in the idea that time heals all things—especially for the young—I felt that Pat would outgrow this phase. But then she brought me to with a start. One night, she came into my room after a school dance and fell to talking about the boy back home. It seemed that he had quit school and gone to work.

"Why didn't he finish out the year and get his diploma?"

"Oh, he's got a good job," she assured me. "He's driving a truck and earns about eighty dollars a week, with overtime."

"That's a lot of money for an eighteen-year-old boy to earn."

"Mother! He's nearly nineteen."

"Well, he should be able to show you a good time this summer."

"Oh, we're saving it to get married."

"Pat—you're only sixteen years old. You have a year to go before you even finish high school!"

"Don't forget, I'll be seventeen this summer. And what's a year anyway?"

This conversation left me shaken, for the idea that these two youngsters were seriously contemplating matrimony hadn't dawned on me. While I had nothing against the boy, he certainly wasn't mature enough to take on the responsibility of a wife—and Pat hardly knew her own mind.

Now I dreaded the thought of allowing her to spend the summer in Utah. But children attach great importance to promises and I hated to break mine to Pat. In my perplexity I called Roy, who was traveling in Idaho, to ask his advice. He felt that the children should have a summer back home, and added that Aunt Gert and Uncle Lije counted on it. When I mentioned my concern over Pat's romance, he said soothingly, "Now, Mother, don't take it so seriously. At their age romance comes and goes. Don't forget, Aunt Gert can handle Pat. Don't you worry about her."

Somewhat reassured, I helped them pack their gear, gave Pat the entire summer's allowance for all three youngsters, and put them on a plane for Utah. Before the plane flew out of sight I was already beginning to miss them and to wonder if it had been wise to let them go. I consoled myself with the thought that it would be good for them to be back in their familiar environment, seeing their old friends and favorite haunts. But nagging doubts continued to assail me. Would Pat be able to resist the blandishments of a persistent beau? And could Aunt Gert cope with a headstrong teen-ager, if she should decide to do something drastic?

XV

THE house seemed so empty that summer.

When I made my way home through the shimmering late-afternoon heat of Washington to our cool brick colonial, I would half expect to hear the phonograph blaring or the noise of young Roy's feet racing up the stairs. But, since even the housekeeper had insisted on going back to Utah, there was no sound to greet me but the echo of the door as I closed it behind me.

Actually, I had little time to feel lonely, for I was at my desk eight hours a day, working hard at my job. After office hours, there was the round of "must" social engagements and the constant demand for speeches at one place or another.

Roy managed to spend weekends with the children at Aunt Gert's and kept a steady stream of "don't worry, Mother" letters coming my way. Pat, I was told, had gone to work at the telephone company as an operator, following her mother's footsteps into her first job.

What I was not told, until a propitious moment much

later, was why she'd gone to work. It seemed that the young-sters had blown their entire summer's allowance, which I'd entrusted to Pat, within a couple of weeks of arriving. They were unable to reach their father readily, and Aunt Gert felt this would teach them a lesson about reckless spending, so Pat got the job. If not provident, she was at least self-reliant, and I was glad to see the children sticking together in an emergency.

I made plans to be in Salt Lake City for Pat's birthday late in August and to bring them home again. A short time before I was due to go west, a committee representing the President's Cup Regatta, headed by Edgar Morris, a promi-nent businessman, came to see me.

They explained that they were charged with finding a young girl, connected with the new administration, to serve as Queen of the Regatta that fall and thought I might be able to suggest the names of some attractive daughters of Cabinet officers.

As I began to name several girls I knew, Mr. Morris spotted a photograph of Pat on my desk.

"Say, that's a pretty girl," he exclaimed. "Who is she?"

"My daughter," I replied.

He picked up the picture and showed it to the others. "Just exactly what we want," he said. "She's a beauty!"

So I promised to ask Pat about it when I saw her in a few days, feeling sure she'd be delighted. Providence moves in strange ways to direct one's life, and this was one of the happy moves. For it was only two days later that Pat phoned.

"Mother!" she said excitedly. "Is it all right if I get an engagement ring for my birthday?"

My heart sank as I recalled the "don't worry" notes from her father. But I came back as cheerfully as I could, "Pat—I've got the most exciting news for you. I can't tell you over the phone, but it's absolutely fabulous. And if you get engaged, it will just spoil everything. Wait until I get there and tell you about it."

She agreed none too willingly and I sighed with relief. My first evening back in Salt Lake, I told her all about the regatta—the ball, the festivities, and the princesses. I tried to make it sound just a cut above the last Buckingham Palace presentation.

"Always used to like *regrettas* when I was a girl," Aunt Gert said helpfully.

"You know, the fastest speedboats in the country compete for the President's Cup," I went on. "It's really an exciting week."

Pat listened with apparent interest, but made no commitment immediately. At breakfast the next morning she said casually, "I've decided that I won't take the ring for my birthday after all. But will it be all right if I get it for Christmas?"

"Christmas is a long way off, my girl," Aunt Gert put in. "Ye may 'ave changed yer mind by then."

"Oh, no, I won't!" Pat said with a toss of her blond head.

"We'll discuss that when the time comes," I said, sighing with relief at this temporary reprieve.

Back in Washington, Pat was swept along by the regatta festivities into a glittering land of make-believe, and she presided with great beauty and poise, I thought, over the regatta and ball.

A new, intriguing life unfolded for her. Her mind, which had been half back in Utah, now focused on Washington and the opportunities it offered for new friendships and interests. These distractions crowded out her romantic notions and she began to talk in terms of college, as her school friends were doing.

I was grateful that a diversion had occurred just in time to steer her away from a premature marriage. For Pat did not react well to parental sternness. There was an independent streak in her that could make her take matters into her own hands, if I put my foot down too firmly.

Once the excitement of the regatta was out of the way, I called a family council with the three children. After homesickness had driven Rosa, our housekeeper, back to Utah, the burden of running a household and filling a nine-to-five job became too heavy. So I suggested a division of labor, with each of us taking something like an equal share. Pat agreed to do the cooking, and Nancy and Roy staked out their claims on dishwashing and ironing privileges.

Each Saturday, we went shopping together. I made out the list and we broke it down by departments. When we got to the supermarket, we would scatter like a school of frightened minnows and go down the aisles selecting favorite items. I developed Aunt Gert's sharp eye for freezer bargains. On one occasion my thrifty instincts ran away with me and I bought twenty pounds of an untried brand of sausage because it was so cheap. This proved penny-wise and pound-foolish, for it cooked up into more grease than sausage.

Nancy, who had acquired a set of lacquer bowls and cups, experimented with Chinese dishes. Her cart was often laden with water chestnuts, bamboo shoots, bean sprouts, and canned chop suey and chow mein. Young Roy's tastes were even more exotic—fried cactus worms and rooster combs, roasted grasshoppers and ants, and pickled quails' eggs piled up in his cart. It was sometimes difficult to keep our household rule of eating everything we'd purchased.

In addition to being required to keep at least a clear path through their own rooms, the youngsters—with the help of a cleaning woman twice weekly—kept the downstairs in sufficient order. Allowing for normal disruptions, our cooperative system worked out pretty well. Nancy would get diverted sometimes when a new Eddie Fisher record came out and, as President of Eddie Fisher Fan Club Chapter 286, she had to assemble the fans for an afternoon of squealing and sighing. I felt that I would go into orbit if I heard that record one more time.

Roy was now repairing his friends' radios for a small fee.

Sometimes he would swap jobs with Nancy, and I would come home to find him ironing shirts near the telephone stand in the breakfast room. He always had plenty of company there, for Pat practically lived on the phone.

As I thought back to the days of summer when the place had been like a mausoleum, I was grateful for all the hubbub and proud that the youngsters could be counted on to do their share.

In November, Roy came east for the holidays. He looked about good-naturedly, issued a few orders, and suddenly the uproar, which I had come to accept as a necessity, subsided and a degree of quiet was restored in the house. Roy wandered around the neighborhood, looking up friends, tradesmen, and repairmen. In Washington, the dinner list might show "The Treasurer of the United States and Mr. Priest," but to find us in our own neighborhood, you asked for Mrs. Roy Priest.

That fall, Mary-Stuart Price, who arranged debutante parties, asked if Pat could make her debut with other daughters of official Washington. Pat was delighted at the prospect, and her father thought it wise to continue to divert her with such girlish interests. But, once we decided to go into the affair, he assumed an attitude of vast indifference to the whole business, and preferred to tie up new fishing flies with young Roy, pausing just enough to admire our butterfly's evening gown.

With the hustle and bustle of deb parties, Pat was having a whirl, often escorted by Pierce Jensen, a Navy flyer and White House aide whom she had met at the regatta. Her own debut party was held at the Shoreham Hotel and, looking at her so radiant and poised that night, I found it hard to believe that this was the same freckled-faced, tousled bobby-soxer who had led the high-school cheering team at basketball games in Bountiful a year before. Roy struggled into his tails, groaning and protesting like any man unaccustomed to wearing this strait jacket. Nancy and young Roy, dressed to the nines, were of course on hand to see their sister "come out"— though they vowed she had always been "in" as far as they were concerned.

Having survived the party season, I was able in January to celebrate the end of my first year in office. Mother, wife, government official—it had been rugged, but I would not have missed a minute of it.

Early in February, I was in Philadelphia to make a speech to the Pennsylvania Bankers Association, when I received a phone call from Soda Springs, Idaho. Roy, who had returned to his territory, had been taken to the hospital with a stroke. Since my experience with Mother's strokes I had terrible visions of Roy lying helpless and alone far from home.

Frantically, I checked flights westward, but it was too late that night to get out. When I went to deliver the keynote speech at the convention the next morning acute anxiety was added to my usual stage fright. Later, the officers of the banking group rallied around, secured a plane reservation, and put me aboard. I stopped over in Washington, where an anxious Pat was waiting with a suitcase she had packed for me.

At the hospital the doctor assured me that Roy had had a minor stroke. Though Roy had difficulty moving one arm and a leg, the doctor predicted he would recover completely.

During the week I spent at his bedside, we had hours to talk about our future, and agreed that, at the age of seventy, it was time for him to retire from business. Naturally, he fell to worrying about what would happen to his customers and how his furniture house would work it all out. My mind was on other things.

We had accumulated some savings, and Roy owned farm property which brought us a small income. Luckily, my pay had been increased in the course of over-all Federal raises. But it was one thing to maintain the position required of a Federal official on two salaries. It would be quite another to do so on only one.

When Roy left the hospital, we returned to Bountiful briefly to arrange the sale of our house—for the time being we would be living in Washington. We said good-by to Aunt Gert and Uncle Lije—for we knew not how long—and there was a lump in my throat, as we headed east, racing ahead of a blizzard.

In the Rockies we had a flat tire, and Roy could only fuss and fidget over his helplessness while I unpacked the trunk and changed the tire. His normal good nature deserted him as we raced on through the night, and he seemed moody and despondent.

"I guess that's the way it's going to be from now on," he sighed.

"How's that, dear?"

"You changing the tires, doing all the driving. . . ."

"Now, Roy, don't be silly," I broke in. "The doctor said you'd be good as new in a few weeks."

For the rest of the trip, I could not be sure whether Roy was depressed or just tired. I kept up a cheerful chatter, but at night after he had begun to snore gently, I lay there thinking about our problems. Here was a man who had been active and successful all his life, reduced by a stroke to being a semi-invalid. I knew he would recover physically, but how was he going to adjust to retirement—and in a completely new environment?

In the past year I had become somewhat adjusted to life in the Capital, while Roy was away working. But how would it be for him? "The Treasurer of the United States and Mr. Priest. . . ." Hours of idleness around the house while I was out earning the family income—how would Roy feel?

But there was no choice. We had young children to educate and launch into the world. We had made it through rough times before, and we would make it again, with God's help—and Roy's stability and great understanding.

The house took on a different atmosphere as soon as Father arrived. Young ladies quit coming to breakfast in their bathrobes and manicuring their toenails while they chattered on the phone downstairs. Young man brushed his hair before dinner and closed doors more quietly. The furnace man, who'd been promising to come for weeks, appeared promptly after one call from Father. Squeaky doors became silent and leaky faucets dried up. The general noise-level lowered to a mere tumult. And, best of all, Roy began to recover complete use of his muscles—especially the ones that crinkled his face into a grin.

Roy appeared to be enjoying what he called his new job as household superintendent. For the first time in his life, he was home—free from the grind of nights on the road, free to hear the children's day-to-day problems and triumphs, and free to do the many things he'd always wanted to do.

A friend of ours, who had reached retirement age and was worried about his capacity to endure leisure, once asked Roy how he could take it.

"Oh, it's not as bad as you think," Roy told him. "There are lots of compensations. In the old days I did all the traveling and Ivy stayed home with the children. Now, it's all turned upside down. You might say I'm just plumb, cold retired, I suppose. But I seem to be busier than I ever was before."

It's true that there are some things he can no longer do, such as engage in strenuous sports or dance, which we both used to enjoy. But there are many interests he's had time to cultivate. Always an avid fisherman, he is no longer limited to vacation angling; he enjoys reading, light gardening, corresponding with the friends he made in his traveling days, and on family vacations he's an inveterate sight-seer.

There was no opportunity to introduce him gradually into the dizzy whirl of Washington social life. As soon as he was well enough to accompany me, he had to take the plunge. And, after that, it was sink or swim.

At our first formal dinner party together I watched out of the corner of my eye to see how he was taking it. He seemed to be perfectly at ease and was chatting amiably with his dinner partner. But on the way home, he said, "I never saw such an imposing array of silver on a table in all my life. You don't see much silver, climbing up on stools at lunch counters. I thought I had figured things out pretty well until they cleared the plates off. I had one piece of silver left over. I was really embarrassed until I noticed that the titled English lady who was sitting next to me had one piece left over, too. But you know what made me feel so good, Ivy?"

"I can't imagine."

"It wasn't even the same piece."

Roy was just a little nervous, anticipating his first dinner with royalty. To allay his fears I told him about the time I became involved in a *faux pas* at a dinner at the Greek Embassy, honoring Queen Frederika.

Wearing long white gloves, I approached the queen in the receiving line. Uncertain about the etiquette pertaining to gloves, I was just a step away when I decided that I should perhaps take my glove off before shaking hands. Frantically, I struggled to get my right hand free of the glove when the queen, seeing my confusion, smiled warmly.

"Don't bother," she said pleasantly, holding out her hand.

There was quite a glittering company at dinner. I was seated next to a Greek admiral, who kept looking at me strangely. I had dressed carefully—in my inaugural ball gown, a champagne satin embroidered with crystals and pearls. Of course, my necklace was probably the only one at the table which wasn't made of real gems, but that hardly explained the admiral's persistent stare. Noticing my discomfort, he finally explained, "Forgive me for staring, dear lady—but I had looked at the seating arrangements and learned that on my right was to be the Treasurer of the United States. Frankly, I'd expected an old man!"

Another memorable event was a dinner at the Chinese Embassy. I had been the guest of Ambassador and Mrs. Wellington Koo several times and we had become warm friends. But it was Roy's first meeting with them. We were presented to Madame Chiang Kai-shek, the guest of honor, and to our Ambassador to Italy, Clare Booth Luce, who was Roy's dinner partner. For a moment I wondered how he was faring with this scintillating woman. Then I saw her chuckle with amusement over something he said. Every time I glanced their way after that, Mrs. Luce was laughing at one of Roy's sallies.

I realized he had been selling Roy Priest along with furniture for forty years, so he'd have no trouble selling himself to Washington. But was he buying Washington? That was the important question.

At cocktail parties and receptions—the most widespread form of entertainment here—I would get so absorbed in talking with friends that I would often ignore the lavish buffet. Roy liked the people, too, but he didn't let conversation keep him from sampling the foreign cheeses and delicacies that were served.

When I would fish a particularly odd-looking piece of

cheese out of the refrigerator at home, he would explain, "That's some of that goats'-milk cheese the Norwegian Ambassador was telling me about the other day."

I often found Roy in the kitchen, helping Pat get dinner. They would be engaged in lively discussions about Hosts and Hostesses I Have Known or Does Caviar Really Need Lemon Juice?

One night, I was writing Aunt Gert and I asked Roy if he wanted to include any description about his life in Washington.

"Tell them that all I do is change my clothes," he said.

A few nights later, we got into our most formal attire for a dinner at the Netherlands Embassy, where Prince Bernhard was the guest of honor. Ordinarily, the Treasurer of the United States sits below the salt at an official dinner. But this time I was seated at the right of the prince, apparently one of the ranking guests. Air Force Secretary Harold Talbot and his wife, Peggy, were also there.

Since Washington protocol dictates that one never leaves a dinner party until the ranking guest has departed, Mrs. Talbot came up to me late in the evening and said, "Harold thinks that you are the ranking guest."

"Oh, no. I think he is."

"Since we're not sure, why don't we leave together," Peggy suggested.

"A good idea. I'll tell Roy."

"You find him and I'll try to locate the prince, so we can say our good nights."

After searching the drawing room, Peggy and I found each other—both looking puzzled.

"I can't find Roy," I said.

"And I can't find the prince."

"They can't have strayed far. Let's look in the library," I suggested.

As we approached the open door of the library, I heard the prince laughing uproariously.

"So this Easterner said, 'Well that's not much of a trout'— I swear it was two feet long—and Dad Turner looked at him and said, 'I know—that's just bait.'" It was Roy's familiar voice relating some of those terrible fishing whoppers of Dad Turner's about the Jackson Hole country. The prince laughed heartily and before we could leave he had to top my husband's story with one of his own.

Roy gave every evidence of enjoying all this. But it was not until we went to a dinner party at the home of Jim and Gladys Black, two newly found friends, that I was convinced he'd made the transition. Among the guests were Irene Dunne, the actress, and her husband, Dr. Griffith. After dinner, various toasts were proposed. The distinguished doctor stood up and, raising his glass, said, "I should like to propose a toast to my beautiful wife—from her trailer."

This produced general laughter. Then Roy jumped up and said, "Hold it, Doctor. Let another trailer join this tribute—to his wife."

It was so spontaneous and amusing that, once and for all, I knew Roy was going to be all right in Washington.

And suddenly my concern for my family was directed elsewhere. One night as Pat left on a date with Pierce Jensen, I noticed their exchange of tender glances. When the door closed behind them, I exclaimed laughingly, "Well! Do we have another romance budding?"

"Oh, haven't you noticed?" said Roy. "Pierce is top man now. But don't go jumping to conclusions."

"Well, you know, my mother jumped to conclusions. And look how right she was!"

XVI

SEATED at the head table at a luncheon given by the dignified Commonwealth Club in San Francisco, I stole a quick
look around the room. The jitters which commonly afflict me
just before a speech were not quieted in the least by this
glance around. For there were several hundred solid business-
men in the room and, except for myself, not a single woman.

"I thought your wives might be here today," I said brightly
to the president of the club.

"Mrs. Priest, you were not invited here today because you
are a woman," he said severely. "We asked you because we
wanted to hear from the Treasurer of the United States."

This did little to tranquilize me, and my heart was fluttering when, after a very proper introduction, I rose to speak.
Looking around at those solemn faces, I knew I would have
to deliver a serious oration and desperately searched for an
ice-breaker.

"Gentlemen, I wonder if you appreciate how glad I am

to be here today," I began, "and to realize suddenly that I am the most beautiful woman in this room."

They exchanged startled glances, craned their necks to check the accuracy of the statement, and—thank heaven—burst into laughter.

Without an opening of this kind, I would have gone down for the count the first time I stood up before the discerning audiences I had to face after I became Treasurer. It is one thing to speak to an enthusiastic crowd of political partisans, but quite another to face a roomful of bankers wondering what I could tell them that they didn't already know.

But public speaking seems to be considered a part of the Treasurer's job, I discovered. Despite a good deal of political speaking, I had never overcome a certain shakiness of knee in advance. But if I could just feel the audience smiling back at me, I picked up confidence.

Although I did not make policy in the administration, I was expected to explain it to bankers and financial groups whose affairs are vitally affected by decisions made in the Treasury Department. To help me with these important speeches, I had the assistance of a young Treasury writer during my first months in office, but he moved on to other work, and I was soon writing some of my speeches on my own.

In addition to talks before professional groups and speeches where I presented awards for savings bonds campaigns, I had many other types of audience, ranging in size from fifty to fifty thousand persons. These talks took me out of Washington frequently and gave me a chance to indulge my favorite pastime—meeting people.

Though I had a special partiality to women's groups, as far as food was concerned the men did better. I have always eaten three hearty meals a day, and the light diet at women's luncheons left me hungry. One day, I was booked to speak at two ladies' luncheons in Washington on the same day. I was to have a main course at one, make my talk, and then dash to the other for dessert and another talk.

Afterward, I walked weakly into the office and rang for Grayce.

"Please get me a sandwich and a glass of milk, will you? One more luncheon and I would have starved to death."

Inevitably, when I appeared as a speaker or guest at a gathering, someone always asked me to autograph a bill. Before I realized the perils involved, I was literally smothered in bills of every denomination. At the close of a St. Louis reception attended by twelve hundred women, the usual autograph party began and before it was over, hours later, I had signed over a thousand bills.

After that, I learned to turn aside requests, while in a reception line, with a light "Mail it to me at the office and I'll send you back a nice new bill with an autograph." At banquets, it's a different matter. I am a sitting target at the head table, and I can't excuse myself on the grounds that it would hold up the reception line.

One night, at a dinner in Chicago, I was besieged for autographs all through the meal, and surrounded after dinner. A friend finally sent a bellboy in to page me for a phone call. I didn't realize that it was just a ruse until I was safely outside. Then I felt a tug at my sleeve. It was the bellboy who had paged me.

"Would you please autograph this bill for me, Mrs. Priest?" he said.

I am asked to autograph all sorts of things, from club cards to Confederate or foreign money—or even blank checks. I decline, however, to put my name on anything other than United States currency or to autograph books.

At another banquet in Chicago I was kept so busy signing bills that I didn't get a bite to eat. When I thought the autograph party was about over, I was amazed to see dollar bills attached to strings showering down upon me from the balcony, which was filled with people who had come only to hear the speech. I proceeded to sign these bills and sent them flying back, to the great amusement of the audience. During this vigorous operation one of the guests at the head table passed a note to me. I did a double take—for it was a $100 bill—and I knew the owner was a Texan.

This gave me an ideal opener for my speech.

"Ladies and gentlemen, you've all seen that I've been doing my bit toward keeping down inflation. Bit by bit I've been taking money out of circulation." Holding up the $100 bill, I added, "Now I've been asked to autograph this $100 bill. You guessed it. It's from Texas. But, as you can see, there are no strings attached to this one."

When the 1954 campaign for Congress opened, I was back in the thick of it, making campaign swings around the country, which alternated with nonpolitical speeches. Sometimes alone, at times accompanied by my secretary, Grayce Abajian, I flew from coast to coast. We would touch down in North Carolina for a day, move on to Alabama where I would shake hands with sixteen hundred ladies at a nonpartisan reception, and then fly on to Tampa to stump for Bill Cramer, candidate for Congress. Then I would head west on a twenty-state swing to the coast—a merry-go-round of riding sound trucks, handshaking, speeches, and autographs.

For swings of this kind, I would pack only one bag and hope for the best. In addition to a suit, cocktail dress, afternoon dress, and nylons, I took an assortment of accessories that could make a costume suitable for any occasion—from a formal tea to a hayride. For I never knew until I got there exactly how I was expected to dress.

On one occasion, Grayce and I flew to Wellesley, Massachusetts, where I had to speak at the fiftieth anniversary celebration of the Babson Institute. Roger Babson had suggested that I make a prognostic speech about the role of women in public affairs fifty years hence.

Grayce and I were guests at the Babsons' home, which had such a formal atmosphere that we wondered whether we were to dress for dinner, but we had no opportunity to inquire. So Grayce hovered at the head of the stairs until she could spot Mrs. Babson strolling into the living room in a dinner dress—and dashed back to give me the word.

One night in Syracuse, I was guest at the state fair. The turkey growers gave me a box with a huge frozen turkey, "as a token of esteem," and asked me to let them know how New York gobblers compared with the Utah variety. Since I was catching a plane for Utah that night and expected to spend Sunday with my brothers and sisters, this would be a welcome gift.

But a close plane connection in Chicago with only fifteen minutes to spare presented a problem. At 1 A.M. I was frantically racing down the ramp, with a suitcase in one hand and the bird in the other. I rushed aboard, panting and disheveled, just as they were about to pull the steps away.

Turning the suitcase and turkey over to the startled stewardess, I fell into a seat and broke into laughter. If the sleepy passengers had noticed my wild dash and undignified entrance they would have thought, "This woman hasn't got all her buttons"—as indeed I hadn't, for a few suit buttons had popped off in the wild scramble.

Back in Washington, when the campaign was over, Roy and I were glad to stay at home on election night. After an arduous campaign tour, I was too tired to do anything but have a light supper, get into a negligee, and prop my feet up on a living-room hassock. The returns that came over TV were certainly nothing to cheer about, for our party lost control of Congress in 1954. There was small consolation in the fact that the candidates I'd stumped for—all but two—had made it.

I was not the only member of the family who had been appearing in public that summer. Miss Pat had landed a job on a Washington television station, taking a pretty strenuous part in an afternoon program featuring interviews and recordings. Loyalty to the sponsors dictated the brands of hot dogs, ice cream, shampoo, and shoes we had to buy. But Pat managed to put aside enough money to buy herself an attractive wardrobe for her first year at Marjorie Webster Junior College.

One night, she stopped in my bedroom after her date with Pierce, whom she was seeing exclusively now. Holding out her left hand excitedly, she cried, "Look what I've got!"

On her engagement finger flashed a diamond ring from Pierce, who would be around to discuss it all with us the next day, she announced.

Roy and I had grown fond of Pierce. And Pat was older now, poised and surprisingly mature. We could see no reason to object to this marriage. Intelligent and capable, Pierce was a graduate of M.I.T. as well as Annapolis. Tall and personable, with dark hair and intense brown eyes, he was several years older than Pat, and we knew he had the maturity and stability to make her a fine husband. Although she was still quite young to settle down, at least she was better fitted for marriage at nineteen than she'd been three years earlier.

"I hope you don't think I put the cart before the horse," Pierce said, when he arrived for the traditional talk with Pat's father. We assured him that we would welcome him into the family, and only hoped that Pat would finish her school year before they set the date.

Pat chose August 20 for her wedding and Pierce announced firmly that she would go back to school and get her certificate the following year.

As it was to be the first "official" wedding in the new administration, it would take some careful planning. Perhaps

I let my enthusiasm run away with me at the outset, for Pat began to bridle and remind me that, after all, it was *her* wedding.

"Well, of course it is, dear," I said, admitting the obvious. "But don't you want it to be just right?"

"As far as I'm concerned," she said airily, "we could just have a simple little ceremony with a few friends."

Her father snorted. "That's all your mother wants," he said. "Just a few friends."

"My gosh," young Roy put in, "Mother's got about a million friends."

"I know," said his father. "We could probably get them into Griffith Stadium if she just invited her intimates."

"Listen, you fellows go tie fishing flies," said Pat, "or build an electronic brain or something. This is girl talk."

With them out of the way, Pat and I sat down to settle the issues.

"Now, Pat, you understand we want this to be just the way you want it. But, you know, we've made many friends here and some might be offended if they were not invited."

"Mother, I don't want a Hollywood production. I just want to get married and have a pretty church wedding."

"Pat, we don't want a big production ... we can't afford it anyway. Why don't we ask Mary-Stuart Price to help us plan it? She's had a lot of experience with these things."

"O.K.," she said, relaxing a little, "but on one condition. There's going to be no publicity, no photographers, no reporters—nobody but friends."

"All right, dear, if that's the way you want it."

From then on, Mary-Stuart handled diplomatic negotiations between Pat and me about the wedding. I told Mary-Stuart how much I thought we could afford to spend and Roy cautiously upped the estimate by half, which he held in a just-in-case fund.

When we started making out the invitation list, what with "musts" in official Washington and friends and relatives around the country, we had a list that touched forty-seven states and resembled a telephone directory. We no sooner cut it down to a thousand guests than it began to grow again.

While Pat and I were going along our merry way, having an occasional summit conference with Mary-Stuart, little Nancy, aged fifteen, was wandering around with a long face. Suddenly, it occurred to me that we had forgotten to fit her into the Big Scheme.

"Couldn't Nancy be in the wedding?" I asked Pat.

"Now, Mother, she's too old to be a flower girl and too young to be a bridesmaid," said Pat.

"That's been the story of Washington for Nancy," I sighed. "She's always either too young or too old."

The next day I called Mary-Stuart from the office and made a date with her for lunch.

"Have you ever put on a wedding where the bride's sister was just a little too old for flower girl and too young for bridesmaid? Could she be a sort of junior bridesmaid?" I asked.

Mary-Stuart was born for the diplomatic service. Smiling in complicity, she said, "I think Nancy would make just an *ideal* junior bridesmaid, Mrs. Priest."

"Now, you understand, Pat is to have the kind of wedding she wants. I wouldn't have her think I was dictating anything. Why don't you suggest this idea?"

Soon after, we were at dinner when Pat came swinging in from a dress fitting. She was all bubbly and radiant, as she took her place at the table, and my heart sank when I realized how much we were going to miss her.

"Nancy," Pat asked suddenly, "how would you like to be a junior bridesmaid at my wedding?"

Feigning complete surprise, I asked, "Oh, do they have junior bridesmaids?"

"Why, of course, Mother," Pat said knowingly. "Mary-Stuart Price says . . ."

And so the plans progressed and the tension mounted. Wedding presents began to pour in and we had to set up long tables atop camouflaged sawhorses in the rec room to hold them all. Young Roy protested unhappily that this arrangement interfered with his newest money-making scheme —the operation of an "electronic brain" by which he was working his friends' arithmetic problems.

Pierce's parents, Dr. and Mrs. Jensen, arrived from Iowa, Dr. Juel Trowbridge, our family physician, and his wife Doris came from Utah, followed by Roy's cousin Gates Priest, of Chicago; and our place soon overflowed with guests. To ease the housing shortage, neighbors generously offered their extra bedrooms.

Since Pierce was a lieutenant commander in the Navy, the traditional military ceremony was planned—with the bridal couple leaving the church under an arch of crossed swords. I assumed that this ceremony would occur inside the church, but on the morning of the wedding I was disappointed to learn that it would be outside, where no one could see it.

At the beauty shop, while sitting under the dryer, I kept worrying about this rite. So I rushed to phone Mary-Stuart to ask if it couldn't be changed. She in turn called Pat. I guess there was an earth tremor that could be felt for miles.

When I got home, the father of the bride met me at the door and stopped me in my tracks.

"Now, Mother," he said quietly but firmly, "Pat's been quite upset all morning. She thinks you're going to spoil everything if you make any last-minute changes. She and Pierce liked the rehearsal last night . . . so let's just let well enough alone and not upset Pat any further. What both of you need is a little rest."

Roy's gentle but decisive way of putting this made me see it in the proper light. Maybe that executive desk and all those telephones had gotten me—but I realized suddenly that I had been guilty of overmanaging. I had promised Pat that she could have the wedding as she wanted it—and here I was butting in on every detail.

Rushing up to her room, I put my arms around her and said remorsefully, "I'm sorry, Pat. I didn't mean to upset you on this of all days."

Then we had a good cry together and one of those traditional heart-to-heart talks—which seem to bring mother and daughter closer together just as they are about to part.

Glancing at her watch, Pat suddenly cried, "Oh, Mother, look at the time! We'd better start dressing."

So I helped her into her white lace gown, a wedding gift from David and Irene Gothe, who had designed it for her. And I rushed into my blue *peau de soie* dress, another Gothe creation.

At the church the nervous bride got an inkling of what it must be like to be left at the altar. The clock crept on toward five but there was no sign of Pierce. The ushers were seating the guests, the pews were crowded. But still no groom.

Pale with anxiety, Pat moaned, "What if he doesn't come? Oh, what if he doesn't come?"

Roy patted her hand consolingly. "Calm down now, of course he'll be here in time. Pierce is never late. Don't worry."

"But, Daddy, he should be here by now," she wailed. "It's almost time—"

The organ then burst into the wedding march. Her eyes darting nervously around the church, Pat slowly went down the aisle on her father's arm. And then her face lighted up radiantly as she caught sight of Pierce waiting at the altar with the minister. Later it appeared that the groom and his best man had been in the vestry all the while, and in the confusion no one thought to tell us he had arrived.

The church was beautifully decorated, with six-feet-high

candelabra entwined with ivy at the end of every pew. As I glanced about, I was delighted to see so many friends there, friends from back home, many others whom Roy and I had met in our years of travel across the country, friends and fellow officers of Pierce. I was particularly pleased to see that besides the Trowbridges other good friends had come all the way from Utah—Eve Ashton of Vernal, the Horace Beasleys of Bountiful, and Mrs. Jenny Wong, the wife of a Chinese merchant who was an old customer of Roy's. Then there were the Cabinet members, diplomats, and other guests from official Washington.

And I must admit that the crossed swords ceremony looked very effective on the church steps.

At the reception in the Sheraton Park Hotel, it was something of an ordeal to stand in line and receive about fifteen hundred guests. When Dr. Jensen took me out on the floor, I was—for probably the first time in my life—too tired to dance. But I perked up when the rapturous bride and groom danced by, and Nancy, the "junior bridesmaid," waved gaily to young Roy, as she floated by in the arms of an usher.

"Mrs. Priest, we've gained a charming daughter," Dr. Jensen said gallantly.

"I guess families don't break up," I said. "They just increase."

When we returned to our table, Roy, with his eyes following the bridal couple, said wistfully, "They're so well matched, aren't they? So bright and handsome together—" I found myself uttering a little prayer that their future would be as bright as this moment.

Later, we watched them take off in Pierce's car which, in spite of all his precautions to keep it in a secret parking place, had been found by exuberant friends and bedecked with the customary trappings.

As they drove away, laughing and waving to the throng of

well-wishers, our joy in their happiness was tinged with regret and loneliness. Roy patted my hand gently and gave me a sympathetic glance. I knew this feeling would pass. Pierce was easy to love as a son—and surely he'd be bringing Pat home for occasional visits.

But the sense of loss which I'd tried to stave off all day now overwhelmed me. Our daughter would not be sleeping under our roof tonight and in all the nights to come. There was no denying that simple fact. We'd have to accept it and learn to live with it.

XVII

THE bride and groom had departed, but somehow the celebration kept rolling along. I would rush home from a long day at the office to pitch in and throw together a buffet supper for fifteen or twenty guests. This went on for about a week, and then the tide began to ebb. One evening I got home to find Roy in one of those disreputable old shirts he was always rescuing "for fishing," and I knew the party was over.

At breakfast the next morning, we held a family council on where do we go from here. We were now short one member of the team. We would all have to pull a bit harder, it was conceded by all hands.

Our discussion was unusually subdued and sober. I suppose we were all suffering something of a letdown. With all the accumulated tension of the period, we were lucky still to be on speaking terms.

For the first time, I fully realized the pressure my job was exerting upon our life. We had tried to keep the family on the same even keel it had maintained in Bountiful. But the demands upon me as a public official had increased immeasurably. The wedding was a reflection of this change in our way of life. It was quite different from the kind we would have had in Bountiful.

Was this all to the good? I asked myself whether the advantages the children enjoyed were offsetting the problems created by my public career.

Looking across the breakfast table that morning, I tried to assess the effect upon the youngsters, to whom I owed an obligation deeper than to any other cause.

Nancy, a chestnut-haired teen-ager, was as quiet and serious as Pat was effervescent and gay. She and young Roy, who was about a year and a half her junior, had always been as close as the freckles on his face. They seemed to be a pair of normal, lively youngsters as they sat there discussing the new division of labor. These two were used to swapping household jobs and young Roy was able to iron shirts, run the washing machine, or make a bed. Any bed save his own, which was usually covered with butterflies or radio parts. They had become responsible young citizens. If this was the result of being the children of a government official, then hooray for Washington.

Nancy suggested that the two of them take turns preparing dinner, and so the new order was established. She cooked on Monday, Wednesday, and Friday, while Roy fixed the evening meal on alternate days. It's my theory that it's pretty hard to damage food to the point where it can't be retrieved, and I usually managed to reach home before smoke began to curl out the kitchen windows.

Young Roy took a coldly realistic approach to fixing dinner. The number of foods really worth eating, he concluded, is definitely limited. His menu ranged from home-cooked spaghetti to hamburgers or minute steaks, invariably accompanied by one of four vegetables—peas, string beans, asparagus, or corn. In his choice of desserts he was more flexible. At times we had vanilla ice cream with fudge sauce, at other times plain vanilla ice cream.

"That's the best dessert there is," he said flatly.

But our home life remained somewhat complicated. Even such a simple thing as taking Nancy to school in the evening to appear in a dance recital could become a problem, if her father was not available as chauffeur. One evening after a late conference, I rushed home to take Nancy to a performance. A flat tire delayed me further and she had to change clothes in the back seat of the car, as we rushed to school. We made it just a second before the curtain went up.

The children learned to take these crises philosophically. When an important dinner prevented us from taking young Roy to a scout jamboree, he commented, "Well, Mother, you have to do your job. After all, it isn't every kid's mother who gets to be Treasurer of the United States."

What are you going to do with a youngster like that? Just everything you can, that's all. In return for the understanding they show about my obligations, I try to take the same interest in their needs. Weekends are set aside for the family. We shop together, attend church together, play together. And, whenever possible, we take them along on trips.

Since I had to make some speeches in the South we decided to spend the Christmas after Pat's wedding in Florida. We drove down together during the holidays and, after my work was done, we stopped at Englewood. The boys wanted to see whether the fish in the Gulf were as big as the average Jackson Hole trout.

We had barely gotten into fishing clothes, when word came that Aunt Gert was in the hospital with a stroke. There it was again—that ominous word on the phone. It took all the wind out of me. Aunt Gert had been like a second mother to me and it was with trembling hand that I put a call through to Uncle Lije in Salt Lake City.

She was in no immediate danger, he assured me, so I promised to fly out as soon as I could, and we left immediately for Washington. After a melancholy Christmas, filled with reminiscences of Aunt Gert, I took a plane west.

Uncle Lije sat like a sad, watchful sentry by the bed where Aunt Gert lay, completely paralyzed. The doctor said there was no way of telling whether she would recover, or to what extent. When I saw her, the once high-spirited Aunt Gert, lying there so helpless and silent—for the first time in her life —I couldn't restrain the tears.

During the days that followed, it seemed that I was almost clinging to Aunt Gert, for she was the last link with my childhood—the period which seemed, in these hours of gloom, to have more reality than the troubled present.

When the New Year came, I was with Uncle Lije and reminded him of his duty to do the first-footing.

He slipped out the back door and a few seconds later I heard his familiar tap at the front door. I opened it to find him, as of old, looking a little like a thin, long-legged bird caught in a spotlight:

"The old year out, the New Year in,
  Please to let the lucky bird in . . ."

His pent-up tears began to flow, as I put my arms around him.

Fixing scrambled eggs a little later, I heard a voice coming over the radio which sounded disconcertingly familiar.

"Thank you, Ivy Baker Priest," said the announcer. "And now a New Year's greeting from the attorney general."

Uncle Lije stood there transfixed, as I continued to stir the eggs. His eyes darted from the radio to me, as if he wasn't sure where the voice was coming from.

"Can't be you! You're here," he said with rare garrulity. "Must be some mistake."

"No, Uncle Lije. I made that recording weeks ago—and forgot all about it."

It gave me a strange sensation for a moment, and I suddenly felt there was something almost symbolic about it. Here was Ivy Baker Priest, scrambling eggs in a modest kitchen in Salt Lake City, and there she was, speaking on a national radio hookup, from Washington. Two different people in one. It was what had been bothering me for so long: wife, mother, civic worker—Utah miner's daughter, public official. I gave a little shudder, as I wondered which I *really* was.

Back at the hospital, I assured Aunt Gert, who could hear with her aid but could not talk, that the first-footing had been done in great style and it should be a good year for all of us. There was nothing I wanted to do more than stay there and nurse her back to health. Her niece Ivy could have stayed —but the Treasurer had to get back to Washington. I left with tears in my heart.

From others in the family, I got regular reports on Aunt Gert, but by February I was back in Salt Lake City for a speech and helped Uncle Lije transfer her to a nursing home.

Some months earlier Roy and I had been invited to make a tour of Greece, where I was to speak to women's groups, and now that Aunt Gert's doctor assured me that her condition was improving it seemed safe enough to keep my commitment.

We sailed from New York that spring, on the Greek liner *Queen Frederika*. We were hardly out of the harbor before I discovered that the suitcase containing my clothes was missing. All I had to wear was one red cocktail dress, which I had put in Roy's bag. There is nothing quite so tiresome, with continuous wear, as a scarlet dress.

After two nights as a lady in red, a friend we'd made

aboard ship chipped in a white sheath of her own, which luckily fitted me—and I did some weird improvisations after that, using scarves and cummerbunds from Roy's dress clothes. Captain Condoyannis, a former admiral in the Greek Navy, whose table guests we were, was amused by my quick changes. One night when I turned up in the same white dress, enhanced by Roy's black cummerbund and a red rose on the shoulder, he was gallant as usual.

"Thank you, Captain," I said. "I'm glad you're pleased with my efforts to look nice at your table. I hope you'll be equally pleased if I suddenly appear in gray satin—for it will be the bedspread from our cabin."

We had just left Gibraltar, when I received a cable from Salt Lake City. Aunt Gert had passed away quietly. Had it come sooner, I could have flown home from Gibraltar, but there was nothing I could do on the high seas. Nothing but sit by the porthole and cry.

A full moon shone on the Mediterranean that night as I sat there, staring at its silver path through the dark waters, reliving all the years from Bingham to Washington. Aunt Gert was the last of her generation. I could see her in our kitchen, while Mother—dressed in a bibbed white apron—fussed over the big, black cookstove in Bingham. I could see Dad raising his eyebrows ever so faintly as Aunt Gert ripped out a "damn," when one of the boys slammed a door. Oh, the memories poured back and the tears poured down my cheeks.

Here I was on a boat, rocking over a limitless sea thousands of miles from home. What was I really doing here? I had the strange, haunting feeling again of being two people. Part of me was back with Uncle Lije, mourning the loss of Aunt Gert. I felt a terrible pang of regret that I was not actually there. But here it was again, the conflict between my two roles in life. I was still sitting there, red-eyed and distraught, as dawn cast its first light on the horizon.

"I know how you feel," Roy said gently. "We all loved Aunt Gert. But hadn't you better try to get some sleep?"

I dozed fitfully for a few hours, worn out from the sleepless night. Later, when we went up on deck into another bright sunny day, it was an effort to get back into the swing of shipboard life. My heart just wasn't in it.

That evening there was a good deal of excitement among the passengers, when the rumor spread that Queen Frederika, who was traveling in Italy, would board the ship at Naples, our first landfall.

When we docked, the officials of the line arranged to have an interpreter take me on a shopping trip to replace my lost clothing. There was also time for a little hurried sightseeing. Naples's steep, winding streets were teeming with exuberant humanity. We stopped to lunch at an outdoor *ristorante* overlooking the magnificent crescent-shaped harbor, with Mount Vesuvius looming in the background and the green island of Capri rising from the turquoise sea.

Our meal of succulent little oysters, pasta, fruit, and cheese was accompanied by Neapolitan songs played by strolling musicians who moved from table to table. The lilting music, brilliant blue sky, sun-dappled sea, and the laughing, chattering people around us lifted my gloom somewhat. It was difficult to think of death in an atmosphere simply bursting with life.

When we returned to the ship Queen Frederika was already aboard, looking as young and captivating as ever, with her modish cluster of light-brown curls framing her winsome face. She invited us to dine with her and her daughter, Princess Sophie, and we reminisced about the Greek Embassy dinner in Washington where her kindness had dissolved my embarrassment over the glove incident.

After dinner she insisted that I must see the great bargain in a fur coat she had bought for Princess Sophie. It was a remarkable coat, made of perfectly matched little bits of fur, painstakingly put together by Greek craftsmen out of discards sent to them from America. But I was even more impressed by the fact that even a queen was first and foremost a mother.

Two days later we sailed up the beautiful Aegean to Peiraeus, the port of Athens, where we were met by officers of the clubs that had arranged the tour. Among them was Mrs. Eftahia Eftaxopolis, a charming, vivacious woman, who was delegated to be our hostess. Since she spoke no English, she brought along an interpreter, Nick Marcopolis, a walking encyclopedia of Greek lore, who had once worked in Chicago.

A caravan of American cars took us on an eight-day tour of the Peloponnesos, the southernmost province of Greece. We drove through rugged mountainous country reminiscent of Utah—in terrain, but not vegetation, of course. For the narrow roads wound through groves of blossoming lemon, fig, olive, and pistachio trees, and vineyards climbed miraculously up the steep mountainsides.

En route we stopped off to see the great amphitheater at Epidaurus, the tomb of Agamemnon at Mycenae, the excavations at Corinth, and the ruins of the ancient arena at Olympia, site of the original Olympic games—now overgrown with a vivid profusion of wildflowers.

At the little village of Steno we paused to wait for the officials of the province of Arcadia to escort us to a banquet at nearby Tripolis. "The president"—as our guide called him— of the village greeted us ceremoniously and took us to his house, a small whitewashed cottage on a hilltop. His wife, a plump, genial woman, wearing a voluminous dark skirt and embroidered jerkin, received us with the hospitality for which the Greeks are famous. It was a rainy day and the entire family was gathered around a potbellied wood stove in the kitchen, where we were served a delicious confection called *loukoumi*. I feared that my appreciation—conveyed by the interpreter—was inadequate. Recalling the bit of Greek I'd learned aboard ship, I pointed to the delicacy and said, "*Parakalo*" (please). Beaming with pleasure, our hostess rushed to pass the dish to us.

When we returned to Athens, the entire city was in mourning for the Archbishop of Greece. The solemnity and grandeur of his funeral procession were in marked contrast to the festivities of Greek Independence Day, which was celebrated as scheduled the next day, March 25. From our balcony at the Grande Bretagne Hotel we watched a marvelously brilliant parade and took color films of the evzones, the palace guards, marching smartly in their white tunics, red-tasseled caps, and pointed red shoes with blue pompoms.

The following day we got a closeup view of the Acropolis, the historic hill that dominates Athens, and the Parthenon standing on its crest. It was a moving experience to see the temple of Athena, the city's patron goddess, with its noble columns framing the deep blue sky. Small wonder that the Parthenon is considered the most beautiful building in the world and has inspired so many Greek-revival homes and public buildings in our own country.

Later, when we went shopping for souvenirs, our past caught up with us unexpectedly. In a dry-goods shop on Hermon Street we found a merchant named Pete Diamantes who was the uncle of one of Roy's old customers in Utah. Overcome at having news of his relative, Mr. Diamantes turned his shop inside out for us, and sent out for heaping trays of delicacies.

My final speech in Athens had me rather worried. At the time feeling ran high about the Cyprus situation, because many people believed that the island should belong to Greece again. Since I am not in a policy-making position, I was afraid of being drawn into a discussion of ticklish political matters.

Ambassador Cavendish Cannon, a former Utahan, whose

mother had been a friend of my mother's, advised me to go ahead with the speech. But to help me over any difficulties that might arise he offered to send along Duncan Emrich, of the Embassy staff.

After my travelogue type of talk extolling the beauties I'd seen in Greece, the chairman rose to thank me. Of course, I didn't understand a word he said, but from his smiles and expansive gestures, I gathered he was making a polite acknowledgment. Then his expression changed. From his determined voice and manner, I guessed that he had launched into a tirade on Cyprus. When I thought the interpreter had concluded the flowery remarks, I quickly extended my hand to the chairman and said, *"Efharisto, Kyrios Abramides. Efharisto para poli. Adio."*—"Thank you, Mr. Abramides. Thank you very much. Good-by."

And I *adioed* my way out of the hall to the gratifying cheers of the audience.

"How did you know he was talking about Cyprus?" Duncan Emrich asked, once we were outside.

"Oh, did I interrupt something?" I said with a show of innocence. "I thought he was merely complimenting me."

"He was—at first. If you had interrupted to thank him in English the audience would have resented it. But your thanks in Greek at the right moment simply delighted them."

After this memorable trip we were soon engulfed again in the routine of home life at Arlington, where Pat and Pierce had stayed to look after the young fry. But our experiences and film showing were topped by the young couple's announcement that they were expecting a baby. Roy and I were delighted by the prospect of becoming grandparents.

That May, I found myself emotionally torn again between the roles of housewife and public official. I had agreed to make the commencement address at Marjorie Webster College where Pat, good as Pierce's word, had continued her studies that year. When I faced the audience, I knew this would be a difficult speech to make. For a mother always has a lump in her throat when a child graduates. As I stood there solemnly telling those young girls about the big responsibilities ahead, I could see my own daughter in the first row. And I knew how soon she would be undertaking her own first big responsibility.

If I dwell upon this sensation of duality which haunted me, it is because it seemed to become more pronounced at this time. The demands upon me as an official and as a mother often met head on, sometimes with hilarious results.

For instance, I was invited that summer to lovely Mackinac Island, in Michigan, to speak to the state Bankers Association. It offered one of those chances I tried never to miss to get off with Roy and the youngsters—so we drove up there together.

We allowed an extra day, which gave the boys time to go fishing before we reached the island. We stopped at a country store, where they invested a mere twenty dollars in fishing equipment. As we were about to leave, the proprietor told us happily that our purchase entitled us to two parakeets, absolutely free. I could not see any place for parakeets in our scheme of things, and was about to tell him to keep the change, when Nancy began to plead

"All right," Roy said. "But what do you keep them in?"

It appeared that we needed a cage, and also some feed. Before we paid for this, we made sure this purchase did not entitle us to another parakeet, which would need another cage, which would entitle us to another parakeet. . . .

The boys had a fine afternoon fishing. They didn't catch a thing, but my husband, who was wearing Bermuda shorts, came back with the most beautiful pair of shocking-pink knees I'd ever seen. The poor man was in agony all night, in spite of a thick coating of ointment. In order to keep his sunburned knees from being painfully rubbed by his trousers, I wrapped them in soft cloth and propped his legs on pillows.

We certainly made a grand entrance at the bankers' meeting the next day. The hotel rolled out the red carpet and, while everyone bowed with great dignity, out of our muddy car came: one freckled-faced boy, carrying a fishing rod and a butterfly net; a freckled-faced girl, with two parakeets in a cage; a red-faced gentleman of middle years, limping painfully; and one harassed-looking mother trying to assume the dignity of her office. The hotel manager stepped forward to greet us. "Good morning—and welcome to Mackinac Island."

"Thank you—we're delighted to be here—complete with bag, baggage, and birds," I replied.

The youngsters sat directly in front of the dais at the luncheon. When I rose to speak, a hush settled over the room, which was shattered by a girlish stage-whisper which, I am sure, was heard throughout the room.

"Make it snappy, Mother. Roy wants to go catch butterflies."

"You've probably heard the orders I just received," I said to the audience. "I don't know why my boy wants to catch butterflies—I've already got them!"

That afternoon came a call from Pierce saying that our first grandchild, Pierce Andrew Jensen III, had arrived. Why did I always have to be elsewhere at times like this? And, even worse, I had a speech scheduled the next day in Los Angeles.

Pierce assured me that mother and child were doing nicely and that he was recovering too. So I flew west, while the rest of the family headed east. The speech over, I flew all night to Washington to meet my first grandchild.

Pat was just home from the hospital when Pierce got orders transferring him to Alameda, California. We brought Pat and the baby home with us and, outside of office hours, I could revel in the new role of grandmother.

It was a joy to bathe the wiggly, pink infant whose tiny, plump fingers wrapped themselves around mine, and to rock him to sleep, singing the half-forgotten lullabies that I used to sing to his mother. As I watched his delicate lids droop with sleep, I dreamily looked ahead to the time when Pierce III would become an active voter in 1987—Republican, of course!

But, alas, these days were all too short-lived. For Pat soon followed her husband to his base at Alameda, taking baby, bottles, and bath out of our all too willing hands.

Shortly afterward, I too left for California to attend the Republican convention which opened in San Francisco in August, 1956. Although I had no real duties—having given up my political posts when I became Treasurer—it was a busy time filled with official calls and a ceaseless round of activities.

San Francisco, which held so many poignant memories for me, was an ideal choice for a midsummer convention because of its cool climate. But the shortage of hotel space for the huge inflex was acute, and I had to drive back and forth to the town of Sausalito. This proved to be a blessing in disguise because of the wonderfully scenic drive across the Golden Gate Bridge and the charm of my hotel, the Alta Mira, perched high above the bay.

The convention at the huge, flag-draped Cow Palace was marked more by showmanship than by political maneuvering. Since Eisenhower had agreed to run again, the only prospect of controversy centered around the vice-presidency. But even this contest failed to develop because of Nixon's popularity.

Although the Cow Palace resounded with the usual hullabaloo, the proceedings were fairly routine. The President was overwhelmingly nominated on the first ballot after a rapid roll call, which gave the spokesman for each delegation an opportunity to extol his state, the President, and the party.

Optimism about the November victory ran high, and when Eisenhower arrived to make his acceptance speech, the hall went wild. He waited on the platform, with a pleased, boyish smile, through the hubbub of all the floor demonstrations, snake dances, confetti-throwing, banner-waving, and horn-blowing. When it finally subsided, he made a particularly rousing speech that inspired us with confidence in his leadership.

Requests for campaign speeches had begun to arrive before I left for San Francisco. But it didn't seem wise for me to plunge in without a short vacation. So after the convention I arranged to meet the family in Minneapolis for a car trip through Canada. We would stop along the road for picnic lunches to allow young Roy to catch butterflies and Nancy to take snapshots.

Driving through Michigan one day, we stopped for our picnic at a lonely, wooded spot about thirty miles from Marquette. We left the car and were just out of sight around a bend, taking snapshots, when I heard a car door slam. I raced back and found our bag of clothes missing from the car.

Roy, Sr., racing right behind me, said, "Did you see their car get away?"

"No, I didn't. But from the way the door slammed it sounded like an old jalopy."

We set off in frantic pursuit, guessing which way the other auto might have gone down the main road. It was a good guess, because we soon came up behind a battered car with an Ontario license, and three rough-looking young men inside it. As soon as they saw us, they turned off and sped down a narrow, rutted, dirt road through the woods.

Honking our horn wildly, we chased them for a few miles along the narrow trail until at last they stopped in a clearing. I asked politely if they had seen anyone take our clothes and they said they hadn't. But young Roy, quick as a cat, jumped out of our car and yelled, "Mother—they've got your clothes on the back seat of their car!"

As Roy, blocked by a tree on his side, struggled to get out, I jumped out of my side.

"Why, you took our bag!" I cried, waving a finger at them. "How could you do such a thing? Haven't you any consideration for anyone else? Give them back."

They meekly started returning the pile of clothing. Nancy had slipped a flashlight out of our glove compartment and passed it over to her dad, who put it in his pocket as if it were a gun. He came around the thieves' car now, as I was demanding that they return my fur stole. One of them started to get out of the car, denying that they had taken the fur. Just then the top of it slipped out of the door and Roy snatched it out.

"All right, you lying thieves," Roy snapped, "get out of here while you're still in one piece." He sounded so much like a TV sheriff that I almost laughed.

We drove off and stopped at the first gas station to report the incident to the police. The attendant listened open-mouthed.

"Great Scott, man!" he said to Roy. "You don't mean to tell me you tracked those fellows into that lonely stretch of woods? They could have killed you all and your bodies wouldn't have been found for months."

For the first time, we began to get frightened. But then young Roy spoke up firmly:

"Don't worry, if they'd tried anything, I would have hit them with a flying tackle."

There is nothing like the protection of a fourteen-year-old son!

Back home after this eventful vacation, there was scarcely time to get the children off to school and catch up on office work before I had to plunge into the election campaign. In September, I set forth on a continuous round of speeches, two or three daily, that took me from Virginia all the way to North Dakota. With police sirens screaming, I was whisked from one place to the next—speaking at lunch in Indianapolis and dinner in Detroit.

In the previous presidential campaign, along with stumping for candidates I had to run the women's division of the party. Now there were the obligations of my office plus a strenuous schedule of speeches. So I shuttled back and forth to Washington, living out of a suitcase while on the road, gulping down hasty meals, sleeping wherever I could lay my weary head for a few hours, and working under ceaseless tension.

In North Carolina, where I stumped for Congressman Charlie Jonas of the Tenth District, there was scarcely time for a shower before we started the rounds of brunches, lunches, teas, receptions, and press conferences, winding up with a big rally every night.

"This is a killing pace, Ivy," Charlie Jonas said. "When you get out of here, you'd better get some rest."

But I was on my way to Tampa, wondering whether Roy would remember Nancy's appointment with the dentist and whether he'd gotten the washing machine fixed. After the customary reception, dinner, and ball, I tumbled into bed in the small hours, leaving an 8 A.M. call.

"You look tired," said Congressman Bill Cramer of Florida for whom I was campaigning. "You'd better get some rest—when you leave here."

The next day, we plunged into the usual series of events— and at the reception alone I must have shaken two thousand hands. When I got back to the hotel, Grayce Abajian, who was traveling with me, took one look at me and sent me off for a rest. A massage got me back on my feet for a dinner speech and two rallies before we flew to Dallas.

Our plane touched down at New Orleans—and there were

television cameras and an interviewer waiting. A half hour later, we were on our way for a hectic two days' work for Congressman Bruce Alger of the Fifth District in Texas. Flying to Chicago, we set up headquarters for intensive campaigning throughout the Midwest.

One day, after gliding into Cleveland airport through gray murk, Grayce and I found an enthusiastic young man waiting to escort us to a political rally in Erie, Pennsylvania. He said we were going to fly to Erie in a private plane, which I accepted without question until I saw the little four-seater waiting for us. Grayce and I exchanged anxious glances. I couldn't help voicing my doubts about the advisability of taking off in black weather in such a small plane.

"We just flew down from Erie," he said confidently. "It's not bad—and there's a big crowd waiting to hear you, Mrs. Priest."

"Isn't there some other way to get there?" I asked.

"Not in time for the meeting. But don't worry—we've got a good pilot."

With a silent prayer, we climbed into the plane, and were introduced to a woman pilot—sitting there as confident as she could be. We didn't say a word, as we headed up into the ominous black clouds—but we kept looking at each other in fright.

"I'm scared to death," I finally confided to the young man.

"So am I," he confessed.

We exchanged sickly smiles and gripped our seats as the little plane, buffeted and tossed by the high wind, gained altitude.

But, fortunately, it smoothed out as we flew above the clouds and we felt that our pilot knew what she was doing. We landed with no trouble at all and thanked her for the fine job she'd done.

As we walked off the field, my young escort said, "Mrs.

Priest, I guess you got really scared when you saw it was a woman pilot!"

"On the contrary, that was the most reassuring thing that happened. Let me tell you, young man, a woman has to be twice as good to earn half as much at anything as a man."

After completing a grueling ten-day circuit of the Midwest we flew to Los Angeles to attend the American Bankers Association convention—sandwiched in between another series of political talks. By this time I was so weary that I couldn't even fall asleep on the plane. The old bounce that had kept me going through the last presidential campaign didn't seem to be there now. Above the hum of the motors I could hear the refrain, "It's a killing pace . . . you must get some rest."

Things became just a little blurred after that. There were breakfast and luncheon talks, and "could you just drop in to our reception for a few minutes?" and then a campaign speech before two thousand in the civic auditorium that afternoon. At dinner afterward I was so hoarse that, for once, I was quite content to keep quiet.

In the morning, I picked up the phone to order breakfast —and discovered that I had no voice left. Grayce took over and called Cal Tech where I was scheduled to talk at a luncheon. At the group's insistence I agreed to go along while Grayce read my speech.

When we got back to the hotel, she called a doctor.

"Her blood pressure's down to eighty," he said. "She's completely exhausted. Put her to bed and don't let her out until I give the word."

Well, there went the rest of the campaign. For three days I was under sedation. Every time I sat up to ask who was going to make my speech in Salt Lake or to wonder whether Roy had remembered to send the rugs to the cleaners, they stuck me with another needle. Finally the doctor let me out —but only to go up to Alameda to stay with Pat.

On Saturday before election day, we located a notary public and, much against her will, persuaded her to stay open long enough to notarize my absentee ballot.

"Oh, Mrs. Priest, wouldn't it have been terrible if I hadn't let you in!" she said, when she learned my name. "Why didn't you tell me who you were?"

Soon it was time to tear myself away from baby Pierce and his parents, and return home. But it was a relief to sleep in my own bed again—and a luxury to have Nancy bring me a breakfast tray in the morning, while the two Roys hovered solicitously over the bed and briefed me on home affairs. Even the charges and countercharges the children tossed back and forth were music to my ears.

On election night we gathered around the television set and watched the cheering returns come in. Eisenhower took an early lead over Adlai Stevenson and won with over 35 million votes. We were also elated over the returns in Utah, where Senator Bennett was reelected and our party ran away with every national and state office.

But it was disappointing to learn that we had again lost the majority lead in the Senate and House. I wondered if the President would have the same difficulty in carrying out his program as he'd had in the last two years, when the opposition was in control of Congress.

Later that night, as we had some hot chocolate and cookies in front of the fire, young Roy piped up gleefully, "Gee, Mom! Now you can be Treasurer for four more years."

"Now, don't be so sure," said Nancy, the cautious one. "Maybe Ike will appoint someone else."

"Not a chance!" retorted her brother with supreme confidence in his hero.

Roy and I exchanged amused glances, as the children blithely disposed of our future.

In the meantime, the immediate past caught up with me,

for the campaign had taken its toll. When Dr. George Dewey, our family physician, came to give me a checkup, he announced that the machine had run down—low blood pressure, low hemoglobin count, low energy.

His prescription of plenty of rest was fine, but how to follow it? Just before I was to leave for a Salute to Eisenhower speech in Michigan I took a sudden chill and went to bed.

"Temperature of 104," Dr. Dewey said. "Cancel your speech. You're staying home."

I had the A-type virus flu—the type which had swept through the country in 1918. It had waited a long time to catch up with me.

Months previously, I had promised to serve as chairman of the 1957 Easter Seal Campaign to raise funds for the National Society for Crippled Children and Adults. I had been active in this organization for years, ever since I'd learned about its excellent work when a nervous disorder of one of my nieces was diagnosed as cerebral palsy.

"I promised to do it," I told the family, when I was back on my feet. "And I just can't let those children down."

We started the campaign in San Francisco with a schedule that began at breakfast and ended at midnight. In Los Angeles we had another crowded day, and toward evening Kay Bauer, publicity director of the society, said sweetly, "There's just one more thing. We've got to make a film tonight with some handicapped children over at the NBC studio."

"I'm sorry," I said. "But I just couldn't do another thing tonight. Can't we make it tomorrow?"

She agreed readily. Then a look of doubt crossed her face.

"It's too late to stop them from bringing in those little crippled children for the film," she said hesitantly. "They're so hard to handle. But I guess they can bring them back tomorrow."

258

"Say no more," I sighed. "I can get around better than they can. Let's make it tonight."

Later, at the NBC studio, we rehearsed the film with ten handicapped youngsters. It was a simple scene, in which I started by putting my hand on one child's shoulder and asking, "How old are you, Danny?"

"I am fourteen," he replied.

Then I made a little pitch for Easter Seals.

We rehearsed the scene a few times and finally the director said, "All right, Mrs. Priest. That sounds good to me. This time we'll take it. Start when I drop my arm."

He gave the signal and I asked the little boy, "How old are you, Danny?"

"I'm fourteen, Mrs. Priest. Just as old as your son Roy. And this is a surprise for you!"

I thought the little fellow had flubbed his lines and I was ready to step in with some improvisation. But he was rushing on, "This is your life, Mrs. Priest!"

At this moment, a door opened and Ralph Edwards, emcee of the television program "This Is Your Life," stepped into the room. But I still thought it was all a joke.

"But this is a rehearsal, Mr. Edwards," I said.

"It *was* a rehearsal," he corrected. "But now you're going across the hall and on to the stage and back through the years."

There are surprises which are so complete that they actually paralyze you physically—and this was one of them. I didn't know whether I was going to faint dead away, cry, or start laughing hysterically. Since a commercial had flashed on the television screen, I had a few moments to collect myself.

Stepping out on the stage, I found myself on the verge of tears again when I saw that, for the opening scene, they had faithfully reproduced the interior of our old house in Bingham

Canyon. There were pictures of Mother and Dad—and then I heard a familiar voice off stage yelling, "Ivy's home, gang!"

It was my brother Fearnley—the one who used to say, "I can't make up my mind whether the Lord has you by the hand—or the devil looks after his own." He dashed into the "living room," that same boyish expression of mischief on his face, leading my brothers and sisters. There was Max, strong and healthy; Lloyd, a six-footer with the deeply lined face of a hard-working man; Gertrude, her brown hair turned prematurely gray; and Keith, the Navy flyer, now a dignified young lawyer. They were all there but sister Lynn, whose husband was ill. Looking at them standing in the replica of our living room, I was overcome by the memory of our parents' struggle to raise their big family. It was Gertrude, of course, who saw the fix I was in and slipped me a handkerchief.

The scene shifted, almost like a kaleidoscope. There was our old childhood friend and playmate John Creedon; the switchboard at which I had worked in Salt Lake City, and my supervisor; the department-store counter, the political associates and friends I had not seen in years and, suddenly, there was Roy with all our children—even Pierce and baby Pierce.

Then the bright lights went off and we were left together for the evening, to reconstruct it all. For the first time in many months, the pressure seemed to be lifted and I felt like one person, instead of two, secure in the heart of my family.

But, after a day or two together, I had to continue with the Easter Seal campaign. The schedule which had been laid out for me on my way back east was as demanding as any political campaign. Again, I plunged into the heady, but tiring, routine of meeting hundreds of people, making dozens of appearances, and talking, talking, day after day.

By the time we reached Indianapolis, I wondered whether I could get through the last few days of the fund drive. I tumbled into bed in my hotel late one night, that familiar hoarse and scratchy feeling in my throat, and left a call for 8 A.M.

When the phone rang next morning, I tried to speak to the operator—but no sound came out. I was terrified. Alone in a strange room in a strange city, completely mute and unable to summon help, I panicked.

The silence on the line must have alerted the operator, for a short time later there was a knock on the door. It was Joe Staples, the Easter Seal representative, who summoned the hotel doctor; he administered sedatives and firmly ordered an end to my tour. Joe Staples put out a press release, explaining the cancellation. Governor Handley of Indiana sent his car to take me to the airport and Roy met me in Washington.

Safe at home in the dark silence of my bedroom, I awaited the arrival of Dr. Dewey.

"Nature has its ways of warning us, Ivy," he said gravely. "It's lucky that you lost your voice before your family lost you. You'd better heed the warning."

There it was, cold and plain.

I could make no reply, but when he left, I turned my face to the wall. It seemed as if I were slipping into some dark gulf of despair. Would I ever be able to speak again—if not publicly, at least to my own people? Perhaps they'd prefer silence, I thought wryly, but for a talker like me it would be a sad fate indeed.

The two parts of Ivy Priest—the public official and the wife-mother—had pulled apart at the seams. In trying to sustain both, I had almost succeeded in destroying each. It seemed that I had nothing left to give either.

And so I lay there in the dark, listening to the children

move quietly about downstairs and hearing Roy answer the phone to assure friends that I would be all right.

I did not even have the voice to cry out and tell him he was wrong. Would I ever be all right again, I wondered despairingly. For I had reached a fork in the road. Which way would I go from here?

XVIII

SELF-PITY is, perhaps, the least becoming of all emotions, and we often indulge in it only because we are too exhausted to resist.

Deep in the dead of night, when I looked back over the long road I had traveled—and wondered whether it had all been worth the effort and whether I had the strength to move on the rest of the way—I recalled again my father's words about how much easier it was if you were not alone. That night I prayed fervently, and I felt that my burden was lifted from me, as if by the unseen hand that had guided my life.

When I woke up, Roy was sitting quietly at my bedside, considerate and encouraging—the engaging twinkle still in his eye.

I made a feeble attempt to say good morning—only to hear my normal voice again. At times it really is good to hear your own voice. The sound seemed to galvanize the family into action. Nancy and young Roy came rushing in.

"Mother, you can talk!" Nancy exclaimed.

And Roy, Jr. said, "Gee, it sounds great!"

"You'd better get ready for school," their father said, his brusque tone hiding a tremor of emotion, "or you'll hear more from your mother—and it won't sound so good."

After school each day, the children came trooping in, Nancy to show off her new charm bracelet or to tell excitedly that the boy she liked was going to take her to the spring dance. And young Roy would consult me earnestly about which butterfly in the catalogue should be ordered for his collection.

Then, as the days went by, Grayce Abajian would come merrily in from the office to consult me on some little problems. And Tracey Petersen, warm and friendly, would bring bundles of cheering get-well messages.

"You're looking better," the doctor said encouragingly, each day.

We seldom stop to think how many peoples' lives are entwined with our own. It is a form of selfishness to imagine that every individual can operate on his own or can pull out of the general stream and not be missed.

Perhaps this realization that people at home and at work were depending on me increased my determination to get back on my feet. When I felt strong enough, I returned to the office on a limited schedule, and it was good to be back at my desk and working with my efficient staff.

One day, I went to the White House to attend the swearing-in ceremony for the new Secretary of the Treasury, Robert B. Anderson, of Vernon, Texas. He and Mrs. Anderson were among the first friends I had made in Washington, when he was Secretary of the Navy. Later he had become Deputy Secretary of Defense. His name would now appear on the money with mine—on bills that would bear, for the first time, the United States motto: "In God We Trust." When the President came in for the swearing-in ceremony, he shook hands all around and said, when he came to me, "You're looking great, Ivy."

"Thank you, Mr. President. So are you," I said, feeling my spirits soar at his friendliness.

"I feel great!" he said. Health and happiness combined to light up his face.

Here was a man who had come back three times after dangerous illnesses and who had worked on at one of the toughest jobs in the world out of his sense of duty. If he could do all that, I told myself, you can surely do your little part.

Any woman who has a career and a family automatically develops something in the way of two personalities, like two sides of a dollar bill, each different in design. But one can complement the other to make a valuable whole. Her problem is to keep one from draining the life from the other. She can achieve happiness only as long as she keeps the two in balance.

My home, it seemed to me, was like the Lord's storehouse of our Mormon faith. Here was a reservoir of love and understanding to which we could all contribute and from which we could then draw. I hoped I had been able to keep that part of my life in order. In our home, we understood each other's needs and rights and we did not ask the impossible.

I had staggered under the load only because I had allowed the public part of my life to overdraw its account. Others could not be expected to place limitations on the demands they made on me. It was up to me to recognize my limitations and to impose the necessary restrictions upon my activities.

This decision made, I began to feel a greater peace of mind and sense of purpose. After all, Washington had done well by us. My family and I enjoyed the kind of life we could never have known under other circumstances. No matter what the future might bring, I had gained experience that would be invaluable either in public affairs or in private business. And I could go on making my contribution—whatever it might be—to the society in which I lived. As a wise friend once said, "The time you give is the rent you pay for the space you occupy."

Life now seemed to stretch before me along a clear and inviting road. I gave a prayer of thanks to my mother again for having encouraged me to get into politics. For it is essential that women play a part in this field—I do not say that as a partisan, because I believe strongly in the two-party system —and I like to see women working for the party of their choice.

When I am asked how much money there is in the Treasury, I am tempted to point out that all the dollars in our vaults cannot buy the devotion of people to the principles of freedom. In this realm of intangible values women play an important role. Ultimately, it's not the gold and silver stored in the vaults that make the nation strong, but it's men and women working together for our mutual benefit.

Soon I was able to resume a full schedule—but one from which I carefully eliminated many of the social activities and public speaking engagements which I had previously undertaken.

However, when an invitation crossed my desk that summer to present a savings bond award to the Kennecott Copper Mine in Bingham Canyon, I accepted with alacrity.

When we drove into Bingham, I was startled and deeply moved to see the streets bedecked with "Welcome Home, Ivy Baker Priest" banners. There were so many changes that I hardly knew my home town. I suppose I had half expected to see Mr. Shea come walking down Main Street, or Dr.

Straupp, our old mayor, his coattails flying and a big cigar in his mouth. But the years had passed. The old Bingham Merc, where the Fourth of July orators had held forth for so many years, was gone. So were many of the other landmarks, including the old Social Hall and the high school. The little town was bright and modern with plate-glass shop windows and neon signs. The mud that used to bother Mother so much was all gone now, and the still-narrow streets were well paved with concrete sidewalks. The Kennecott Copper hill, where we used to play as children, was now completely electrified —and was still the biggest open-pit copper mine in the world.

I managed to steal away from the welcoming committee for a few moments to pay a sentimental visit to our old homestead. But it too had disappeared. And in its place stood the Gemmell Memorial Clubhouse, a recreation club for miners. Father would have liked that, I thought.

As I stood there in a bemused state, the present faded away, and I could see our old frame house and the big yard filled with laughing, boisterous children, and Mother in the doorway, admonishing us to "get down off that shed beforre ye brreak yer young necks!"

Then I saw Father coming down the canyon off his shift, swinging his lunch bucket, as we broke into a mad race to reach him first and be rewarded with the few scraps he'd saved from his lunch for us. And there was the noisy confusion at the dinner table, after a few moments of silence while Dad said grace, when the hungry horde of youngsters took up the chant of "Please pass the meat—potatoes—bread."

Then came the family hour, common to Mormon homes, when the littlest children nodded sleepily as we listened to Dad read his much-thumbed Bible in his quiet, grave voice. He would intersperse these readings with lessons from the Mormon Church books, adding his own homey bits of wisdom, which often came back through the years to strengthen and sustain me in moments of trouble and self-doubt.

"When in doubt, don't," Dad would say, and "To follow the line of least resistance makes both men and rivers crooked." And the saying that perhaps best demonstrated his generous, open-minded point of view, "No matter how weak the crutch a man leans on may seem to you, don't take it away unless you can put a stronger one in its place."

I smiled to myself when I recalled Mother's customary remark: "And now we'll close the family hour by singing some songs, with Ivy on the piano and Fearnley on the violin." She beamed with pride as we stumbled through her favorite tunes. And I could almost hear her clear soprano ringing out above our inept accompaniment in "Then You'll Remember Me." Yes, Mother, we'll always remember.

I'm afraid I was a little red-eyed when I rejoined my hosts, who immediately marched me off to jail. For the old Western spirit was still alive and they were celebrating "Galena Days," when men were allowed to appear clean-shaven only if they had a permit. I was held in the mock cell until I bought a permit to appear without whiskers.

Then a young reporter came up to ask for an interview. "Can you give me a brief outline of your philosophy of life?" she said.

"Will four words be brief enough?"

"Can you really sum up your philosophy of life in four words?" she asked skeptically.

"Perhaps philosophy is too ambitious a word. Call it a credo, if you like. But it has great meaning for me. It used to be 'Live and let live.' But the years have taught me that it should be 'Live and *help* live.' "

I went on to explain that my parents had instilled in me the importance of responsibility and cooperation. From their Mormon faith I had imbibed the belief that, when the spirit of God dwells in a home, the problems and vicissitudes of daily living are easier to overcome. And if we live by this faith ourselves we are better able to help others live.

Later, there was a little welcoming ceremony in the center of town, where the Bingham Merc had once stood. Mayor Ed Johnson, a boyhood friend of my brother Max, announced that they were going to present me with a token of esteem, something that would serve as a link to the days when my Dad was a miner there.

"It gives me great pleasure to present you with this diamond . . ." the mayor said, pausing as I caught my breath. Then he finished the sentence ". . . drill bit."

They had made up a charming little scarfpin with one of the industrial diamond drill bits which miners use.

We went on to the Kennecott Copper works, where I stood before an audience of miners, who looked pleased at the prospect of receiving a Treasury award. But their pleasure must have been increased by the fact that they'd been given time off, with pay, to attend the ceremonies with their families. Looking around, I saw the familiar faces of men and women who had been children when I lived there. Before opening my speech, I singled out old friends in the audience and reminisced—much to the amusement of the newcomers —about the days when we had swung from the crane across the canyon, jumped from tramcar to tramcar, and played tag on the bridge girders.

Mingling with the crowd later, I had a strange feeling. I could remember back to school days, when I was by no means the most popular belle. I recalled my dream that one day I would come back and they would be glad to see me in Bingham. I had hardly dreamed that the streets would be decked with banners, but I hoped to do some little thing that would make them proud of me.

As I made my way back to my car, a group of youngsters

gathered around, to have me autograph the inevitable bills.

"Mrs. Priest, did you really live in Bingham when you were a kid?" asked one little pig-tailed girl.

"Indeed I did," I replied.

An Italian girl edged up shyly and asked:

"Do you think I could ever be Treasurer of the United States?"

"Why, of course you can be Treasurer," I answered, with the absolute certainty that this was true. "If I could be, you could be. How's your handwriting?"

"Not so good," she laughed.

"Well, you'd better get busy and practice. If I had known when I was a little girl that I was going to sign all that green money, I would have practiced in order to have a pretty signature to put on the bills."

As we drove away, I looked back into the setting sun and saw the "Welcome Home, Ivy" banner on Main Street waving good-by.

The old town had certainly changed and grown. Widening levels of green-hued copper ore were spreading over the mountainside like green-growing ivy struggling upward. Perhaps it was the sun in my eyes—but my sight grew misty as I strained for a last glimpse of the little valley in the Canyon in order to fix it forever in my memory.